SURVIVING A THOUSAND CUTS

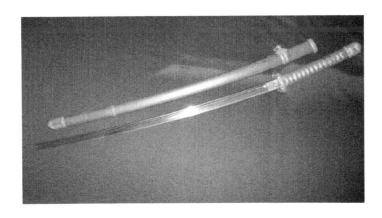

Copyright 2021 Wim Wetzel
Published by Wim Wetzel at Smashwords

Smashwords Edition License Notes
This ebook is licensed for your personal enjoyment only. This ebook may not be re-sold or given away to other people. If you would like to share this book with another person, please purchase an additional copy for each recipient. If you are reading this book and did not purchase it, or it was not purchased for your enjoyment only, then please return to Smashwords.com or your favorite retailer and purchase your own copy. Thank you for respecting the hard work of this author.
Printed in the United States of America
ISBN: 9780463558638

WimPen Publishing – West Palm Beach, Florida

Wim H Wetzel

Table of Contents

Acknowledgements
Prologue
Chapter 1 – The Rebels Attack
Chapter 2 – A Mercenary Soldiers Life
Chapter 3 – My Roots
Chapter 4 – Return To the Homeland
Chapter 5 - Voyage to America - 1956 - Age 9
Chapter 6 – Our First American Home – Age 9 and 10
Chapter 7 – Paper Boy – Milk Man – Thief – 10 Years Old
Chapter 8 – The Birth of a Kung Fu Dynasty In America - 1958
Chapter 9 – Family Skeletons
Chapter 10 – Stranger On the Couch – 1959 – 12 Years Old
Chapter 11 – Lifelong Friends – 1960 – 13 Years Old
Chapter 12 – Time To Go
Chapter 13 – Basic Training
Chapter 14 – First Military Leave (Furlough)
Chapter 15 – Training for War
Chapter 16 – Countdown To Combat
Chapter 17 – Vietnam - My Introduction To Manhood
Chapter 18 – "Quan Cahn – Di Di Mau"
Chapter 19 – Brothers in Combat
Chapter 20 – Da Nang to Dak To
Chapter 21 – Return To Da Nang
Chapter 22 – The Khe Sahn Siege
Chapter 23 – Going Home
Chapter 24 – Dover AFB
Chapter 25 – Korea
Chapter 26 – McGuire AFB
Chapter 27 – The Pilot
Chapter 28 – My Friend Ken and Skydiving
Chapter 29 – Hickam AFB, Hawaii
Chapter 30 – Death By A Thousand Cuts
Chapter 31 – The Trial
Chapter 32 – Return to Hawaii
Chapter 33 – Stupid Is As Stupid Does
Chapter 34 – Edwards AFB
Chapter 35 – Double E-Ticket Ride
Chapter 36 – Blue Eyes
Chapter 37 – Wedding Bells and the Ex From Hell
Chapter 38 – Newly Weds
Chapter 39 – Air Force Officer Commissioning Program

Chapter 40 – Time To Move On
Chapter 41 – The Rocky Road to Chief Master Sergeant
Chapter 42 – Out Of My Comfort Zone
Chapter 43 – What the Hell Did I Get Myself Into?
Chapter 44 – Tides of Change
Chapter 45 – The Job Interview
Chapter 46 – Roy's Final Year
Chapter 47 – "Call 911 – I'm Having A Heart Attack!"
Chapter 48 – Third Job's A Charm
Chapter 49 – Celebrating and Honoring A Life Well-Lived
Chapter 50 – Betrayed
Chapter 51 – "Doctor. How Do You Fix a Broken Heart?"
Chapter 52 – Christmas at Five Guys
Chapter 53 – My Post-Traumatic-Stress Disorder (PTSD) Trigger
Chapter 54 – Does This Mean That I can Get a New Car?
Epilogue
Roy's Actual Defense Testimony From His Trial
The Veterans Administration Battle Every Veteran Endures
Never, Never Teach Them Everything You Know
In Memory of TSgt Robert (Bob) Leavitt 1948-1984
The Mooney Mite N4140 Warbird Final Ferry Flight
About the Author

ACKNOWLEDGEMENTS

This book is dedicated to the most important people in my life. My deceased wife of 32 years Zee, my current wife Vikie, my deceased son Wim who tragically left this world at the young age of 27, my grandchildren; Kali, Tyler, Carlie, and Edward and to the memory of my mother Gerry, my father Willy, and my brother Roy. A special acknowledgement goes out to my beautiful sister Jane who always inspired me as a wonderful devoted and loving mother to her children. Jane died in November 2018 after heroically battling many medical problems. To my brother Jim I want to say how proud I am of you for your indomitable spirit and strength to meet and exceed all the challenges and barriers that life put in your way.

I would like to thank my wife Vikie for supporting me in my efforts to write this book. It has been difficult for her to deal with a veteran suffering from PTSD and numerous Viet Nam service-related medical problems, but she loved and stood beside me all the way. Even though we have only been together six short years at the time of this writing, she never failed to encourage me to write.

Additionally, this is dedicated to all the wonderful people who made a significant difference in my life and were there when I needed them the most. Without their support, guidance, and unconditional love I would not have survived my often troubled but full life.

They include Marilyn (Penny Krepps) Brumbaugh who brought joy, love, support, and inspiration for me to be the best that I could be during my teenage years. Lt. Colonel George Prewitt and his beautiful wife Jane and phenomenal children Lori, Lisa, and Phillip. I cannot forget my colleague and devoted friend Alberto (Al) Capone who came through with financial assistance to support my son and me when I was destitute and did not have a pot to pee in.

To Jim and Nancy Thompson, Blain and Linda Sheppard who helped, encouraged, and kept my spirits up through my recovery from open heart and 360 radical back surgery. Jim never left my side and often fed me for three weeks while I recovered from the heart surgery; Blain for always watching my back in Viet Nam and continuing to do so today. You are 'my brother from another mother' Blain and I am eternally grateful for your friendship and love; Master Sergeant Mike Black who always inspired me to be a better leader and manager during my last four years in the Air Force.

Last, but certainly not least, Steve Fisher at NEC, and one of my dear friends who inspired me to develop, build and launch the NEC National Training Center in Texas. Without Steve's dogged and intense drive to obtain the financial resources to develop the training center and NEC's support for my training team led by Leigh Wolfer. Without my highly professional training team I would not have been successful in that endeavor. The advanced and modern technology Steve and I introduced, deployed, and maintained will give NEC the valuable edge it requires to increase its business worldwide.

With the trepidation that I am forgetting so many other great and influential people in my life, I apologize to all those great people who I have missed in this acknowledgement. You are not forgotten. You are always in my heart, thoughts and prayers and I dedicate this book to you as well as all the great people who have crossed my path, and whom I have had the honor and privilege to meet.

I want to thank my mother for her strength and surviving her terrible over 4-year incarceration in the World War II Japanese concentration camps only to bring me into this world. I want to thank my father for teaching me to never give up, to seek and obtain my life's goals with a sense of honor and backed by our good name and word. I also want to thank him for teaching me what not to do and how not to behave through his often-terrible examples. I thank God that I was wise enough in my early youth to be able to determine the difference between right and wrong and, more-often-than-not choose the correct paths to follow throughout my life.

PROLOGUE

This memoir, written in novel form, includes family pictures and exclusive historical photos. It brings transparency and truth to a complicated family history and will disparage past vicious rumors and attempts to rewrite the history of the Wetzel family.

The untimely brutal death of my father, Willy Wetzel, was 45 years ago but stories on the internet, written publications and an unauthorized movie continue to circulate concerning my family and the circumstances surrounding Dad's death. They are all based on personal opinions and speculation intended to glorify his death and aggrandize the writer's tales about a family of whom they have little factual knowledge.

This is the true story of our legal immigrant family. We had a price on our head, a dream in our hearts and a chance to come to America. We were Dutch-Indonesian colonists living in South East Asia until 1950 when we made a harrowing escape from Muslim rebel insurgents and fled back to Holland.

Our journey brought us from Holland to the United States in 1956 where my father, the family patriarch, built an American dynasty around a successful family business introducing mainstream America to a previously close kept secret of Indonesian style martial arts. As children my two younger brothers, my sister and I were trained and groomed by our father to become the first Poekoelan Tjimindie karate instructors in the United States. As Willy's oldest son it is my privilege to walk you down the unique tumultuous path through history and my family's footprint in it.

There were personal challenges and triumphs over a brutally dysfunctional family, undiagnosed dyslexia, typhoid fever, and the Vietnam war. My brothers and I came of age while serving in some of the bloodiest battles of the Viet Nam war. We all returned home with life altering physical and mental combat injuries which ultimately caused Roy's early death, Jim's and my ongoing battles with Agent Orange-related cancers and Post Traumatic Stress Disorder. Upon our return we were greeted by a family in crisis so intense that Roy was ultimately forced to brutally take our father's life in order to save his own life in self-defense and to protect his beloved daughter. This is a story of family love and forgiveness and as the Willy Wetzel's oldest son, this is my story beyond my father's death and my journey through the good and bad choices I made throughout my life.

Included at the end of this book are four bonus chapters:

1. An excerpt of the original transcript of Roy's murder trial.

2. I share my personal experience in dealing with the Veterans Administration (VA) to receive the medical and other benefits I earned with the goal to give other veterans hopes and directions on how to expedite their benefits awards.

3. A first-hand glimpse into the secret world of Poekoelan Tjmindie.

4. Another harrowing civilian airplane adventure.

CHAPTER 1 – THE REBELS ATTACK

The explosions and gunfire sent Dad catapulting from his bed. He looked out the window as armored insurgents and rebel vehicles entered the compound. Two soldiers and a young officer advanced quickly across our yard towards our front door. Dad grabbed the Samurai sword hanging on the wall and stood behind the door and waited.

I was sound asleep. Mom leaned in close to me and whispered anxiously "Wim, get up! Come with me!" Through my sleep crusted eyes, I looked up and saw Mom holding my two-year-old brother Roy tight to her breast and Dad standing with his back planted tightly against the wall, holding the sword that he had confiscated from the Japanese prison camp a few years before. His eyes darted from us to the door and back again and he gave us a hand signal to halt and then put his index finger up to his lips to silence us. He gingerly moved the curtain back to observe the three men approaching our house with guns drawn. They fell into a single file at our front door and the first Indonesian rebel banged on the door and roared "Buka Sekarang!" "Open up! NOW!" Dad shook his head at us and again held up a hand warning us to remain quiet.

When the rebel did not get a response, he kicked the door open and rushed in. When he crossed the threshold of our home Dad brought the sword down with both hands slicing through the man's neck and diagonally through his torso. His body separated and fell into two pieces causing the second soldier to stop abruptly. Dumbfounded by the sight of his comrade still twitching on the floor he made a quick about face knocking his commanding officer to the ground as he ran into the dark shadows of night. The stunned officer sat on the ground perplexed and confused by the spineless action of his fleeing subordinate. He spotted the bloody scene in the doorway, scrambled to his feet, and followed his cowardly companion.

Dad ran after them fearing they would brutalize other families in the compound, but once they disappeared from sight he retreated. Splattered with the dead rebel's blood and out of breath from the pursuit he charged back through our front door, stepping over the rebel's severed remains and slipping on the soldier's half clotted blood and entrails that were still releasing remnants of his last meal. Mom stood rigid with Roy in her arms while I clung to her leg burying my face in her robe.

"Wim!" Dad yelled "Rennen uit de terug deur. Nu!" "Run out the back door, NOW!" Confused and terrified I looked up at Mom for assurance. She nodded towards the door and kept her voice calm but stern trying not to alarm me. "Gaan Wim" "Go Wim."

Sensing the gravity of her tone I released my grasp and scurried toward the back door. At three years old I struggled to turn the knob and Mom followed me while still clutching Roy. She opened the door and pushed me outside into the night. "Go Wim! Get out!"

She put Roy down and pushed him out behind me. "Wim, take Roy's hand and go to the jungle path." Then she returned to snatch Jane from her crib and quickly followed us. We were all scantily dressed having abandoned every possession, we made a dash for a gap in the backyard fence and Dad followed us still brandishing the bloody sword. We made our way through the precut emergency escape jungle path. When we reached the Royal Dutch Army post there were armed guards and soldiers swarming everywhere like bees protecting a hive.

The following day we were packed onto trucks with hundreds of other European fugitives. The trucks were quickly surrounded by a swarm of armored tanks that escorted us to the seaport where the humming of ship engines could be heard before they came into view. When we approached the seaport, there was a huge fleet of gigantic ships giving off an acrid smell of exhaust from their diesel fuel. The thunderous roar of their great engines penetrated the air as they waited in the harbor prepared to carry out the mass evacuation of Europeans fleeing for their lives.

When we reached the port and disembarked from the trucks, we were met by armed soldiers who loaded us onto one of the ships like precious cargo. The Wetzel family along with hundreds of others had just escaped a planned and calculated massacre and were safely on our way to the Netherlands escorted by heavily armed British and Dutch naval vessels.

***

It was a grueling and tedious trip for all of us. Mom remained quiet during the days at sea. She tried to hide her fear but Roy and I could sense that she was worried and frightened. She held Jane close to her breast during the entire voyage and Roy and I huddled next to her in an attempt to calm our fears and hers. Fighting the flashbacks of being chained in the hold of the Japanese prison ships, Dad stayed on the deck, getting little sleep, chain smoking cigarettes, exchanging stories, and gathering information about the whereabouts of friends and fellow soldiers.

Dad and Wim on the Evacuation Ship's Deck

The ships were marginally equipped to transport Europeans out of harm's way. There were minimal supplies to sustain the huge number of passengers and there were no provisions for babies and children. With no milk or food available, seventy-five per cent of the infants died enroute to the Netherlands.

CHAPTER 2 – A MERCENARY SOLDIER'S LIFE

This story began in Germany in 1850. The Dutch occupied the East Indies (Indonesia) and my great-great grandfather was one of many soldiers recruited from Germany by the Indonesian Royal family to serve as a paid-mercenary soldier. Their job was to defend the Dutch colonists from the numerous rebel factions who were fighting for control of the coveted islands. My father, Willem (Willy) Johannes Christoffel Wetzel, was the fourth generation of Wetzels to become part of the Dutch colonialists living in Indonesia.

Holland gave my paternal grandparents charge over a substantial spice and rubber plantation along with a sizeable staff of servants and countless plantation workers, most of who were Chinese and Indian indentured servants working for little or no pay and held the lowest status in Indonesian culture. Besides running the plantation my paternal grandfather owned a successful storage and export business that distributed the plantation's products worldwide.

On most plantations, the servants worked under deplorable cruel and inhumane conditions but under my grandmother's watch they were treated with respect and dignity. In appreciation of their loyalty and hard work she often threw them festive parties and was esteemed for her generosity and compassion throughout the community

For Dad, life was not perfect growing up in a world of privilege. He endured his father's tyrannical episodes of explosive anger and cycle of physical and mental abuse prompting my grandmother to be very protective of Dad and creating a strong bond of love between them.

My Paternal Grandparents Before the War

A Master of Poekoelan Tjmindie (the Indonesian style of Kung-Fu) lived near the plantation and mentored and taught Dad the closely guarded secret skills and mysteries of this style of Kung-Fu when Dad was only ten years old. Studying under this master he achieved the rank of 9th degree and never revealed his knowledge of martial arts to anyone. In 1938 when he was about to reach the ultimate rank of 10th degree or Master status, the abuse at home escalated and at seventeen Dad decided the only way out of his abusive situation was to join the Royal Dutch Army.

Using his martial arts expertise, he quickly became the sports and military discipline and strength instructor, or drill instructor (DI), for the Royal Dutch Army. He held this position for seventeen years and gained the respect of every soldier from new recruits to the highest-ranking officers.

In 1941 the Japanese invaded Indonesia and toppled the Dutch sovereignty over Indonesia turning the tide drastically. Thousands of Europeans, including dad were captured and taken prisoner by the Japanese. After being interned in a Prisoner of War (POW) camp in Japan for two years Dad and hundreds of other allied POWs became human slave cargo. Being herded onto three slave ships known as Hell ships, they were transported to Thailand and used as slaves for the growing Japanese empire.

They were packed into the sweltering ships' holds and fed rotted meat, fat scraps, and gruel made from spoiled rice, drinking their urine to stave off dehydration and wallowing in their own excrement. Over the course of their journey many emaciated corpses were tossed overboard like discarded garbage after dying from heat strokes, and routine beatings.

A few days into the voyage, allied bombers attacked the fleet forcing the slave ship crews to make risky maneuvers attempting to evade the bombers. The ships pitched and groaned in protest tossing the prisoners about like rag dolls.

The neighboring Hell ships sailing alongside Dad's came dangerously close, threatening a collision with his ship until finally the sister ships were hit by Allied aircraft bombs sending flying shrapnel in all directions and raining down on their vessel and slamming against their hull. The impact from the bombs splashing into the water transformed the surrounding sea into a tsunamic shockwave that dangerously listed their ship from side to side. Some men were crying and calling out for their mothers, some were vomiting, still others prayed and cried out to God.

The smell of smoke and burning flesh permeated their ship's hold as they listened powerlessly to men outside moaning in agony and screaming in terror while the surviving crew and prisoners jumped overboard to abandon the sinking ships. Prisoners from their neighboring ships were grabbing on to whatever floating debris they could find. Dad and his companions listened hopelessly and waited for their own floating coffin to capsize or be destroyed by a bomb. But instead, there was silence. The water continued to churn from the aftershock but the bombers had emptied their deadly loads and retreated.

Looking around the ship's hold in disbelief that they were still alive the men began to breathe easier but no one spoke. Their few minutes of silence was interrupted by a faint humming sound that grew into a loud roar as allied fighter planes flew over strafing and killing the surviving prisoners and enemy sailors bobbing in the water then the planes quickly abandoned the scene. Their floating Hell and human cargo was spared and investigations after the war found the pilots of the allied fighter planes were unaware of killing allied prisoners of war.

After many grueling days Dad and his fellow prisoners were relieved to find out they had reached their destination and would be freed from their stench filled floating coffin. Exhausted, hungry, and thirsty, they shuffled weakly down the gangplank as their emaciated bodies were poked and prodded by gun butts and bayonets.

They stepped onto land to join the other POW slaves who were selected to build the bridge over the River Kwai. Dad soon joined forces with some of the other prisoners who plotted to kill as many Japanese prison guards as possible. The missing remains of these Japanese soldiers were buried under several layers of freshly poured concrete and their captors never knew what happened to their missing comrades.

When Dad and the other slaves were no longer useful, they were relocated to POW camps scattered throughout southeast Asia. After almost two years the prisoners woke up one morning and noticed that the guards were milling around the camp and seemed to be indifferent to them. The daily beatings and torture ceased completely and the prisoners began to notice that the number of guards was dwindling until they were ultimately abandoned to their own survival devices. The guards were gone.

It was August 1945. The confused prisoners began to walk around the camp freely, scrounging for nonexistent food and supplies. Allied aircraft dropped leaflets announcing the end of the war and the Japanese had surrendered allowing the prisoners to go home to their families. The planes returned dropping food and supplies to sustain them until arrangements were made to evacuate them. Some of the prisoners gorged themselves with the plentiful food causing their painful death before they were able to taste freedom.

While waiting to be evacuated the men wandered around the prison yard and scavenged artifacts left behind by their captors. Dad found a Samurai sword that he recognized as belonging to one of the cruelest guards. It was distinctive because of the slightly bent blade and small chunk of metal missing from the blade near the handle. He made a promise to himself that if he ever met the guard that owned it, he would use it to kill him.

The movie Bridge on the River Kwai was technically and historically incorrect but while watching the movie with Dad the memories of his imprisonment flooded back into his consciousness and I watched him shed the only tears he ever shed in public.

After the war, the Dutch regained their foothold in Indonesia. But the Muslim rebels and separatists were becoming more aggressive in their quest for independence from Holland. Their violent acts were intensifying and they were brutally murdering Dutch colonists at an alarming rate.

After leaving the POW camp Dad returned to Jakarta as a career soldier and continued to serve in the Royal Dutch Army. Upon returning to his home, he received the news that while his mother, Erma, was hosting a celebration party for her servants, the rebels attacked their plantation home. She was brutally murdered and her body was cut into pieces and strewn throughout their plantation home as a warning for other Dutch colonists to leave the country. Over one hundred servants including men, women and children attending the party were slaughtered as well. My grandfather was away on business at the time of the massacre.

Dad's rage was inconsolable. He recruited several of his best fighting soldiers and went on a rampage. They hunted down the terrorists responsible for his mother's death, killed them, impaled their heads on bamboo poles and displayed them on stakes in front of their jungle-thatched homes.

CHAPTER 3 – MY ROOTS

I loved to hear my mother's stories about how my parents met. But it was not until we were adults that Mom told us how angry my grandfather was when he found out they had gotten married.

Mom and Dad (secret) Wedding Picture

Not long after my grandmother's brutal murder Dad stopped by a local Royal Dutch Air Force dance for a beer. He was an accomplished ballroom dancer and enjoyed the limelight of showing off his skills to the many friends who attended the event. His martial arts skills contributed to his agile and graceful dancing skills and the lady's loved dancing with him. Dad was a lady's man and he always had a roving eye for new conquests. As he sat at the bar during a musician's break, he scanned the room hoping he would see someone new.

While sitting at the bar Willy felt a tap on the shoulder. "Willy Wetzel, Hoe gaat het met je? How are you?" He immediately recognized the beautiful Dutch blond as Ina, whom he had dated before the war.

She hugged him and continued "Ik heb over je moeder gehoord. I heard about your mother. Ik vind het zo erg. I am so sorry."

"Hallo Ina dankjewel, ik doe het goed." Hello Ina thank you I am doing well. "Hoe gaat het met jou en je moeder? How are you and your mother?" Ina's mother was his mother's best friend.

"Ze is verdrietig." She is sad. "Ze mist Erma." She misses Erma.

"Willy, I want you to meet someone." Ina took him by the arm and guided him to a table in the corner.

Sitting alone at the table was the girl of his dreams, a strikingly beautiful red head smiling with every part of her face, enjoying the music, and watching the dancers glide across the floor.

Ina proceeded to introduce them. "Gerry, this is Willy Wetzel from the plantation that I was telling you about."

Willy smiled and nodded. "Gerry. Aangenaam kennis te maken. Gerry. Nice to meet you." Willy said with his typical mischievous sparkle in his eyes.

"Hallo Willy. Leuk je te ontmoeten. Ga alstublieft zitten " Hello Willy. Nice to meet you. Gerry motioned towards the empty chairs across from her. "Please join me, Willy. You too Ina."

"No thank you. I have to go. I promised Mother that I would be home early. You two have a good time and I will see you tomorrow Gerry." Then Ina turned away and dodged her way through the dancers and towards the exit door.

Willy sat down and turned his attention to Gerry. "Ina is a nice girl. Her family has been friends of my family for a long time." Willy said. "Ben je Nederland?" You are Dutch?

"Ja." Yes. Gerry said. "My parents came from Holland but I was born in Indonesia. My mother died when I was young. They came here because my father was a high-ranking policeman in Holland and was transferred here and promoted to Police Commissioner in Jakarta for many years."

Mom, Opa and Oma Nyland before the war.

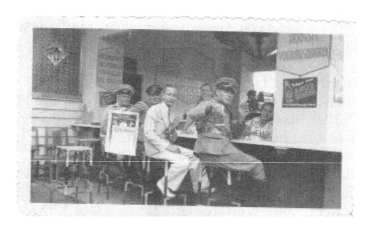

Opa – Far Right with his men.

Willy raised his eyebrows in surprise. "Your father is Herman Nyland?"

"Ja." Yes. "Do you know him?"

"Is there anyone that doesn't know him?" It was a statement in awe more than a question.

"So, you were here during the Japanese occupation?" Willy asked.

"Yes."

"I heard your father was badly injured and brutalized during the Japanese occupation because of his high position."

"You heard correctly. He will never be the same. They tortured him and broke his back and did not allow him to have medical care. They did not kill him because the Japanese needed a high-ranking Dutch official to maintain control of the population. His position as the regional police superintendent filled that requirement. Fortunately, he will be retiring soon and we will be moving back to Holland. He is looking forward to that. It has been awfully hard for him during this time of unrest as the rebels are getting harder to control. I have mixed feelings about moving to Holland. As unstable as it is, this is the only home I have ever known."

Willy said: "My Dad was spared an execution as well." He was overseer of the largest plantation and all of the storage warehouses in the region. Rubber, fruit, and all matter of critical supplies were stored there and the Japanese needed someone to manage and ship the supplies needed to support their homeland. He was treated with great respect and much differently than your father was."

"Where were you during the war Gerry?"

"That is a long story Willy."

Willy reached in his shirt pocket and took out a pack of cigarettes and offered one to Gerry. "I have time. Go on."

Gerry pulled a cigarette from the pack. "Dank u wel." Thank you.

Willy pulled out his lighter and lit her cigarette. Gerry inhaled and exhaled slowly using the gesture to gather her thoughts.

"There were seven of us. When my mother died, Dad's job took him away from home for weeks at a time. He married an Indonesian woman because he needed someone to take care of us. When the Japanese invaded Indonesia she did not want to be branded as a Dutch sympathizer so she abandoned us and married an Indonesian man even though she was still married to Dad. My older sister was captured and interned immediately. I was the oldest one left at home at fourteen and my brother Hank and I sold everything we had to buy food for all of us.

When we thought things could not get worse my stepmother turned us over to the Kenpeitai for the financial reward and assurance that she would not be interned."

"The bitch turned you in to the Japanese secret police. How did you survive?" Willy asked.

"Yes. And we were all interned for four and a half years."

"What did they do to you? I know they were very cruel to young girls."

"I was fortunate to have a nun befriend me and tell me to pretend I was not right in the head and then they would leave me alone. She was right but that did not stop the beatings, cruelty, starvation and hard work involved in serving them." Gerry suddenly grew quiet. "Willy, do you mind if we change the subject? I am not ready to talk about it yet.?"

"I understand. May I have this dance Gerry."

***

"Dad, you can't make me stop seeing Willy. I am an adult. I can make my own decisions."

"Gerry, you have got to stop seeing him."

"Why Dad?"

"Gerry, I had him investigated. Even though he comes from a wealthy and prominent family he is no good for you and he is definitely not good marriage material. He is a career soldier and a womanizer. The Muslim rebels have a price on his head for God's sake. His brutal retaliation of the rebels for butchering his mother put him in grave danger. The insurgents want his head and you would be in danger too."

"Dad, we will be fine."

"No, when I retire you must go back to Holland with me."

"I can't do that."

"Of course, you can Gerry!" He shouted in frustration.

"We are already married."

Herman's face reddened in anger. "What did you say?"

"Willy and I are already married Dad."

"Where do you intend to live? How can I protect you? What were you thinking?"

"We will live on the military compound. I will be safe there?"

Herman pounded his fist on the table. "I can't believe this." he roared. He took a deep breath to gain his composure. "You have been through so much and I wanted so much better for you. Can you let me at least provide your housing while I am still police commissioner? Willy will be gone a lot with his military duties and I want to make sure you are safe when he is gone."

"Naturlik (naturally) but I'll ask Willy. I would like that Dad, thank you."

My maternal Dutch grandfather (Opa) had access to whatever he desired as the Dutch police commissioner so until he retired and moved back to Holland, we remained heavily guarded and protected by his police. Mom and Dad lived in a beautiful home with servants and had access to anything they needed. Soon after their marriage I was born in 1947, my brother Roy was born in1948, and Jane came along in 1949.

Dad, Wim Wearing a Designer Dress and Mom

Our Bandung Home and Mom's Designer Clothing

Soon after Jane was born Opa retired and moved back to Holland. When Opa returned to Holland our family moved to the Royal Dutch Army compound located near Bandung.

During January 1950, the Netherlands officially transferred sovereignty over to Indonesia causing an explosive rebellion including an unsuccessful attempted coup by a group of Dutch sympathizers led by a former Dutch colonel Raymond Westerling. Complicating matters, the Islamists were also fighting to make Indonesia an Islamic state while rebels and insurgents were determined to purge all Dutch and European inhabitants living in the region.

The account of my family's escape and evacuation to Holland has been told by my parents in written and verbal accounts and confirmed by my aunts and uncles. At the time of our escape, I was three years old, my brother Roy was two, and my sister Jane was one. Any error in this account is not intentional but God's merciful gift of fading memories.

CHAPTER 4 – RETURN TO THE HOMELAND

Our escape and grueling voyage from Indonesia ended when our ship docked at the Port of Rotterdam, Holland. Mom and Dad were stunned by the extent of Holland's devastation. The Dutch were working diligently to reclaim and rebuild what the Nazis had destroyed, but Holland had lost her global financial domination and the economic dike kept springing leaks.

A layer of thick damp fog and the sulfur acidic smell of diesel exhaust fumes hovered over us from the never-ending parade of ship traffic moving in and out of the harbor. The port buzzed with a flurry of activity as reunited families were hugging and talking excitedly. Dock workers scurried around us barking orders to each other as mountains of luggage and bags of all shapes, colors and sizes were pitched carelessly onto the dock waiting for their owners to claim them.

Dad spotted my grandfather walking towards us and we followed him as he rushed up to shake Opa's (granddad's) hand and thank him for meeting us. Carrying Jane on her hip, Mom walked slowly down the gang plank towards her father who rushed to meet her. Giggling, Roy, and I watched as he clumsily maneuvered in a futile attempt to hug all of us at one time. Jane nestled her sleepy head in Mom's neck.

Calling our names one at a time Mom put her hand on our heads one at a time. "Wim, Roy, dit is je grootvader Herman" "Wim, Roy, this is my dad, your Opa Herman.".

Opa smiled and put his hand on Jane's back. "Laat me raden. Dit moet Jane zijn" "Let me guess: This must be Jane" Jane looked at Mom through eye lashes wet with tears and whimpered in protest "Ik wil naar huis." "I want to go home."

The adults all laughed but I saw no humor in Jane's pronouncement and silently agreed with her.

Attempting to draw Jane out of her shell Opa said "You are home. And I am glad that all of you are here and safe. We will be good friends."

Opa and I did become best friends. He was kind and understanding and my best memories of Holland are connected to the special times I spent with Opa. He was our connection and lifeline as we got settled in our new country and with six mouths to feed on Dad's military pay, he was there to take up the slack. Opa became our personal protector but he had no fondness for Dad. At the risk of wearing out a cliché, the feeling was mutual. At best they stayed at arm's length and tolerated each other for Mom's sake. When times were difficult and money or food was scarce or cold weather showed no mercy, Opa made sure we had extra coal to heat our home and food on the table.

In Holland Soon After Jimmy Was Born - 1951

After moving into the military housing compound our brother Jimmy arrived unannounced. At four and five-years-old, Roy and I assumed the position of men of the house when Dad was deployed. Living in the nearby town of Deventer, Opa was always available if we needed something.

While living in the island nation of Indonesia we enjoyed an abundance of fresh fruits, vegetables, succulent meats, and aromatic rice dishes. Now in Holland, bland starchy potatoes, turnips, and bits of flavorless meat adorned our table. In Indonesia we played under palm trees and thrived on sun warmed gentle breezes. Now we played under dreary skies and unforgiving winters.

Our light colorful tropical clothing was replaced with drab heavy bulky coats, scarves, mittens and, "Yes", "klompen" or wooden shoes. It took some time to adapt to the inflexible footwear but we grew accustomed to it over time. Wearing heavy socks and stuffing newspaper into our klompen provided insulation and extra warmth for walking in the snow. Snow would build up under our shoes as we walked and we would join in the neighborhood competition to see who could grow in greater height by walking on the snow in our klompen. Roy's driven competitive spirit usually meant that he won.

Roy and I were always on the lookout for ways to help. We quickly figured out we could add to our coal supply simply by gleaning lumps of coal that fell from the coal trucks on delivery days. We turned every chore into a sports event including who could collect the most coal and who found the biggest chunk of coal? Roy usually left me choking in his coal dust.

***

One winter morning the family awakened to find all the doors and windows completely blocked by snow. Dad broke a window and dug his way out to the top of the snow level. He led us out through the window and we dug our way back into the front door. We found out later that several people in the neighborhood were stranded in their homes and died from carbon monoxide poisoning when their coal-fired stove pipes became blocked by snow and ice.

By observing the best ice skaters, Dad taught himself to skate and was soon successfully competing with other good skaters and winning many local racing events. Lack of money never hindered Dad's ingenuity so after fashioning homemade ice skates for us, he taught us to skate. Roy and Dad's unspoken rivalry may have begun then. Roy had a raw determination to be the alpha male which compelled him to be better than Dad at everything.

I do not remember celebrating Christmas in Indonesia but In Holland the celebration is a major national and family event. The traditional Christmas tree in Holland is fashioned from branches cut from available local trees. The tree branch had to have a lot of small branches or a small tree with branches still attached would also suffice. We leaned the tree or tree branch against the corner of the living room and since it was already dead it required no water. We decorated it with homemade bulbs, popcorn, mementos, and real wax candles. The lit candles were clipped onto the branches making house fires common during the Christmas season.

Dutch Christmas Tree

In preparation for Sinterklaas's (the original Santa Claus) visit the children put their klompen (wooden shoes) on the front stoop with the anticipation that they would be filled with gifts the next morning. If you were good you got a present but if you were bad you received a lump of coal.

On the eve of December 5th, we put snacks and milk under the tree for Sinterklaas and his helpers who were ominous little people or midgets in black face, known as Black Peter. When Sinterklaas showed up in public, he brought his helpers. If children had been bad, the scary black faced helpers would throw them in a burlap bag and take them to Madrid, Spain to teach them how to be good. Their name, "Black Peter", came from the black faces they acquired from going down chimneys. In recent times the black face has been replaced by more festive colors in an attempt to be politically correct. I can only speculate that since none of the kids in our neighborhood were ever carried off to Madrid that we must have been particularly good children.

***

Our house was located near a small restaurant on our street. The owner took notice of how industrious Roy and I were in our efforts to provide food for our hungry family. He taught us to grow worms in used coffee grounds and other organic material that he would have otherwise discarded. We grew healthy and big earthworms and sold them to local fisherman for pennies, that we gave to mom. Despite the meager amounts we were proud of our contributions.

Assen, Holland Canal

There was a canal across the street from our home in Assen. Our interest was piqued as Roy and I watched people fish and asked the fishermen lots of questions. We could not afford fishing gear so we hand-lined for fish by collecting and re-using scrapped or snagged fishing line, hooks, and anchors on the canal bank. Fisherman would scavenge most of the expensive discarded lead and steel anchors so most of the time we had to resort to small rocks for anchors.

Our sister Jane had a vitamin deficiency that the doctors could not find a cure for. One day while Roy and I were collecting our worms to sell to a local fisherman we discovered Jane sitting next to the bait can with a mouth full of the slimy wiggling mud coated worms. Some of them were only partially in her mouth attempting to escape. We found it amusing and gave her more.

Hearing our muffled giggles, Mom came out to see what we were up to. Jane was still sitting on the ground shoveling handfuls of worms into her small mouth. Horrified and against Jane's will, Mom picked her up and forced her to spit them out and rushed her to a nearby doctor. The doctor told Mom that the worms would not hurt Jane. He explained how a Royal Society study found that earthworms contain significant amounts of calcium, similar to what you would get from cow's milk and cheese. Earthworms are also a source of iron, magnesium, potassium, phosphorus, and copper.

Jane continued to enjoy her diet of fishing worms and Roy and I were happy to support her habit. But we did become more sophisticated, cleaning the mud off the slimy delicacies before serving them to her. To everyone's amazement her vitamin deficiency was resolved, and Jane regained her health never relinquishing her habit until 1956 when the worm farm closed down and we moved to America.

***

My most harrowing experience occurred when I was seven years old. I attended grade school in a building that served as a Nazi headquarters during the war. The building was huge, surrounded by a high fence, barred windows and large boulders at its base. One day I had been detained after school for a minor infraction that I do not remember today.

The teacher put me in a large room and closed the door. After a while I remember going to the windows trying to see the street below. Pulling a desk close to the wall I climbed up and looked outside. I watched parents waiting for their younger children to be released to go home. The older children in my class, including Roy, walked home on their own.

I watched the teachers leaving for the day and banged on the windows to get someone's attention. I jumped off the desk and ran to the door and finding it still locked I banged on it finally collapsing on the floor in a heap. There was one thing left to do, I began to panic and cried out loud. "Helpen!" Help!

Returning to the desk I pounded on the heavy windows again with my shoe and leaned on the sill for a long time looking for someone to save me. It was almost dark when I spied Mom and Dad standing at the locked gate outside. I could tell that they were concerned and talking frantically to each other. But they walked away without glancing back.

Soon after that I watched a police car stop and a policeman getting out of his car. He walked slowly around the building appearing to be looking for something or someone. He finally got back into his car and disappeared into the night. In the darkness of the room, I finally fell asleep from sheer exhaustion, waking up occasionally to check out the window for a rescuer.

As the dawn hour awarded me with sunbeams streaming into the windows, I awakened to the sound of someone opening the door. When the cleaning lady opened the door, I jumped to my feet as she jumped back in shock. We both stood speechless gaping at each other.

"Wat doe jij hier?" What are you doing here?

"Slapen." Sleeping.

She picked me up, wrapped me in her arms and carried me downstairs to the office instructing me to sit down and assuring me everything would be alright. She called the school administrator and advised him about finding me. A few minutes later the unshaven headmaster, dressed in unkempt clothes and disheveled hair rushed through the door and pulled up a chair and faced me.

"Wat is er gebeurd zoon" What happened son?"

"Wat dee je daaboven?" What were you doing up there?

"Iedereen was naar je op zoek?" Everyone has been looking for you.

My face was flushed and drenched with tears and my hair was wet with nervous sweat. I recounted my tale with convulsive sobs. Then he called the police and my parents. A short time later Mom and Dad arrived by police car to take me home. I think I got the day off school that day.

***

The Refugee Relief Act of 1953 was an act of legislation passed by the 83rd United States Congress. It permitted the admission of immigrants from numerous European countries but the act was going to expire in 1956. The opportunity for a new beginning for his family was stronger than the lure of a secure military retirement. When he discovered that the Act was going to expire soon, Dad wasted no time in applying for immigration to the United States. Applying for immigration required us to have a sponsor in the United States who guaranteed that we would have a home, transportation, and a job upon our arrival.

The United Methodist Church in Rochester, Pennsylvania (PA) sponsored our family and committed to have a fully furnished home, car, and a job. After months of waiting anxiously, we received immigration approval to America. Dad had completed eighteen years of the twenty needed for army retirement when we left Holland. But moving to America for a better life was more important than staying in the army for two more years. Dad considered this opportunity as winning a lottery ticket and he was not about to give it up.

In order to purchase tickets on the next transport ship out of Rotterdam, Holland, Mom and Dad sold everything they had except for his children and his prized Samurai sword. When we departed Rotterdam on the SS Waterman on the eight-day sea voyage at the end of September 1956, the number one song on all the Dutch radio stations was "The Yellow Rose of Texas." It is still my favorite song.

CHAPTER 5 - VOYAGE TO AMERICA - AGE 9

Turning over our plates to examine them more closely she asked Mom "Waarom verkoop je alles mevrouw Wetzel?" Why are you selling everything Mrs. Wetzel?

"We verhuizen naar Amerika," We are moving to America. Mom told her.

"Wat geweldig." How wonderful. The lady said.

Roy and I watched the lady walk around the house and look at our furniture. She stopped to examine a lamp. She turned it over and put it back on the little table. "Hoeveel voor dit?" How much for this?

Someone knocked at the door and Mom asked him to come in. He walked around looking at everything in our house and spied Dad's sword. "Hoeveel voor het zwaard?" How much is the sword?

"Is dat het enige dat mijn man niet verkoopt?" That is the only thing my husband will not sell.

Strangers came in and out of our house all day giving Mom money and leaving with our furniture, dishes, pots, pans, and lamps. In a few days we were sitting on the floor to eat dinner from the last plates and slept on the floor because our beds were gone. Mom said we would have new ones when we got to America.

Dad's sword was wrapped securely in a blanket and placed at the bottom of a trunk that was then filled with our clothes, everything else was left behind. Roy and I only had one point of reference about ocean voyages and it was not a very pleasant one. But this time it appeared that we may be taking a change of clothes.

When we arrived at the dock a man came up to us and put a numbered tag on the trunk handle and disappeared along with our trunk. I sighed in despair. *So, we are not taking any clothes after all.* Lucky for me I wore my favorite shirt because we walked up the gang plank of the S.S. Waterman with nothing but the clothes on our backs.

Dad had a paper in his hand with the same number that was on the tag and told us to follow him. He stopped at a cabin door that had a number that matched the number on the paper. When he opened the door

Roy and I were amazed. There it was, our trunk was in the middle of the floor, and there were sleeping bunks with clean sheets, pillows and even a clean bathroom.

Suffering with a severe case of seasickness, Dad remained in bed in our cabin during the entire trip. His only relief was to lay in bed and to draw the curtain to lie in darkness. The rest of us soaked in the whole luxurious experience with full abandon.

Our native language was Dutch but we were also fluent in several Indonesian dialects. The ship's crew and the Indonesian kitchen help quickly adopted us because we could communicate with them in their unique and disparate dialects. The dining room staff lavished us with our favorite Indonesian dishes and huge bowls of oranges were available all the time. Oranges were an unfamiliar fruit to us and we binged on the delicious citrus globes until the acid gave us mouth ulcers. Roy and I explored every nook and cranny that we were permitted to enter and sometimes where we were not.

On the last day of the week-long voyage Dad had a miraculous recovery and abandoned the confines of our cabin. This was the day that he dreamed of and he wanted us to beat the crowd to the ship's railing. We had arrived in America and he was adamant that we be the first passengers to view the Statue of Liberty. When Lady Liberty came into view many of the immigrants cried openly and thanked their God for bringing them safely to America. We were lined up at the ship's rail and with great pride Dad announced, "We kunnen dit beeld vandaag zien omdat Amerikaanse soldaten hun leven riskeerden om ons te bevrijden uit Japanse gevangeniskampen. Vergeet nooit dat we dit land dank verschuldigd zijn." We are able to see this statue today because American soldiers risked their lives to free us from Japanese prison camps. Never forget that we owe this country a debt of gratitude.

***

We were immediately herded through the drawn-out immigration process to get the coveted green card. But first we were humiliated with a public medical evaluation in front of all the other immigrants. Folks that failed were taken to a private room for a more extensive evaluation. Failure to pass the second examination meant that they were denied entry and were scheduled to return to Holland on the same ship they had just disembarked.

There were a lot of heart-broken families who were forced to decide whether they would return to Holland with the sick family member or stay in America and let the ailing family member return to Europe alone. The men usually stayed behind with healthy family members, sending their wives back to Holland with the sick children because the men were more likely to get jobs.

Mom was given all our green cards and we discovered that the immigration officer had changed my name from Wim to Bill because he thought the name Wim was short for William. I started to tell the man that he was wrong but Mom quickly grabbed my hand and pulled me away.

"Mam, mijn naam is geen Bill." Mom, my name is not Bill I protested and pulled away to go back. "I want him to change it."

"Come on Wim. We will get it changed later."

The processing room was a huge open building with long lines and rows of baggage waiting for inspection. We were all getting very hungry and tired but we still had to wait for customs to clear our baggage. Some people's baggage was taken away and I prayed that they would not steal our trunk again. In my nine-year-old mind, everyone seemed to want our clothes.

When they finally allowed us to pick up our trunk a man came and grabbed it from Dad signaling us to follow him. Following the stranger out to the street Dad had to pay the man when he returned our trunk to us.

A genuinely nice lady from the Rochester, Pennsylvania First Methodist Church, named Mrs. Wilson met us at the curb. She spoke Dutch and asked to see our green cards. Mom handed her my card and I said "Dame, mijn naam is geen Bill." Lady, my name is not Bill. She ignored my protests and signed some papers so we could go with her.

Since we had a long wait before the train would take us to Beaver Valley, Pennsylvania she found a place for us to leave our trunk while she took us on a stroll through downtown New York City. The buildings were so tall that it hurt my neck to try to see the top of them. There were lots of men in suits and ties hurrying in every direction and ladies in high heel shoes and beautiful dresses impatiently rushed past us. There was a deafening roar as car horns blared, people yelled, and tires screeched. To my relief, Dad asked Mrs. Wilson to take us back to the train station to get something to eat.

In front of Grand Central Station street vendors were lined up offering all sorts of strange sandwiches, snacks, and drinks. We all chose hot dogs and sauerkraut as our first meal on American soil because it was the only food, we recognized similar to the Dutch version (hotdog en zuurkool).

Mrs. Wilson gifted us an envelope containing American currency to use in any way we wished for our train trip to our new home in Pennsylvania.

We boarded the train for our last leg to our new home in Rochester and out of sheer exhaustion we all collapsed into merciful sleep.

CHAPTER 6 - OUR FIRST AMERICAN HOME-AGE 9 AND 10

We were met by a large group of very friendly people from the First United Methodist Church led by our new Pastor Dr. Fisher. The large convoy drove to the church where a wonderful welcoming ceremony and dinner awaited us. It was an overwhelming event that scared us because we were not used to such attention. Mom and Dad were presented with several housewarming gifts, keys to our new home, keys to a Ford station wagon and numerous gifts were provided to the kids.

Upon arriving at our new home on First Street near the church in Rochester we discovered a fully stocked refrigerator, clothing, and a bonus gift of a thirteen-inch black and white television with an antenna wrapped with aluminum foil for better reception. Dr. Fisher gave Dad an envelope containing enough cash to keep us going until he received his first paycheck at the Westinghouse plant in Beaver.

Before leaving us alone in our new home Dr. Fisher introduced us to a man who worked at Westinghouse and told Dad that he was responsible for getting us settled into our new home. He was going to help Dad get his new driver's license, familiarize him with getting around town, to his new job, set up bank accounts and anything necessary to make our transition as smooth as possible. The man's name was Duke and would become one of our closest friends.

The TV was a big hit but there was only one channel - KDKA in Pittsburgh, the home of the first radio station established in America and except for the flickering static and vertical lines we had great reception. Dad made Roy and me take turns holding the antenna at various angles to get rid of the continuously scrolling vertical lines. We learned a lot of English from watching Popeye cartoons, Gunsmoke, Dragnet, and I Love Lucy.

The Wilsons ensured that all of our needs were met, including the financial support to sustain us through the first few weeks. There are no words to adequately tell someone with that much generosity, kindness and selflessness how appreciated they are. The entire Church congregation was an amazing example of walking the Christian walk.

***

We went to church every Sunday and my first experience in Sunday school was a painful one. A strange adult took my hand and led me to an age-appropriate Sunday school room. A small group of boys and girls were sitting around a table giggling and talking to each other in a language that I did not understand. When I walked into the room, silence filled the air and all eyes were on me.

The teacher put me on display in the front of the room and began talking to the class in a language I could not understand and when she finished her speech the class obediently murmured "Hello Bill." My name is not Bill. I was overcome with panic and dread. All I could hear was the sound of my heart pounding in my ears growing louder and faster and I imagined everyone in the room could hear it.

The teacher pointed me towards a chair at the end of the table and ten pairs of eyes followed me to my seat in gawking wonder. Dad was considered Eurasian because his German ancestors had married Indonesian women and I had inherited some of Dad's Asian features so most of the children were seeing an Asian for the first time. I sat forcing myself not to make eye contact with anyone in a desperate attempt to ignore their stares. One of the girls spoke to me but I could not understand her so I just shrugged and shook my head. She rolled her eyes at my rudeness then turned and whispered something to the girl next to her.

I considered bolting from the room and out of the building, but I knew Dad would punish me severely for embarrassing him. I sat there willing myself not to cry, but I could feel the tears forming in the corners of my eyes. The teacher smiled sympathetically and handed me a book. Again, I shook my head and shrugged unable to verbally communicate that I could not read English any more than I could speak it. She proudly opened the book to an inscription on the first page. I could only read the name that someone had filled in. It read: PRESENTED TO: Bill Wetzel.

***

Dad was grateful to be in America where he could control his future for the first time in his life. He proudly swept floors and cleaned bathrooms at the Westinghouse plant in Beaver.

Many of the employees at the plant were WWII combat veterans and they associated Dad's Asian features with the brutal Japanese enemy. Dad tried to ignore their cruel racial slurs such as chink, slope head and zipper head but one man of considerable bulk and a head taller than him constantly goaded him by bullying him on a grand scale. With his martial arts skills he could have easily taken the bully down but he remained composed. He quietly ignored the man's insults for weeks but Dad's indifference only fueled the man's venomous verbal attacks.

Dad understood more English than he could speak but he knew what the man was saying. His patience was wearing thin until one fateful day he dropped his broom, walking calmly towards the mocker, poked his finger in the man's chest and roared, "You dead!" He then made an about face, walked back to his broom, picked it up and continued sweeping, leaving the rest of the employees speechless and staring at him.

A few hours later there was commotion on the factory floor. People were scurrying about hurriedly and barking orders that Dad could not understand. Others were running towards a man lying on the factory floor. People were blocking his view so Dad could not see who the man was. Not wanting to get involved he went back to his sweeping. Sometime later he spied someone being taken away on a gurney. Curious to see who it was, he made his way closer to the scene. No one was more surprised than Dad. It was the bully. The aggressor had suffered a massive heart attack and dropped dead on the factory floor. Dad's mystique became a legend and he was never harassed at work again.

***

A few months after our arrival we experienced our first American Thanksgiving. We were not accustomed to eating meat except for a few thin slices of lunch meat on a piece of bread so none of us was prepared for this royal banquet. The church members lavished us with a huge roast turkey and more trimmings than anyone could ever ask for. We gorged ourselves on the rich, traditional Thanksgiving feast. But our gluttony came with a price.

We all had bloated bellies and formed a line at the bathroom door if we could make it that far. I did not. We called our friend Mrs. Wilson to find out if we could get some medicine. She came to our house immediately and being fearful that we may have food poisoning she loaded us all in the station wagon and took us to the hospital emergency room. The diagnosis was a serious case of overindulgence. We were given something to relieve our misery and sent on our way.

***

In Pennsylvania target shooting and hunting are immensely popular father and son activities. Dad was determined that Roy and I would be able to fit into the local American hunting culture so he bought us 22-caliber rifles, taught us gun safety, and took us to target practice regularly. Roy and I disappeared into the woods at every available opportunity to hunt for squirrels and rabbits, returning home hours later with conquests that we hoped to see on the dinner table. It was one more opportunity for us to have some friendly competition and this was the one category that we were well matched. We both became expert marksmen.

*****

Dad's stature was deceiving and at five-foot six inches he was lean, muscular, and amazingly strong and agile and as a martial arts expert, pity any person who might challenge his ability to defend himself. He usually took Roy and me with him to translate when he ran errands.

One winter night we drove into a full-service gas station and pulled up to the forward fuel pump. Since it was near closing time the station owner told Dad to go ahead and pump his own gas while he finished closing up. Dad removed the gas cap and inserted the fuel nozzle as a car pulled up behind us bumping against our rear bumper.

Roy and I watched out the car window as the scene unfolded. A huge hulking African American man well over six feet tall and seemingly more than double Dad's size opened his car door, jumped out and thundered "Get out of my way!" His expression turned more ominous when he realized Dad was Asian. More infuriated now, he bellowed "Get the Hell out of my way you Gook!" Dad shrugged his shoulders and pointed to his ear attempting to let the man know that he could not understand what he was saying.

The enraged man became bolder and he advanced towards Dad like a bulldozer. Dad dropped the gas nozzle and assumed his karate defensive stance for balance. As the man continued to advance, Dad did a flying sweeping round-house kick to the right side of the attacker's head. In a nanosecond the left side of the man's temple slammed into the fuel pump, his eye popped out of its socket and he slammed to the ground.

A local policeman monitoring traffic nearby witnessed the incident and called for an ambulance while the stunned station manager stood frozen and confused.

My English was only slightly better than Dad's but I understood well enough to translate the English back to Dutch for Dad. Between Roy and me, we explained to the policeman that Dad was concerned that the incident would get him deported but the officer assured us not to worry. He said Dad was clearly responding in self-defense. However, Dad did get a $15 fine for disturbing the peace.

***

Dad had a difficult time grasping the nuances of the English language. Some of what he was picking up came from what he heard from the blue-collar coworkers at Westinghouse. He was progressing slowly and he took every opportunity to practice his new English words and phrases.

He never missed a bible study and used the opportunity to be able to hear and speak English in the nonthreatening environment. One day not yet understanding that some phrases may be inappropriate, he was proud to make an important announcement to the class.

"I'll be right back; I have to go take a crap."

***

"Bill, come up front and let me introduce you to the class." It was my first day at school in America and I remained planted in my seat not understanding what the teacher wanted me to do. She came to my desk, held my hand, and walked me to the front of the room. I stood wide eyed, frightened, and confused as she announced "Class, this is Bill Wetzel and he has just arrived in America from Holland." My name is not Bill.

The group gawked at me curiously and the teacher grew impatient with my lack of social response and interaction. Realizing her efforts were futile she prompted me to return to my desk.

Having been taught never to turn my back on an adult when they were speaking to me, I walked backwards to my seat as she continued to speak. About half-way to my desk, I screamed out in pain. I had a sudden stabbing sensation in my buttocks and I turned to see what happened. A boy wearing a smug satisfied smile was holding up a bloodied pencil stub and blood was soaking my pants. The tip of the pencil had contacted the bone and broke off before he pulled it out.

Grabbing the malicious offender by the scruff of the neck the teacher dragged him to the front of the room while telling another student to get the school nurse. My humiliation was intensified when the nurse took me to her office, pulled down my pants and laid me on my stomach to examine the wound. She judged it to be beyond her skill to stop the bleeding or to remove the remnants of the pencil so she called the school doctor. He arrived quickly, removed the pencil remnant, and dressed the wound. No one notified my parents about the incident and I was too ashamed to tell them.

***

I could understand English but I was still afraid to speak it at school because when I tried the older kids called me dummy and stupid. I remained silent, kept my head down and avoided eye contact with everyone. I hated that everyone called me Bill instead of Wim. I hated that I looked different than my Caucasian school mates and I fantasized about ways that I could hide my face in school. Most of all I hated that they called me chink and gook. It was my first experience with racial discrimination and it affected me throughout my life.

I was a very passive and shy child but desperate to fit in. Often the boys in my class used my naive vulnerability to exploit me for their entertainment. One boy in my class, I will call Joe, pretended to be my friend, and help me with my English. He told me to ask the teacher about a word and in a secret huddle he helped me practice it with him for a few minutes. I was so excited to have a friend and I wanted to please him so I dutifully approached the teacher and asked her "What does f_ _k mean.?"

"Bill where did you hear that word?" I looked out at the class and proudly pointed to my new friend. She called my friend up to the front and told me to go back to my seat and she hurried him out of the room. She finally returned alone. I never did find out that day what the word meant.

While leaving for the day and walking past the principal's office I noticed his door was open. Joe was sitting alone slouched down in a chair in the corner of the office with his arms folded tight across his chest. The principal was sitting behind his desk talking to two adults facing him who I assumed were Joe's parents.

I continued out of the building to go home and was ambushed by Joe's buddies waiting to retaliate against me for being a snitch. They followed behind me most of the way home yelling derogatory Asian remarks and some other names that I did not understand.

***

I yearned for Opa and slept with his picture under my pillow to feel closer to him. I began suffering headaches, stomachaches, bowel problems and bed wetting issues, and became quiet and withdrawn. I refused to go to school and cried at the most trivial offenses and sometimes for no reason at all. I wanted to be with Opa so bad that Mom and Dad started a savings account to send me back to live with Opa in Holland.

Dad eventually sat me down and asked me to tell him what was going on. I poured out my story an uncontrolled flood of tears. "Can you show me where you got stabbed Wim?"

When I pulled down my pants and he gasped at the sight of the black lead pencil mark wound. His eyes darkened with anger. He pulled up my pants and hugged me. "I will resolve this Wim."

Dad had a motto that he instilled in us for as long as I can remember. If you don't ask, you don't get. He reached out to the school principal who brushed him off with an arrogant condescending attitude and an insulting offensive retort. "Boys will be boys."

Incensed by the principal's response he called our pastor who scheduled a meeting with the principal, the district superintendent, key teachers, the school nurse, and Dad. A long contentious meeting ensued but they finally came to a mutual agreement about what may neutralize the situation.

A school assembly was scheduled and the student body, their parents, and all the teachers were required to attend. With the aid of an interpreter, the principal asked our whole family to join him on the stage. He introduced us and giving a pep talk about respect for others and the virtues of having good manners. He added "Many of you know the Methodist Church and its parishioners, including some of you in the audience, supported the Wetzel family and welcomed them to the United States. I am pleased to invite everyone here today to come up and join me to meet the Wetzel family, shake their hands and welcome them to their new country and new home."

Everyone in attendance came on the stage and shook our parent's hands and many of the women hugged all the Wetzel children. But for me the cruel acts of bigotry had already caused irrevocable emotional damage and I retreated further into my protective shell. I reached a point so low that I no longer wanted to live. Bullying is one of the most painful and most vicious experiences anyone can imagine. When I hear about a young person that has taken her or his own life because of bullying I feel their burden as if it were mine.

***

After Thanksgiving there was a flurry of excitement building up for Christmas Day. School classrooms were decorated, and a massive Christmas tree illuminated the town square. Houses were draped with multicolor lights and front windows exhibited elaborate decorated trees. The store window displays were competing for everyone's attention and people were bustling everywhere filling their carts with gifts and enough food to feed our family for months. We had never experienced anything to compare to this and we were bursting with the anticipation of our first American Christmas. Mom and Dad had promised us that we would go buy our own tree and on Christmas day we would have lots of presents under it.

The day we planned to go find our special tree Dad came home from work with the news of a labor union strike and he had been summarily laid off. We were penniless. We all knew to not expect anything for Christmas. And the money they had been putting away for my return to Holland had to be used to sustain us until Dad or Mom could find work. Dad took every available job no matter how menial or how little it paid.

The week before Christmas a local tree farmer offered him $40 and his choice of any tree on the farm if Dad would hand-trim 4,000 Christmas trees. By the end of the week Dad's hands were raw, blistered and covered with cuts. Two ladies from the church brought us some decorations and lights for the tree and we strung some popcorn and made a few of our own decorations. On Christmas eve Mom and Dad put us all to bed and told us that next year would be a better Christmas. We knew there would be no gifts under that tree, but at least we had our first American Christmas tree.

We had no expectations when we woke up on Christmas morning and wandered into the living room one by one getting ready to watch our favorite morning TV show - Captain Kangaroo. None of us had bothered to look towards the tree. Dad and Mom were sitting on the couch flashing us a playful grin. I do not remember who noticed first but chaos ensued as we realized that there were wrapped gifts under the tree. Dad had bought us some clothes that we sorely needed but there were also some new children's books and toys that the church had sent. As we frantically tore open our gifts, I noticed bloody fingerprints on the wrapping paper. Dad had helped Mom wrap the gifts with his battered hands.

Dad was determined that we would celebrate a traditional Christmas in our first year in America. It was not the gifts under the tree that made that Christmas so special but the hope that it gave us for a better future in our newly adopted country. The gifts we received that special Christmas are all long forgotten but the love that came with those bloody fingerprints will be cherished forever.

I have had a lot of nice Christmases since then but Mom and Dad were wrong, there will never be a better Christmas.

CHAPTER 7 - PAPER BOY - MILK MAN – THIEF - 10 YEARS OLD

We never worried about what we were going to eat the next day; the question was always if we were going to eat the next day. Life was not a day at a time, it was a minute at a time. Where would Dad find the next odd job? Would we pay the rent on time? Should we pay for heating the house or buy groceries? We all wanted to pitch in where we could and even the kids were trying to think of ways to make some money.

There were not a lot of job opportunities for ten-year-old boys but my opportunity came out of thin air. The neighborhood paper boy wanted to give up part of his route and I jumped on it and soon discovered why he was willing to forfeit that part of his route. The territory was hilly and the Sunday edition of the Pittsburgh Times was heavy laden with advertisement inserts. I was smaller than most kids my age and the winter weather was unforgiving but the money was too good to pass up.

I had 40 customers, most of them with overdue accounts. I liked math and grasped the money concept quickly. The route manager was amazed with my success at collecting all of the overdue accounts and my diligence in keeping them current. I did not share with him that I was very motivated by six empty stomachs.

***

We moved to more affordable housing in the nearby town of New Brighton where Roy started second grade and I started third grade. The principal branded me as a slow learner because my English-speaking skills were weak and sent me back to second grade in the same class as Roy. Roy had a photographic memory and caught on to speaking English quickly. It was a devastating blow to my self-esteem. But with stubborn tenacity I approached the English skills challenge with a vengeance and became quite proficient and fluent.

As a desperate means to get attention I became a petty thief, stealing small amounts of money from Mom and Dad. My plan to gain attention surpassed my expectations but the punishment for getting caught well exceeded the seriousness of the crime. But I learned my lesson.

There was a dairy delivery company within walking distance of our home. During the summer Mom and Dad were hired to clean the spilled-spoiled milk accumulating on the delivery truck floors every night. Sometimes Dad recruited Roy and me to help them so they could get home and to bed earlier.

The summer heat created a putrid, gut wrenching foul odor. The stench was so bad we had to stop periodically to step outside to vomit - if we could make it that far. Mom and Dad meticulously cleaned those trucks as if our lives depended on it. And it did.

Recognizing that Mom and Dad had more potential than cleaning smelly trucks the owner of the milk trucks pulled some strings and arranged for both of my parents to be re-hired at Westinghouse with substantially better paying jobs.

***

Every Saturday night was family night when Dad roasted chestnuts, Mom made popcorn and we watched The Lawrence Welk Show on our new black and white TV. We rolled back the carpet and Dad and Mom would dance to the music on the television. They were graceful ballroom dancers and effortlessly floated around the living room, laughing, and gazing into each other's eyes as if no one else were in the room.

They often invited friends and neighbors over on Saturday to play Charades and we watched the adults act out their selected phrases, movie, and book titles. The titles became racier as the night wore on and Mom refused to participate sending us upstairs to bed. Sending us to bed just raised our youthful curiosity and we snuck out of bed and peeked through the stair railing at the top of the stairs. We learned a lot about what adults do when children are not around.

We had little thought of the trappings of financial success and always felt loved, safe, and secure. But success came and it was devastating.

CHAPTER 8 - THE BIRTH OF A KUNG FU DYNASTY IN AMERICA - 1958

Mom was practicing her English by reading the local newspaper when a headline caught her attention. "Willy, a local policeman is in the hospital. He was nearly beaten to death by a street thug last night. Don't they get training to defend themselves?"

"I don't know Gerry. Nobody knows karate in this community."

"You could teach them. Willy, they should be trained to defend themselves. Why don't you talk to the police department and volunteer to train them to defend themselves against these hoodlums?"

"I do not speak good English so no one would understand how much I could help."

"You could try. Take Wim with you and let him explain it to them."

Dad's interest was piqued and he pondered the idea for a long time. Finally, the desire to give back to the country that gave him so much won over his fear.

I called the police department to make an appointment with the New Brighton Chief of Police. My first challenge was convincing the police department to take an eleven-year-old seriously about making an appointment with the Chief to offer a training program for the police force on how to defend themselves. My persistence finally wore them down and after a lot of reluctant skepticism the Chief hesitantly agreed to see us.

Not confident in my own English skills we boldly walked into the police chief's office. He got up from his desk and introduced himself and politely shook dad's hand and then mine and returned to his desk chair and smiled. "Okay son, now what is this all about?"

I inhaled deeply and in one breath I blurted out the offer that Dad wanted me to translate for him. "Sir, my Mom read about the officer that was beaten to death. My Dad is an expert in Jujitsu and Karate and he is volunteering to teach your police officers for free. He would only need the police department to supply workout mats, punching and kicking bags, and a place to teach the classes.

The chief leaned over his desk with squinted eyes, furrowed brows and spoke. "Well Son." He paused and raised his eyes to the ceiling and bit his lower lip. He remained quiet for quite a while and the only sound was the ticking of the clock. I was sure he was going to throw us out of his office. My mind began to race. Will Dad be angry at me? Will he think it is my fault for not doing a good job translating? Will he punish me for not convincing the man?

I felt Dad nudge me on the shoulder to signal me to say more to him. My breath caught in my throat and the blood drained from my face. I swallowed hard took a deep breath and squeaked "Yes sir?"

Speaking slowly so that I would understand he continued "Ask your dad when he can start."

The classes were held at the New Brighton National Guard Armory (NGA) and the news spread quickly to every Beaver County police department and the Pennsylvania State Police in the Beaver Valley area. With no financial compensation, over the next three years Dad taught hundreds of police officers how to defend themselves. Some of them became instructors.

He earned the respect of the police officers in the tristate area, including Pennsylvania, Ohio, and West Virginia. One of the policemen was so grateful for Dad's mentoring and teaching program that he offered to help him get started opening his classes to the general public to generate some income for our family.

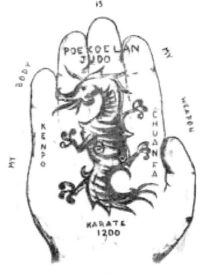

Our School Name and Logo

Dad

Roy

Roy and Jimmy

While still offering free lessons to police officers in the New Brighton National Guard Armory, he rented another building in Rochester. Advertising classes for $3 a month in the local newspapers brought a new audience through the school doors. If a potential student was unable to pay for the classes Dad waived the fee. He had been training Roy and me since we were eight and nine years old and by ten and eleven years of age, we were teaching adults to defend themselves. So much for child labor laws.

Classes were held on Saturdays and Sundays, but the school was open every night for workouts and practices. Roy and I were required to be there every night after school to provide additional training to anyone who needed it. Although Jim was not teaching yet, he was being groomed for the same fate. We slept at home, went to school, but lived at the Karate school.

The crux of martial arts is not in a person's strength or size but leverage, agility, and the ability to identify body pressure points. The opponent's momentum and weight are used against him or her. Some of the new adult students were skeptical about two scrawny pipsqueaks teaching them how to fight.

One anecdote that became a classic in our family was about an adult student who outweighed me by well over one hundred pounds. He had just begun the program and was clumsily practicing some basic moves. I noticed that he was not using proper body mechanics so I walked over to him and offered to give him some instructions. He looked down at me and began to laugh. "What do you think you can do little man? Tell your Dad that I want a grown-up instructor."

Roy was close by helping another student and noticed what was happening. He sauntered over with a wide sly grin "No – just attack him any way that you want and let's see what he can teach you." The student gave Roy an exaggerated eye roll and came at me attempting a choke hold. He was so much bigger than me that I simply grabbed his thumb and bent it backwards and let his momentum and weight carry him over my small body. He hit the mat with full force and while still holding his aching thumb I rolled over on top of him and gave him a simulated Karate chop across his throat.

***

By the age of fifteen I was a seasoned martial arts instructor and Dad often assigned me to teach the younger students and women in our school. It seems I had an affinity for working with those students the other instructors did not want to or choose to work with.

One day a mother walked in with her eleven-year-old boy that had been beaten up by some neighborhood bullies at school. She said, "Make him tough and make him strong!" It almost seemed as if she were expecting us to melt him down and pour him into a Superman mold.

His name was Bill Dobich and he appeared to roll from place to place rather than walk. I gave him the nickname of Butch. The new handle of "Butch" seemed to inspire him and we noticed a slight increase in his self-confidence immediately.

Butch was willing to stand up for himself but lacked the skills to do so. The first order of business was to slim him down and increase his physical endurance. No matter what I required of him to improve his fitness he always did more than asked. As I watched him build confidence, skill, and stamina it became obvious he would not have a problem with bullies much longer. Bill was well on his way to excellence and by the time I graduated from high school he was a champion martial artist.

CHAPTER 9 - FAMILY SKELETONS

Mom had a horrific start to married life for which she never recovered. She was well into her first pregnancy in September 1946 and was coerced by Dad to take a herbal jungle potion known to induce premature labor and then endured a painful delivery of my stillborn brother. Ten months later I was born on July 8, 1947 in Bandung, Indonesia.

Mom was of Dutch ancestry and Dad was of German stock. Over several generations the Wetzel men married Southeast Asian women. As a result, I inherited Dad's diluted Asian features with only a splash of Mom's western European characteristics. All my siblings had distinctive western European characteristics with a subtle hint of Asian.

Thirteen months after I was born, on August 9, 1948, my brother Roy came into the world. He was bright, charismatic, and athletic with a myriad of unique talents and skills. He had a photographic memory and an IQ that was off the charts. Roy had all the attributes that Dad wanted in a son but he continuously challenged Dad's authority, opinions and demands.

Then one year later on August 5, 1949 Jane was born. She was a refreshing ray of sunshine in our testosterone filled house. She blossomed into a beautiful girl and an artistic genius. She had the natural ability to memorize scenes around her and then replicate them in pencil art drawings. One day while Jane was washing dishes a colorful bird landed on the windowsill and quickly took flight again. She finished washing the dishes, picked up her artist pencils and drew it from memory. Of all her artistic treasures it is my favorite art piece. She was the apple of Dad's eye and his reason to smile. Her relationship with Dad and Mom was uncomplicated and loving. And even Roy and I treated her like a precious jewel. She grew up to be a graceful, selfless, unspoiled wife and mother that anyone would be proud of.

Soon after our escape to Holland Mom became pregnant with my youngest brother Jim. When Dad found out that we were going to have a new Wetzel in the family, he cold-bloodedly ordered Mom to drink some potion again to eliminate the problem. This time she refused to cower to his demands. Dad's response was "If you have this baby you will both suffer the consequences for the rest of your lives." This time Mom held her ground.

Jim was born in Holland on September 16, 1951 and throughout his life gave us nothing less than joy and love. He is every bit as bright as Roy and is a gentle and loving spirit with a passion for life. As a music prodigy, he started playing the piano at four years old and became an accomplished self-taught violinist as well as a drummer and guitarist. His favorite genre is heavy metal and he has a strong base of fans in Beaver Valley. Jim continues to successfully run the family Karate school and I could not be prouder of Jim for continuing that historic family legacy.

***

Financially, family life improved exponentially and a whole new world opened up for Mom. Her driver's license expanded her horizons and she was no longer at the mercy of others to drive her where and whenever she needed to go. She found new freedom in running errands, grocery, and clothes shopping for the family. She took us on picnics at Brady's Run Park, fishing and canoeing at local lakes and just spur of the moment trips around Beaver Valley.

Dad used his martial arts skills to build a thriving successful family business and formed strong networks with influential people throughout the community. He made great sacrifices for us in our early childhood. I saw him as a man of integrity, honor, courage, and strength. But over a short period of time something happened to change his entire demeanor and how he interacted with our family.

He began to have violent nightmares of his days in the bowels of the Japanese slave ships, the torture he witnessed and what he personally endured in the POW camps. He began to drink heavily, flew into violent impromptu drunken rages, and manipulated and controlled the family through violence and terror.

Despite strong ties to the Christian community, he became a dichotomy of good and evil attending and participating in meetings, ceremonies, and rituals of witchcraft and voodoo. He claimed to possess magic powers and was successful in brainwashing his friends to believe he could change their lives if they followed him. He memorized the bible and quoted whatever verse suited his needs at any moment or situation that required it.

Under his self-appointed tyrannical dictatorship, we became spit polished, well behaved, and respectful children. Maintaining the facade of a perfect father and family man, he became a highly regarded pillar of the community. The outside world saw us as the .9999 pure gold standard of the Great American Dream. But we were "pot-metal" sprayed with a thin layer of cheap gold paint and over time we became unstable, bent, cracked, shattered, and pitted, unable to be glued, soldered, or welded back together.

Jim's life consisted of Dad either denying his existence or loathing his presence by locking him in a closet for hours at a time. Jim suffered relentless verbal abuse and severe beatings that we were forced to watch. Dad got a macabre pleasure from requiring Jim to do bizarre things. He ordered Jim to wear his shoes on the wrong feet causing permanent painful malformation in the growth pattern of his bones and cartilage and leaving Jim with a painful tangible lifetime reminder of days he would rather forget. Jim never uttered the endearing term Dad and always refers to him as Willy.

Dad required nothing less than 85% grades on tests and school report cards. Arriving home from school one day with an 84% on my report card I fearfully anticipated the punishment I was about to receive at Dad's hands. When I walked into the house, I was shaken to the core to see the refrigerator toppled on its side with the door open. I found myself standing in in a puddle of melting ice, remnants of broken eggs dripping down the kitchen walls and food strewn about in every direction.

Dad came staggering in from the living room, shit-face drunk and ready for a fight. He spied the report card in my hand and snatched it away. I stood frozen holding my breath. His eyes darting down to my grades then back to me, then down at the offending report card again.

Finally, the silence was broken with a deafening roar "Get your brothers and go up to your room NOW!" I darted up the stairs struck with terror and dread and warned Roy and Jim about the upcoming doom. We lined up at attention and waited for Dad to come in.

He barged through the bedroom door dragging Duke, our beloved border collie by his choke collar and chain. Duke was twitching and jerking convulsively trying to escape the painful choke hold with his front paws off the floor and his back paws barely touching the floor. Dad's voice bellowed over Duke's shrill squeals of pain. "I warned you about coming home with bad grades and now you will suffer the consequences when you do!"

We watched in terror as we stood at attention forcing ourselves not to show emotion or react as he dragged Duke to the steam heater under our bedroom window and tied the leash to it. He raised the window and hurled the screaming dog out, leaving him to dangle from the second story window wildly contorting and gagging. When Duke gave up the struggle and stopped moving Dad dragged his lifeless body back into the bedroom and dropped him on the floor in front of us. While ruthlessly kicking Duke several times his lifeless body heaved and began showing signs of life.

"This is what I can do to each one of you. Do not forget it and never bring failing grades home again!" With that proclamation, he walked out of the room slamming the bedroom door behind him as we stood staring after him, paralyzed with fear.

By the time Dad was recalled to work at the Westinghouse plant, the Karate school was financially successful and he had become a highly respected member of the community and by law enforcement. He could not wait to return to his job to receive the admiration of his fellow employees and gloat over his new financial and public community status. Several of his Westinghouse peers were now his students and they let everyone know how proficient Dad was as a karate instructor and businessman. Westinghouse management received that message and Dad rapidly moved up the management ladder.

He became a division manager overseeing 250 women and a small number of men. Noticing the women were charmed by his European accent he began to exaggerate it while spinning anecdotes about his war experiences and details about his hand-to-hand combat. His erotic prowess and exotic mystique attracted lonely and vulnerable women to him like bees to honey.

Since Mom was also employed at the same plant, she was made aware through the rumor grapevine of every encounter and illicit interlude Dad had. Dad saw nothing unusual about his decision to take advantage of his many sexual opportunities. From his selfish self-aggrandizing perspective, he believed Mom had no reason to protest his infidelity. He was the perfect husband and father who provided a roof over our heads and food on the table.

To keep track of Mom he made me keep a written record of the odometer mileage on our car whenever Mom left the house and again when she returned. I hated doing it because I knew it was wrong but my options were limited. I had to decide to betray my loyalty to Mom or accept the no holds barred wrath of Dad if I did not comply. Every day Dad checked the mileage log and if the mileage even minutely exceeded what he had allotted for her he would interrogate Mom about her whereabouts that day. The verbal abuse for the wrong answers escalated to physical abuse.

***

Together Mom and Dad built a financially successful business but the price tag for that success resulted in the total destruction of their sixteen-year marriage.

Dad often made it clear he wanted to kill us all and we understood it was not an idle threat. His increasing violence was a constant reminder that we were all in genuine danger of losing our lives. My brothers and I were beaten for the slightest infractions but Jim was abused relentlessly simply because he existed. Jane was spared the physical abuse but the emotional and mental abuse permanently broke her spirit and took a tremendous toll on her sensitive nature. She became increasingly withdrawn as she was forced to watch Dad's brutality against Mom and her brothers.

None of us ever shed a tear or screamed out in pain during our own beatings but our eyes were flooded with tears as we stood by helplessly watching him inflict pain on whoever he had chosen to victimize at that moment. Attempting to protect us, sometimes Mom would stand between us and Dad and silently endure the violent beatings that were meant for us. She braved his wrath and infidelity while working full time, taking care of the house, and tending to the family,

Through the eyes of the students and instructors at the karate school Dad's persona was faultless. He continued to be enchanting, charming, and charismatic. Omniscient to his students and a pillar of the community, he relished every minute of the spotlight. His best students became instructors and he began to stay at the school every spare moment. He was running a successful business, having affairs, and holding down a full-time job. At home we enjoyed the peace that we were afforded by his absence.

CHAPTER 10 - STRANGER ON THE COUCH – 1959 – 12 YEARS OLD

It was a Sunday afternoon. I was about eleven years old and just returning from a weekend camping trip with my neighbor friend and his parents. They dropped me off at my house and I could hardly contain my excitement to tell Mom about my fun weekend. Sweaty, tired, and lugging my bag of dirty clothes I sprinted up the sidewalk, flung the door open and charged into the house. I stopped abruptly dropping my bag on the floor. My breath caught in my throat as I stood frozen in place with my mouth agape staring at the stranger on the couch. I gingerly crept towards her but she never looked up. Burying her face in her hands all I could see was her tangled red mane matted with blood and her shoulders convulsing up and down keeping rhythm with her breath catching sobs.

"Mom?"

She dropped her hands from her face and snapped her head up with a start. I held back the vomit forming in the back of my throat as I surveyed her battered face, bleeding nose and the disfigured purple flesh preventing her from fully opening her eyes. She looked at me confused and struggled to focus, then slowly turned her head away in shame but she failed to hide the bruises swelling up on her arms. I wanted to hug her but I was afraid it would cause her more pain.

"What happened Mom?"

Refusing to look at me she whispered under her breath.

"Your dad got mad at me. It will be okay Wim."

Jane, Roy, and Jim came bouncing in from playing outside anticipating one of Mom's special Sunday dinners. We had all witnessed this before but never this severe. We huddled on the floor at her feet, and tearfully put our heads on her lap wishing we could ease her pain. Mom could no longer hide the truth from us and finally told us what happened. Dad was having an affair with a student from the school who also worked at the plant and Mom confronted him. His response was self-explanatory and if we were home, he would have included us in his rampage, just to teach Mom a lesson.

The next day after Dad left for work, Mom told us to get dressed and follow her. We walked a mile to the Justice of the Peace (JP) office that was located directly across the street from the New Brighton National Guard Armory where we had our Karate School. Sporting her battered, disfigured swollen face, blackened eyes, crooked broken nose and the four of us in tow, she limped into the JP's office.

He sat at his desk absorbed in the work before him. Hearing the door open he glanced up from his work and over his reading glasses with a ready smile. As soon as his eyes met Mom's he pulled off his glasses and dropped them on the desk. His friendly smile turned into a slack jawed wide-eyed serious questioning stare. He started to say something but the words would not come out. He did not verbalize it but his expression said it all. "What the Hell happened to you?" Gaining his composure, he politely asked, "Can I help you with something?"

We all began talking at once but Mom put her hand up motioning for us to let her talk. When she introduced herself as Mrs. Willy Wetzel, there was a hint of recognition on his face that Mom ignored because most people in the community knew our family name. Without explaining the details of what happened she pressed on through painful swollen lips. "What do I need to do to get a restraining order against my husband?"

"He did that to you?" he asked.

"Yes, he did." Mom answered.

"Well! What did you do to deserve to get the beating Mrs. Wetzel?" the JP responded.

Left speechless, Mom started to cry uncontrollably as we gathered close to her like baby chicks to a mother hen and began crying along with her. It was obvious that the JP was one of Dad's friends or an admirer. In a soft condescending voice and a mocking sympathetic smile, he gave Mom some final advice.

"Mrs. Wetzel, I have work to do here so I suggest you leave my office, go home and behave yourself.

***

Mom eventually filed for divorce and we moved from our middle-class home into a low rent housing project called Van Buren Homes. The residents of our specific area of the "Homes" on L Street were considered to be the lowest socioeconomic inhabitants of the entire area. It had a mixed minority of Italians, Irish, African Americans and now Dutch/Asians. We all shared a common bond that transcended bigotry and hate – we were all poor.

Mom's salary at Westinghouse was barely enough to sustain the five of us but we were squeaking by. It was an era when society dictated that women should be home raising their children instead of denying a man a job. Dad was in the good old boy world of management, where he was admired, well-liked and respected. His management status gave him a lot of latitude for hiring and firing. In an act of revenge against Mom for filing for a divorce, he used his influence to have her fired.

The lost income brought us down to subsisting on welfare and government food surplus which consisted of Velveeta cheese and powdered milk. We were all lactose intolerant, narrowing down our options to peanut butter and jelly sandwiches. Dad did leave us two things; our 22 rifles and the skill to hunt with them. The woods behind the hood occasionally provided rabbit or squirrel meat. Since it was Mom's decision to end the marriage, Dad felt he had no obligation to pay child support. Mom did not press the issue because the brutal retaliation just was not worth it.

He worked the evening shift and every night after he left work at eleven P.M. he would walk into our house at will for the sole purpose of striking terror with any manner of verbal abuse, including continuing threats to kill us all.

One day I decided that I was not going to allow him to terrorize us any longer. I was going to kill him. So, one night with my rifle pointed out the second-floor window towards where he always parked, I waited for him at my bedroom window ready to pull the trigger as soon as he got out of the car. I waited for two hours. He never showed up that night and I fell asleep with the rifle beside me. Like so many instances in my life God was watching over me saving me from myself.

Dad soon remarried and lost interest in his late-night visits. He and his new bride moved into a nice home across town, bought a white Corvette to show off their financial status while enjoying the lucrative comforts of two incomes and the profits from two extraordinarily successful Karate schools.

***

One of my most trusted friends in the hood was an Afro-American - Adolph Ellis. He was a star player for the Beaver Area Senior High School Bobcats and had a bright future playing professional football. His eyes were set towards becoming the Pittsburgh Steeler Fullback and anyone who saw him play was sure he would make it.

Our friendship transcended race, color, and creed. It was a tough neighborhood and the boys were always in competition for the alpha male position. But one day it got out of hand.

Normally Adolph was not a scrapper but one of the neighborhood teenage bullies made a mistake of referring to Adolph by the "N" word. Every kid in the neighborhood watched in shock as Adolph knocked him down, sat on his chest and pissed in his face. I would say that made him "Alpha" Adolph.

Our Irish neighbors, the Keenens, had a lasting influence on our lives. Mrs. Keenen was a gifted musician and taught Jim and Roy how to play several instruments including the piano and guitar. Her sons, Dave, and Shawn became my life-long friends and Shawn introduced Roy and me to scouting. We joined the Boy Scouts and went on to become Explorers. Our Scoutmaster, Mr. George Wildman, and his wife offered us a safe haven whenever life became unbearable at home.

I am not a confrontational person and I was literally sickened by the situation that Dad had put us in. I responded by becoming withdrawn and quiet. Roy and Jim were more outgoing and animated and I became an easy target for them acting out their anger about our circumstances. It became a personal challenge for them to try to call me out through intimidation.

It began as teasing but it soon escalated into cruel taunting about my unruly jet-black hair and calling me Hitler. My protruding and obviously visible cow lick invited another nickname "Alfalfa" of the Little Rascals television and movie fame. When I did not respond to their insults, they ramped up their rhetoric and became more ruthless and wounding. Mom was still feeling betrayed by my forced spying on her by tracking her mileage. She began to join in, saying that I was just like my dad, looked and sounded like him and that I should probably move in with him. Even saying." Sometimes I wish you were dead!"

All I could do was cry which gave them more ammunition, leaving me no outlet for my pain and no way to defend myself. They read my silence as confirmation that I had betrayed them and they took my lack of response as a sign that I must be siding with Dad. My inability to be able to communicate my hurt or explain my feelings created an inconsolable wedge in our relationship.

CHAPTER 11 - LIFELONG FRIENDS – 1960 - 13 YEARS OLD

We all eventually mastered the English language but the word "love" was not in the Wetzel family vocabulary. We became separate anchorless islands, floating in an angry sea of grief, pain, and frustration. Our lives were as empty as Mom's check book. I volleyed back and forth from Mom's place and back to Dad's. At barely twelve years old, I did not care if I made it to thirteen.

The divorce agreement included a clause that the children had the option to choose to split their time living with each parent for six months at a time. At the time none of us wanted to take the judge up on that choice. But after continuous badgering from my siblings and Mom I walked the mile to Dad's front door in tears and he opened it without question. My stepmother, Peggy, showed me to my new room and consoled my emotional wounds and broken spirit.

Life was so peaceful that I began to let my emotional walls come down. I felt loved. I was doing better in school and more relaxed. I thought things could not get better, then one day I came home from school and walked into my bedroom and was greeted by the most beautiful German Shepherd I have ever seen. He was as glad to see me as I was to see him.

His name was King. He was a retired K-nine police dog that a karate student had given to Dad and he gave him to me. I was euphoric on two levels. Dad had made the beautiful gesture of love and King was instantly my best friend. We bonded at first sight. Every day when I came home from school, he was waiting at the door his entire body gyrating with excitement and uncontrolled sloppy kisses. His tail thumped against every piece of furniture in his path as he followed me to my room. He never left my side and slept at the foot of my bed. Every morning Dad would tap on the door before he entered to wake me up for school.

One fall school day after turning thirteen I was late getting on the school bus to go home. All the seats were taken except one next to this absolutely gorgeous twelve-year-old girl; Penny Krepps. My insecurity prevented me from asking her if I could sit in that seat. She noticed me eyeing the empty seat and flashed a hospitable smile.

"This seat isn't saved. You can sit here." she said.

That seat had my name on it for the rest of the school year. We developed a kinship as we talked, laughed, and shared stories about teachers and classmates. Penny lived only two blocks from Dad's which meant we could be together going home from school every day.

She never pried into my dark family life or made fun of my unruly hair and did not notice or just did not care that I was part Asian. Except for a few scouting friends it was the first time I had a friend that I could trust to be myself with.

Things were stable living with Dad and by meeting Penny I had found a "happy place". She was the first person to ever utter "I love you." to me. She was the first girl I ever kissed and who recognized my birthday as a special day to celebrate. I had to be at the karate school on Sunday afternoons and she started taking Karate classes so we could spend more time together. Dad and my stepmother Peggy recognized the positive impact she had on my state of mind and accepted her with open arms.

One morning Dad opened my bedroom door to wake me up for school without his usual warning knock and King did what he was trained to do - protect his master. Dad slammed the door closed to prevent being bitten and told me to put the leash on King. I walked King out of my room and handed the leash to Dad. I When I returned home from school my buddy was gone never to be seen again. I was devastated. and crawled back into my protective shell.

Dad began his own brand of mockery. "You are soft. No guts and all you can do is cry. You are a weakling like your mother. Why don't you go live with her?" And so, I did.

In a sense, there were two divorces in our family, my parent's divorce, and my whole family's divorce from me. Dad was using me as a go between with Mom and my siblings and both parents were manipulating me to get revenge on the other. They both considered me as a spy for the other one but all I wanted was a home. I was a stoic introvert living in a world of terribly angry extroverts and a living ping pong ball without a net to stop me from bouncing.

The turmoil of living with Mom was intensifying and my grades began to deteriorate in direct proportion to the chaos. By age fifteen, I spent so much time at Penny's house that I had become as much a part of her family as their beloved regal collie, Duke and Penny's sister, Charlene. Six years younger than Penny and me, Charlene was an uncomplicated, lovable, funny vivacious tomboy pest who made me laugh at every turn. She became as much my sister as she was Penny's. Charlene reveled in the fact I referred to her as Baby Sister.

Once again Dad asked me to move in with him. At Dad's request a friend of his hired me to work part-time in his lawn mower shop in Bridgewater. I walked three miles to get there or used my bike. My mechanical skills left a lot to be desired but I was eager to learn and I was excited to have a paying job. About a week after starting the job I was fired without any explanation.

Dad seemed smug about my job loss and hinted that he was responsible for my dismissal. He never told me why he had me fired and told me that I had to leave his house. The roller coaster ride of life with Mom and Dad was reaching an uncontrollable speed beyond my ability to hang on any longer.

I had no choice but to return to Mom's house. My siblings did not hide their disdain about me moving back in. The only acknowledgement they gave me was to raise the bar on their cruel rhetoric and bullying. This time there was no escape since Dad had closed the door to his home permanently.

The cacophony of overwhelming mixed emotions sent me into a deep depression and suicide began to cross my mind all too often. My moodiness turned most of my friends away but Penny stayed the course. She was not just my girlfriend; she was my best friend through the good, bad, and ugly. I doubt that I would have survived my teenage years if it had not been for her unconditional caring and compassion. Meeting her was the life-altering turn of events that changed the course of my life.

***

Penny's mother, Mrs. Bryner, was the manager of the Beaver County Humane Society Shelter. The summer I moved back in with Mom. Mrs. Bryner offered me a job at the shelter cleaning the cages and feeding the animals. I could not start soon enough. My passion for the work was over the top. I loved animals and no one could ever have taken better care of them. I loved the job even though I started my days at 4:30AM Monday through Saturday.

When the new school year started, I began to experience fatigue, exhaustion, decreased appetite, significant weight loss and painful bowel issues that I assumed were just one of my routine flare ups.

One rare Sunday afternoon in early September I was too sick and weak to teach at the Karate school and Penny and I were watching television at her house. As I laid on the couch my body began a series of temperature changes going from chills to hot spells. I suddenly became very hungry, so Penny made me a bacon, lettuce, and tomato sandwich. I took one bite and my body became wracked with unending waves of nausea, painful vomiting, and unbearable cramping. Then the vomiting ended as quickly as it began.

It was a hot end of summer day but I again began to tremble with teeth chattering cold, vacillating back and forth from beads of perspiration rolling from my forehead into my eyes and back again to Penny piling blankets on me in an attempt to stop my convulsive shivering. She wanted to take me home but I refused to go. I never talked about my life at Mom's so she did not know the last thing I wanted to do was to go home to endure more of the incessant bullying.

Penny's mother walked in to find me lying on the couch covered with blankets and shaking uncontrollably. "What's the matter Wim?" She touched my forehead and said "You are burning up. I'm taking you home." By that time, I was too weak to argue.

Penny's mom drove me home and dropped me off. I opened the front door to find my siblings glued to their favorite Sunday TV program, Wonderful World of Disney. Mom was sitting at the kitchen table and barely glanced up.

"Where have you been? You missed supper again."

"Mom, I don't feel very good."

"Then go upstairs, take a bath and go to bed!"

I made it halfway up the stairs and fainted, tumbling back down to the first-floor hallway. I recovered and crawled up the stairs and fell into my bed. Asking for assistance would have been futile because they were all convinced that I was either exaggerating my plight or feigning illness to gain their attention.

I woke up Monday morning feeling worse and it was impossible to get my body to move from the bed. School was an escape and my mind wanted to go to school but my body refused to obey. Still convinced that I was exaggerating my plight Mom chastised me for not getting up and ready for school. When I did not respond she let out a sigh of frustration, closed the bedroom door and left the house. The last thing I remember was the front door closing and the sound of her car as it pulled away from the house. I lapsed in and out of consciousness the rest of that day.

Penny dropped by the house after school to bring me my homework and Mom met her at the door.

"Wim's upstairs in bed, still pretending to be sick."

"Mrs. Wetzel, I don't think he is pretending. He was really in bad shape at my house yesterday. I want to go up to see him." Without being invited in, Penny walked past my mother and ran up the stairs.

She knelt by the bed and asked, "How are you feeling?"

Not realizing how much time had passed, I was wandering what she was doing there when she should be in school.

"Not very well." I mumbled.

"I'm going to take your temperature." She left the room and came back with a thermometer and had to wake me up to put it in my mouth. Mom was now standing in the doorway watching the scene. The thermometer read 106. She thought it was a mistake and shook the mercury back down and took it again.

"My God! Look at this temperature and tell me again that he's pretending." Penny watched Mom's stunned expression as she looked at the thermometer then continued

"Mrs. Wetzel if you don't have a way to take him to the doctor, I will call my mother and ask her to take him."

Mom started to cry and hug me, but I was to hurt and angered by her previous indifference and in my delirium, I pushed her away. Penny saw first-hand why I hated going home every day.

Mom drove me to the doctor's office. He introduced himself as Tom Jones. In my hallucinatory state it occurred to me that Tom Jones was the current box office hit singer and I tried to make sense of why this famous singer was going to be my doctor. I began to laugh hysterically at the prospect a famous singer being my doctor before passing out.

My next recollection was opening my eyes seeing nurses and doctors hovering over me wearing masks and protective gowns. IV bottles were hanging from poles with tubes that attached to my arms, ice packs were being tucked under me and someone was wiping me down with cold cloths and rubbing alcohol in an unsuccessful attempt to reduce my 106.6 body temperature. I was then submerged in a tank filled with ice until the IV antibiotics and ice bath brought my body temperature down to a safe level. I remained in an isolation room in the intensive care unit for about thirty days.

The conclusion was that my immune system was compromised from being malnourished and not taking the proper precautions while feeding and handling my furry friends, I had contracted the first case of Typhoid Fever reported in Pennsylvania in eight years. Once Typhoid goes from the intestinal tract and into the cells of the organs, there is little chance for survival. I had come awfully close to that point and my prognosis was not good.

Everyone who entered my hospital room had to wear a protective mask and gown. The doctor exempted Penny from the precautions explaining that we had spent so much time together that if she were going to get it, she would already have it.

When I was no longer in critical condition Mom entered my room and I told her that I never wanted to see her again. She tried to make amends by visiting each day but I was so weak and emotionally devastated by her previous indifference that I did not care to ever see any of my family members again. As a juvenile I had no choice and after thirty days I was pronounced cured and sent home emaciated and weaker than when I went to the hospital.

Mom seemed hurt by my rejection but after returning home she made no effort to defend me or attempt to stop the cruel taunts and comments of my siblings. The paradox was that the toxicity of Typhoid gave me a thirty-day reprieve from the toxic situation at home. For thirty days in the hospital people cared for me and about me. I was in a safe place, away from the verbal abuse and shunning.

When I regained some strength, I made the decision to run away from home. Since I was still too weak to return to school, I waited for my brothers and sister to leave for the day. After Mom left for her job and I was certain no one was home, I crawled out of the second story bedroom window and climbed down the waterspout between the apartments in our building. Then I broke into the empty apartment next door and passed out. When I woke up, I walked the two miles to the Humane Society office to turn myself in.

Gasping for breath from the ordeal I walked into Mrs. Bryner's office and almost fell at her feet. She looked at me without a hint of recognition. Her first response was irritation that a stranger would rudely barge into her private office unannounced. Then she realized who I was and her expression turned to panic. She had not seen me since the Sunday when she dropped me off at my house and now, I was a walking skeleton with sunken dull eyes and clothes two sizes too big.

"Wim?"

I stood in front of her defiantly and blurted out; "I am turning myself into the Humane Society and am never going home again."

I continued to explain what had prompted my decision and asked her if I could just live there and sleep on the cot that was in the office or in one of the kennels.

Her response was "Wim, I promise no one will ever hurt you again."

She put me down on the cot, covered me with a blanket, grabbed her purse and keys and told me to stay put and wait for her return. I was too weak to protest or ask questions.

The Humane Society was established for the prevention of cruelty to children, elderly, and animals. Mrs. Bryner was a sworn county officer of the Humane Society and if she had proof of abuse, she had the authority to have perpetrators arrested and jailed. I had seen her use this power in the past and now she was more than ready to do so on my behalf.

She met with Dad and explained to him where I was and why. She told him if he did not resolve this problem, she would take legal action against him and my mother to remove me to foster care. Dad had no doubt she had the authority to do so.

No one ever dared to stand up to Dad like she did that day and whether it was fear of losing face in the community or fear of going to jail, he admitted his contributions to the situation and promised to take me in and care for my needs. He committed to never mistreating me again and was good to his word. I moved back in with him and my stepmother. Mrs. Bryner's crusade to resolve my familial problems more than likely saved my life.

Peggy was kind and hospitable and made sure that I had a good breakfast every morning before school. Dad made every effort to be the mentor and teacher that he had been in days gone by. Each day I woke up in a peaceful nonthreatening house with no hostility or chaos and no longer dreaded coming home from school.

As good as it was, it was not perfect. I did not see Mom for the next two years and I still had bouts of depression and sadness over the loss of Mom and siblings. Maintaining my grades to meet Dad's standards was still a huge challenge but I managed the achievement. My high school guidance counselor was not helpful. She counseled me about my collegiate and scholastic aptitude test scores being below average and I should not expect to be accepted to any college. Dad was never told about that conversation.

During those rough spots Penny was my unwavering friend. For five years while both of our family lives were drenched in turmoil, we stole every possible minute to just enjoy being kids together in the midst of an adult war zone.

But the summer between our junior and senior year Penny's mother was invited to be a keynote speaker at a National Humane Society conference. While at the conference she was offered a lucrative job offer in Port Jervis, New York and she saw it as an opportunity to escape an unhappy marriage. Penny, Charlene, and Mrs. Bryner moved 350 miles away to begin a new life.

Three of the most important people in my life were suddenly gone and the loss was overwhelming. A few days after they left, I reached an all-time emotional low and sat in my car for hours feeling a sense of loss and grief that was overpowering. I did not know it was possible to feel so hollow inside. I decided to travel to Port Jervis to visit Penny before my senior year began.

With Dad's permission and financial assistance, I drove nonstop on the longest road trip I had ever taken alone. Nothing was going to interfere with me seeing Penny again. I was shocked, enchanted and enthralled at how gorgeous and mature Penny had become in the short time that we had been apart. We had a wonderful week together but I knew in my heart that she had outgrown me and was forever going to be out of my reach.

Penny's Senior Yearbook Photograph

Later that fall in my senior year of high school, I received a letter from Penny telling me that she had met someone else and I should move on with my life. She had been my best friend, my anchor and compass for so many years. Moving on was not that easy and I never recovered from the loss of my dearest friend and first love. The rest of my senior year was spent just surviving long enough to get the Hell out of Pennsylvania and to never return.

CHAPTER 12 - TIME TO GO

I poured myself into finishing my last year of high school. Roy and I were senior instructors at the karate school on weeknights and weekends. One of our students, Dick Keating, owned the Rollerena in East Palestine, Ohio. He was having problems on Friday nights with some local high school football players coming into the Rollerena after the games and starting brawls and destroying property.

Dick asked Roy, me, and a few of the other senior instructors to help him by being bouncers on Friday nights. Our mission was a success and Dick was incredibly happy with the results, but the football players were not. The perpetrators had remained unchallenged for a long time and the Wetzel brothers treaded on their long-held territory.

***

I had been preparing for many years to stand before a judge to proudly take the oath of citizenship to the country that I loved. Along with several other legal immigrants I fulfilled my dream by taking the final oral exam and answering all the oral exam questions perfectly. With tears on my face and pride in my heart I swore the Oath of Allegiance as a citizen of the United States of America. It was the proudest day of my life but no one in my family attended. My Scoutmaster, mentor and friend, Mr. George Wildman, was my witness and sponsor for the ceremonies.

March 15, 1966 my friend and fellow scout Larry Welsh and I signed up for the Air Force delayed enlistment program, also referred to as the Buddy Enlistment Program. The recruiter assured us that we would be stationed together after Basic Training. I had not yet received my ID card and the recruiter requested proof of citizenship. My only proof was my citizenship certificate and I handed it over to him and never saw it again.

***

By my late teens Dad and I developed a bond where he began confiding in me about the conflicts he was having with Roy about the schools' management. Dad used an old school business approach. He believed through the networking efforts of his students the school would blossom without any formal marketing. Roy saw the merits of professional marketing and planned advertising strategies. He was so engaged in his vision that he planned to pursue a business degree at the University of Pittsburgh to maximized the school's potential and run the school more efficiently. But Dad was not about to change so he formulated his own solution to their management differences.

Dad had a well thought out plan for my life that did not include the Air Force. He offered to pay my full tuition to Penn State University to become, what he had always dreamed of for himself, an Industrial Engineer. The offer came with a caveat. I would assume full control of managing the karate school while going to college full time then pay full college tuition for my two-year- old half-sister and one-year old half-brother when they came of age to go to college. From my perspective the offer was more akin to indentured servitude.

The war in Vietnam was heating up and it was inevitable that my brothers and I would end up going into combat in the same country where Dad had been a POW. He did not want any of us to face the torments of war still festering inside him like a gangrenous sore. Every healthy male of draft age was receiving a formal invitation for an all-expense paid trip to Vietnam but college students were automatically deferred. My decision to not accept his offer was a devastating blow to him. For the first time in his life someone denied him his wishes and the reality that it was his first-born son was devastating.

I had four good reasons for not taking Dad up on his offer.

First: Roy had a vision for the school, a flare for business and a passion for martial arts and I had no intention of interfering with Roy's dream. Dad was relentless in his determination to have me run the school instead of Roy. No matter how much I protested, I could not convince Roy that I had no aspirations to wrest control of the Willy Wetzel empire but regardless, Roy saw me as Dad's co-conspirator and was convinced that I had betrayed him. My world was shattered knowing he could not get past the hurt and the situation created a long-lasting rift in our relationship.

Second: I knew my high school grade point average met the minimum requirements for college admission. But a high school career counselor had closed that door by further lowering my self-esteem and squelching any self-confidence I may have had left.

Third: My sights were planted squarely on serving my adopted country by joining the Air Force and becoming a pilot. Nothing was going to get in my way.

The fourth and most important reason I did not like Dad's plan was I wanted to- NO! I had to get the Hell out of Dodge.

***

Like all high school graduates had done before us, Roy and I walked across the graduation stage and picked up our diplomas. But Roy did it in style. He walked across the stage and accepted his diploma with his graduation cap on the back of his head and his robe open to proudly display a noticeably short, tight, and colorful bathing suit. The audience responded with a mixture of raucous laughter and gasps of horror. That is my bro.

High School Senior Year-Book Graduation

Roy and I remained estranged for some time and our younger brother Jimmy suffered enormously from the family turmoil. My leaving meant Jim would be left holding the hot potato of the conflict between Dad and Roy as well as enduring the tension between Mom and Dad. When I left for the Air Force, Jim felt I betrayed and abandoned him. Cutting the chains from my family was the most painful and most freeing decision I ever made but it was time to go.

CHAPTER 13 - BASIC TRAINING

On June 10, 1966 Dad lost his death-grip on me. He drove me to the Greyhound bus stop in New Brighton in complete silence and without saying goodbye dropped me off and left me standing there alone and bewildered. I was unable to fulfill his dreams for me and I suffered deep remorse for it. Regardless, I donned my freedom-wings, flew out of my prison, and never looked back.

***

At the induction physical most of the recruits were there by special invitation from Uncle Sam and they were amazingly creative at trying to prove that they were unworthy of the honor. Some were dressed as women, others flirted with the medics. Still others could have won an Academy Award for their rendition of being mentally challenged, psychotic or anti-social. The cast of Maxwell Klinger look-a-likes would have been funny if it were not so disconcerting that these were the guys that might have our backs in a combat situation.

***

I passed every aspect of the physical until the very last part. Then the doctor ordered, "Stand straight up with both feet flat on the ground as if you are standing at attention."

I proudly obeyed as he watched my arches hug the floor. "You have flat feet young man. I cannot qualify you to enter the military. You must go home as a 4F." I had waited for this moment all of my life and now he is telling me to go home.

"No sir I am not flat footed! Please check again." He was probably thinking that I was the only one there that was not faking insanity.

"Are you questioning my professional judgment.?"

"No sir but I am not flat footed."

"Yup - you are flat-footed."

"Sir, may I speak to you in private?"

We entered a small, secluded cubicle. "Doctor I just became a citizen of the United States and I want to serve my country to repay it for what it has done for my family and me. Please do not write me up as being flat-footed and destroy all the dreams I have had to serve." I continued by explaining my family's story from the POW camps to our escape from Indonesia and our immigration to America.

He looked at me with a blank stare and seemed to be contemplating his decision. I was holding my breath knowing that my fate was in his hands. Finally, he answered "In that case let me check again. Stand at attention and curl your toes inward as if you are trying to pick something up from the floor with them." he said.

"Hmm…you are right. I misdiagnosed you and you are not flat-footed. Please get dressed and move on to the Oath of Enlistment room and induction ceremony."

As I was about to enter the room where the enlistment ceremony was being held the doctor pulled me aside. "Young man, I appreciate what you are doing but understand that there is a reason that men with flat feet do not serve in uniform. You will suffer greatly during the time you serve, and I want you to remember what happened here today." He was right. I experienced many instances of foot and leg pain but I never regretted the decision.

Taking the oath shoulder to shoulder, my enlistment buddy Larry and I were sworn in and given our written orders and airline tickets to Lackland Air Force Base (AFB) in Texas (TX) to begin basic training. We could not wait to start our new lives.

At nineteen, I was the senior citizen on the list of new recruits. That qualified me to be the official adult supervision and take the responsibility of keeping everyone together. When we arrived at the Pittsburgh International Airport, we were notified that due to a major outbreak of spinal meningitis at Lackland AFB we were being sent instead to basic training at Amarillo AFB located in the panhandle of Texas.

We were keyed up, eager and ready to go. For many of us this was our first commercial flight. We were captivated by the "Barbie Doll" perfect stewardesses and more experienced passengers dressed in their Sunday best and packing their best manners. We had an overnight layover in St. Louis, Missouri (MO) and time to waste while waiting for our final flight to Amarillo.

The majority of us had never been away from home without parental supervision and we acted accordingly. I kept everyone together as ordered and we hit the streets without realizing that we were not in a socially acceptable part of St. Louis. Wide-eyed and free from family bondage we had been let loose in a sea of burlesque houses and strip joints. The details of that adventure are best left to the imagination.

The next morning's flight to Amarillo went as would be expected for a gang of teenage hungover jetsetters. To enhance our experience, the flight was extremely turbulent and we all took full advantage of the complimentary air sick bags.

In 1966 Amarillo was a desolate, depressing, dreary Hell hole. When we stepped onto the tarmac, we eyed each other curiously to see if anyone else noticed that this was not what we were expecting. Someone in the group finally broke the spell. "Well guys, at least it can't get worse." But he was wrong. Vacation was over.

An Air Force bus took us to Amarillo AFB to be processed. We stepped off the courtesy bus to be greeted by a welcoming committee that had no training or experience in the nuances of the hospitality industry, AKA, Drill Instructors or DIs. But they did take great pleasure in preparing us for our future in the military.

I was caught off guard when during my processing I was asked again for proof of citizenship. My heart sank. I had given my only proof to the recruiter. They gave me a grace period to produce a new certificate before graduation. I contacted Mr. Wildman and asked him to help me obtain a duplicate citizenship document. His political connections made it possible for him to expedite the processing of a new certificate. After four agonizing weeks the new one arrived and this time it went into a bank safety deposit box.

We all had to self-identify our nationality. Of the choices available to me I selected "Asian/Pacific Islander" because I was born in Indonesia and my father was Asian/Caucasian and my mother was Caucasian. But the Air Force waved a magic wand and declared me Caucasian.

I was informed by my sister Jane that while Mom and I had been estranged over the past two years Mom had a baby girl, Cindy Jo, and that I should call Mom. I could not believe that no one told me that I had another sister and that Mom was in a financially desperate situation.

A key responsibility for every military service member during in-processing is to fill out next-of-kin information and to identify beneficiaries for their military death benefits and life insurance. I immediately completed a military finance pay allotment for $50 per month to be sent to Mom. It was a tough thing to do because a new recruit's salary in 1966 was about $80 per month. But since I was getting three hots and a cot every day without paying for them, I felt it important and appropriate to do so. That allotment remained in effect for two years. Before returning home for my first military leave, I visited the base exchange (BX) and bought Mom a congratulatory card and a small gift in the form of a small child's ring containing the official Air Force crest for my new sister.

Boot camp was not much different than Dad's years of putting us through grueling work outs and training in martial arts so I adapted easily. But my attitude had not yet been adjusted. While standing at attention in the chow line the DI got into my face and screamed: "Are you having fun yet boy?"

"No Sergeant! Boy Scout camp was rougher than this Sergeant!" For some reason he took offense to that answer so, he gave me an attitude adjustment through extra pushups and latrine duties for the rest of my days of basic training.

The physical training could not take me down but enduring the blistering 110 plus-degree summer temperatures and sleeping in an unairconditioned barracks threatened to do me in. I made it through but some of the recruits did not fare as well and for various reasons were disqualified from service and sent home.

My high school guidance counselor failed to consult with the college admissions board because two weeks into basic training I received my acceptance letter from Penn State University. I showed the acceptance letter to the drill instructor. He handed it back and made me an offer "You know this is your ticket out of Vietnam?" I declined and I am sure my refusal to the request a deferment possibility crossed his mind that I was eligible for a mental disability discharge.

Wim and Larry Sewing on first stripe - Airman Third Class

Larry and I survived "Boy Scout Camp" unscathed. We received base unit assignments, new job titles and Air Force Specialty Codes (AFSC). Larry became a welder at Strategic Air Command Headquarters at Offutt AFB, Nebraska (NB) and I was assigned as an Air Freight Specialist at the Tactical Airlift Command Headquarters at Langley AFB, Virginia (VA), ending our Buddy Enlistment. Somehow, we missed the part that the Buddy Enlistment Program was only applicable through basic training.

First Day Free in Amarillo

    We were issued a long Air Force cardboard "Blue Tube" containing our personnel records, train tickets for home, and a bus ride to the train station in Amarillo and some cash. We were headed home for one last glimpse of our youth. With all its warts, it was still home.

**Wim and Larry Graduation Picture –
Wim is the only graduate with a Karate Stance.**

CHAPTER 14 - FIRST MILITARY LEAVE (FURLOUGH)

Larry and I spent our combined meager funds for overpriced food on the train while on our tedious two-day trip to Chicago, Illinois (IL). Tired, broke, and famished, we hit the streets of the windy city in an attempt to forget about our empty stomachs during our long layover. We wandered around downtown Chicago to show off our brand-new Air Force uniforms and as we walked across one of the city's many bridges a strong gust of wind gently lifted my Air Force wheel hat from my head and over the bridge rail. I watched in shear horror as my official military service hat floated gently down the river and out of sight.

Hungry and hatless I shook my head in disbelief and I turned to Larry with an exasperated grin "What else could go wrong Larry?" We burst into hysterical laughter and I prayed out loud that my recruiter would not see me out of uniform.

Walking around the strange city made us more anxious about our empty bellies and penniless pockets, so we headed back to the train station. Dad's words came back to me in my hour of need.

Because of the not-so-peaceful anti-military and anti-Vietnam demonstrations, asking a stranger for help while wearing a military uniform was a dangerous thing to do. But I put on my most pitiful face and let my eyes search the train station for someone who might have some compassion for a couple of young starving Airmen. I spotted a well-dressed man with a pleasant demeanor and relaxed swagger, took a deep breath, and walked up to him. "Excuse me sir, do you have a minute?" At first, he appeared puzzled by the intrusion but then he smiled "Sure, what can I do for you Airman?"

All in one breath I blurted out "My name is Wim Wetzel and this is my friend Larry. I am sorry to bother you but we are on our way home on furlough from Basic Training and we had to use all our funds to by a meal on the train from Amarillo. We have run out of money for food and we live in Pennsylvania and still have another day's travel." I took a breath and paused while trying to read his expression and then I dove right in. "We realize you don't know us but if you can loan us a few bucks for food I promise to repay you with interest as soon as we get home."

He reached in his back pocket for his wallet while introducing himself. "Nice to meet you. I am Al (Mark) Payne from Fox River Grove, Illinois. How much do you need?"

He handed us what we asked for and told us there was no need to pay him back but I could not let myself accept such a generous proposal. After some coaxing, he finally conceded and we exchanged addresses, phone numbers and my military ID number. Thanks to the generosity and kindness of this stranger Larry and I were able to enjoy some much-needed nourishment to get us through the rest of the trip.

When we arrived at home Dad *loaned* me the money to send to Al and I sent him a thank you letter. We remained in touch for many years but somewhere in between Air Force deployments I lost Al's contact information. Al set the example and precedence for how I would treat strangers the rest of my life.

When I arrived home, despite the anti-war and anti-- military mood of the country, I wore my dress blues everywhere with pride. I felt like a decorated hero with my two ribbons on my uniform, one for Expert Marksmanship and one for Basic Training graduation.

During my visit home I returned to the Karate school and was welcomed with a standing ovation by the instructors and students. I donned my Karate instructor Gi and resumed teaching as if I had never left. I wanted to see Roy and reconcile our differences but he was nowhere to be seen. I found out from one of his students that he had enlisted in the United States Marine Corps and was at boot camp in Parris Island. The head instructor pulled me aside to tell me that Roy told him "I'll be damned if Wim thinks that he will be the only son to serve in Vietnam." He was carrying his competitive nature a little too far.

I had not seen Mom since my typhoid episode and I needed to connect with her. I was overcome by the reality that she was drowning in the indignity of poverty while struggling to support my new baby sister. Her cupboard contained a small box of cereal and a small bag of rice. The refrigerator was wasting electricity on a lonely jar of mustard and a few ounces of milk. I was financially powerless to come to her rescue but we had a long painful discussion, settled our differences, reconciled, and started to rebuild our relationship.

Mom knew that I would soon be going to Vietnam and she was still wrestling with her own wartime demons. My new sister was as beautiful and perfect as I knew she would be. I put a tiny Air Force crest ring on her tiny finger and prayed that she and Mom would be all right. I left with a heavy heart knowing I could not help her by staying but I may have a chance to help by leaving.

Since Roy was not home, I cut my leave short and decided to report to Langley AFB early.

CHAPTER 15 - TRAINING FOR WAR

Before being deployed to Vietnam I was assigned to Langley AFB, the Headquarters for Tactical Airlift Command known as TAC. There were twelve newbies, including me assigned to receive intensive training to become airlift aircrew members and mobility experts. There was an astronomical amount of information and training to absorb during the short seven months.

We trained in every aspect of preparing for airdropping critical supplies to Army and Marine Corps troops front-line battle fields. I learned everything about mobility operations, cargo handling and conveyor systems for loading cargo and how to rig and prepare cargo loads and equipment on the C-130 military cargo planes. We learned how to assemble and build an endless variety of airdrop pallets and cargo bundles to be used for the packaging of heavy equipment such as jeeps, trucks, tanks, bulldozers, and survival supplies to be airdropped to the troops on the battlefield. But nothing was as difficult as the extensive training and instructions we received on the respectful handling of our fallen comrades.

We travelled to designated remote locations that were set up as airdrop zones, would wait to recover the airdrop loads and equipment and then return back to Langley. We repeated the process countless times to ready ourselves for the combat zone drops to come. Our seven months at Langley, although grueling, were a positive experience that we all mostly enjoyed. It built enduring relationships, wonderful memories, and our confidence. We learned skills that we would use throughout our lives.

***

We all came from different backgrounds and I was the serious naïve kid in the group and that made me a prime target for practical jokes.

During a late-night combat exercise on the flight line tarmac, we had just unloaded one of the C-130s and were awaiting the arrival of the next one. Some of us sat on our forklifts, while others either sat or lay on the black asphalt because it was warm from the daylight sun during those chilly nights. I was resting against one of the forklifts and noticed what appeared to be an oil slick or some other type of leak. I made a comment, to no one in particular, that the forklift was leaking fluid. A couple of the guys looked at the leak and tried to find the source.

Gary Torres said: "Stick your finger in it, Wim, and see if it's oil." I did and as I slowly rubbed it between my fingers, I said, "It doesn't feel like oil." Gary responded with a blank look and said: "Put some more on your finger and taste it, to see if it feels or smells oily, or if it may be hydraulic fluid or MOGAS." I started to do just that when my sixth sense kicked in, and I looked suspiciously at Gary. He laughed sarcastically and walked away. The liquid was his pee. He had peed against the tire on the opposite side of the forklift, which then flowed downhill to where I was sitting. Everyone laughed uproariously. I became wiser that day and I never took anything Gary said at face value after that.

We lived on the second floor of an open-bay barracks that could accommodate about 20 people. There was no privacy and personal belongings had to be put in assigned storage lockers that could not be locked. Money and other personal belongings left on the bunks or in the foot lockers were mysteriously coming up missing. Those of us who had been pilfered were stumped about who in our group would do such a thing.

The mystery was solved after I returned to the base from a weekend at home in Pennsylvania. I opened my clothes locker to find that my Karate uniform and belt along with a couple of other items were gone. I gathered a couple of my trustworthy friends, and we opened every locker until we found my belongings.

There is a code of ethics in every branch of the armed services where you simply did not cross that line. We decided to take matters into our own hands. That afternoon we found the culprit napping on his bunk and threw a blanket over his body, and we pummeled him senseless; a process known as a *blanket party*. Someone opened the second-floor window and we threw his mattress outside and a couple of the guys picked him up and threw him down the stairwell.

Somehow, he ended up with most of his sticky little fingers and one thumb broken and he ran to report the abuse to the First Sergeant.

The First Sergeant came to the barracks to investigate what happened. We explained the theft of our belongings and one of the guys shrugged innocently and said "Gosh, I guess he must have broken his fingers while falling down the stair well."

The First Sergeant said "Hmmm! That explains it! Carry on Airmen!" We went about our business as ordered and the thief never returned to the barracks and was never seen again.

***

My roommates knew that I was a Karate instructor and beseeched me to give them some classes. I knew Dad would not have a problem with me holding small classes for these men. His only rule was that when I used my skills that I must use great restraint against others except in extraordinary circumstances.

One of my Airman buddies did not take time to attend any of my classes but was constantly goading me to show him some Karate moves. One day we were all relaxing in our bunks at Fort Campbell, Kentucky and when he hassled me one too many times and I finally relented. "All right, attack me in any way you choose."

He came at me directly from the front, and from a standing position I jumped up and completed a cross legged, scissor kick across his upper body. He flipped over, under the grasp of my legs and landed on top of his head. He never asked for another demonstration.

***

On a late Sunday afternoon. I was just getting out of the shower after returning from a relaxing outing with the guys. We heard a muffled "pop" coming from the barracks next to us. We looked at each other, silently questioning "What was that?" We shrugged it off and went back to the business of enjoying the rest of our day off.

A little while later one of the guys came running up the stairs to our second-floor quarters. "Hey guys, something is going on downstairs. The base security police and an ambulance are parked in front of the next-door barracks."

The area was buzzing with activity and one of our guys saw the ambulance attendants pushing a gurney out of the barracks with a body covered with a sheet. After some inquiries someone finally told us what happened. An Airman had gone home for the weekend and had brought a pistol back with him. He was opening his duffle bag to show off the pistol to his buddy in the next bunk. While he was wrestling to get the gun out of his duffle bag the gun went off shooting his buddy in the head and killing him instantly. We joined the Air Force as naïve teenagers going to scout camp but we were getting our first realization that we were not immortal and we were about to grow up really fast. We were so stupefied by the event that none of us could talk about it again.

We were sent to the Army parachute packing and cargo rigging training school at Fort Lee, Virginia to be certified for airdrop rigging and parachute packing skills and procedures. We learned to pack and repack every parachute that was used on cargo airdrop loads including heavy cargo such as tanks, large trucks, and bulldozers. It was a precise, intense, demanding and physically rigorous program in Army territory and Army personnel were not always happy about the Air Force weenies treading on their turf.

We all received graduation certificates, but more importantly we received the honor of wearing the coveted red riggers hat with the rigger wings emblazoned on the front, a distinction that set us apart from the rest of the airman.

After graduation we all visited the Base Exchange (BX) proudly wearing our new red hats. An Army Lieutenant (Lt) wearing a red hat approached us in the BX parking lot. We dutifully saluted him, but he did not return the honor and reached out to rip the hat from my head. My conditioned response was the Karate defensive stance. Whatever his reason, the Lieutenant backed off ordering us all to remove our hats at once and adding "Airmen, only Army riggers are authorized to wear red hats!"

I regained my composure and answered, "We cannot do that Sir since these are official parts of our Air Force uniforms and as such, we are fully authorized to wear the rigger hat by our commander Sir."

Taking offence to my explanation he responded "Airman, disobeying an officer's direct order is grounds for court martial. What is your name and who is your commander?"

I obliged him with all the information, saluted him respectfully and we all marched away. None of us heard anything further about the incident but I will not deny that it was an undies-changing experience.

***

One of my dreams had always been to become a pilot. We had only been at Langley for a short period when an Army officer visited our unit with an enticing offer to recruit us for Army UH1 Helicopter pilot training. We would attend helicopter school and have immediate promotions to Warrant Officer status. The only catch was that it required changing our branch of service to the Army. It was tempting but I did not want to sell out on my dream of being in the Air Force. I could not abandon that. Being a pilot could wait.

One of the guys in our group accepted the Army offer. He was shot down and died in the crash within a few weeks after reporting to Vietnam. The life-expectancy for helicopter crews ranged from 13 – 30 days. I have often regretted and wandered if I could have beaten those odds and taken the short cut to becoming a Warrant officer.

***

A good dose of ego or complacency or both can stand in the way of safety. We were on the drop zone recovering airdropped heavy equipment, including jeeps and trucks, at Fort Campbell, Kentucky (KY). We saw a quarter-ton utility truck racing towards us and as it got closer, we could see the driver was an Army Second Lt. (often derisively referred to as a Butter Bar) It was apparent that he was unaware of the safety procedures on how to drive on the drop zone (DZ). I drew the short straw and was appointed to give him some instructions. I had two points against me right out of the gate. He was an Army officer and I was way below his prestigious station as an Air Force Airman Third Class, AKA a one-striper.

We all gathered near him and saluted. I approached him as he sat in the truck. Annoyed, he blew out an exasperated breath and rolled his eyes. "What is it Airman?"

"I am Airman Wetzel Sir. It is my duty to brief you on DZ safety protocol, Sir."

He raised his eyebrows and gave me a condescending smirk but I plowed through my speech. "Sir, if you are on the DZ when the airdrop equipment is under parachute, DO NOT drive away from the load. Drive parallel alongside the cargo load or directly towards it to prevent it from dropping on you. That way you will not lose sight of it and it will decrease the chances that it will land on you. However, Sir, safety protocol restricts you from being on the DZ until all airdrop loads have landed.

He gave me a dismissive wave and ordered us to "Carry on."

As we stood on the edge of the DZ watching the C-130 cargo planes fly overhead dropping all sorts of heavy equipment the Lt. drove onto the recovery area before the airdrop loads landed on the DZ. His attention appeared to be focused on one of the biggest heavy equipment loads.

No one knows if he ever saw the airdropped jeep landing from behind his vehicle but the impact crushed it leaving him critically injured. Miraculously he survived the initial impact and was medevacked but we never heard if he survived.

***

The jeeps we used and rigged for airdrop were WW II vintage and notoriously unstable and dangerous. We watched as a jeep sped down the flight-line and the driver suddenly initiated a turn without slowing down. The Jeep flipped over several times throwing him out and sending him sliding across the tarmac flaying and crushing his face beyond human recognition. He was killed instantly.

***

Another incident involved a guy that wore his wedding ring on the flight-line against regulations. He jumped out of the right paratroop door of an aircraft and while holding onto the door frame. I heard a loud scream. While exiting the plane his left hand slid down the door catching his ring on a sharp edge on the door frame ripping his finger out of its socket. He laid on the ground a few feet from us, holding his hand screaming. His twitching finger still hanging on the door frame by his wedding band. From that point on the married guys hung their wedding rings around their necks next to their dog tags.

***

Riding on a forklift as a passenger is strictly prohibited. But one of our guys decided to jump on one to catch a ride while it was moving. He grabbed the right vertical roll bar beams as he boarded the vehicle and the driver increased his speed. They were both laughing as the vehicle increased speed until the driver made an unexpected sharp left turn throwing his passenger off the forklift. The passenger flipped over landing on his head with full force, crushing his skull and exposing brain tissue. Unfortunately, he survived the accident but was permanently disabled and was medically discharged from the Air Force.

In a short space of nine months since graduating from high school and before I had even entered combat, I had already experienced unthinkable brutal deaths and injuries. It was finally sinking into me that military service was not a game and it could have dangerous and deadly consequences. If this was just training, what were we in for as we made final preparations for Vietnam? I had not yet been to a combat zone but I was already accumulating a mental file for future flashbacks as if I had.

***

We finished our training and had become expertly trained members of a synchronized mobility operations team. We felt ready for any role or contingency that we would face in that capacity. We had packed cargo parachutes, loaded all manner of cargo on C-130s, airdropped and recovered all sorts of supplies and equipment from drop zones all over the USA. There was one detail we could not adequately train for; performing these duties while being completely exposed to snipers, rockets, mortars, and bombs.

February 1967, not yet twenty, nine months out of high school, not old enough to drink legally or vote for the president of the United States, from different backgrounds and cultures and no longer wet behind our ears, we would soon be in Vietnam and serving our country on numerous major and remote bases throughout the war zone. We were a microcosm of American society and reflected the characteristics and backgrounds of the idealistic young men from every corner of our nation. We had become lifetime brothers from different mothers and had each other's backs as we still do today.

Blain Sheppard, Gary Torres, John Becker, Bill Brice, Carroll Rhodes, Eugene Camarota, Dave Moody and so many others became lifelong friends and brothers.

CHAPTER 16 - COUNT DOWN TO COMBAT

We received our deployment orders to Vietnam in late February of 1967 and my reporting date was March 15. Before reporting to the port of embarkation at Travis AFB, California (CA) I spent two weeks of leave time at home. Some of the Karate students told me that Dad was bragging about me joining the Air Force. It would have meant so much more if he had told me that himself.

Despite the fact that it was unlikely that an Air Force Airman would ever face the same situations that he had endured in combat, Dad gleaned from his own experiences as a Japanese prisoner of war and gave me sound advice on jungle survival techniques and how to evade capture. He trained me on efficient and effective martial arts defensive and offensive killing moves that he had never shared with anyone before.

He engendered in me a sense of self-confidence and boosted my preparedness to face any contingency that I might face in combat. He showed his love to me the only way he knew how. He prepared me for the Hell of war; a concept I would not understand until I personally experienced the trauma that came from being in harm's way.

Then he hit me with the 'coup-de-gras'. "Wim, for my own sense of reality I have to tell you this. When I take you to the airport to fly to 'Nam, I do not expect to ever see you alive again. For you, the truth of combat has not yet hit home. For me it is very real. I have to expect that you will die in that shithole. If you expect to survive then you must approach every day that you are in combat this way. Do not expect to come home alive and live each day as if it is your last."

"Wim listen carefully. Keep your mind and body focused on the hostile environment and volunteer for anything that can develop your combat survival skills. Do not hesitate to volunteer for those hazardous duties that can get you killed. It is the difficult things that will develop and fine-tune your sense of survival in any situation. It will develop a sense of confidence to face any situation in war and in life when you return home. Those skills will follow you for the rest of your life. Wim, if you want to return home alive, instead of in a body bag, you must do as I say! Do you understand?"

"No Dad, I don't understand."

"Trust me," he said. "If you go over there looking over your shoulder and around every corner expecting the worst, the worst will happen to you. Don't look over your shoulder, look only ahead and do whatever must be done to survive so you can come home in one piece, instead of in a coffin."

I was shocked. I could not believe what he was telling me. In one breath he was telling me that I was going to die and in the next he was talking about my future when I returned home. It was morbid and confusing advice. But when I did put my boots on the ground in Nam, the reality of war hit me as rockets hit Saigon AB, Vietnam all around us and I finally got it. He was preparing me for what I was about to face and how to face it. Focus on staying alive and do not let the fear distract me from that goal. No father has ever given his son more loving advice.

***

The twelve of us were now a well- trained synchronized team deemed ready to serve our troops. We received our orders to deploy from Travis AFB in early March. A team member, Gary Torres, arranged for us to meet at his parents' home near San Francisco before we were deployed.

Gary's family was warm and hospitable. His parents were determined that our last three days in what we referred to as the world were not spent in a lonely cold hotel room. His parents could not accommodate all of us but they had collaborated with Gary's aunts and cousins who lived nearby and we were all welcomed into their homes as part of the family. We set up camp and crashed wherever we could find a spot.

We feasted on authentic Italian meals prepared by Gary's mom, aunts and several of the neighborhood women and Mr. Torres arranged for an all-expense paid deep sea fishing excursion in Oakland Bay. Our coolers were too small to carry the massive fish so Mr. Torres paid extra for the fishing charter crew to fillet them.

Everything I had heard about the love and open-hearted welcome of an Italian family was demonstrated by Mr. and Mrs. Torres. They treated us to three days of our life that none of us will ever forget.

On the morning of our departure the entire family and all the neighbors, who had been so kind and hospitable came to the Torres home to say goodbye. All of us learned more about unconditional sacrificial love in three days than most people learn in an eternity. If tears were money, we could have paid off the national debt. The Torres family will never know the lifetime of memories they created for all of us as we faced our unknown fate.

CHAPTER 17 –VIETNAM – MY INTRODUCTION TO MANHOOD

Several years before I was deployed to Vietnam the Viet Cong communist forces were initiating hundreds of terrorist attacks in South Vietnam and the United States had been sending a few troops there in an advisory capacity to counter that activity. Over time the government of South Vietnam became more corrupt and lost interest in fighting against the insurgency but the United States continued to stay the course. Our government determined that if we let Vietnam fall to communism then the other Asian nations would follow like dominoes falling one after another.

As the insurgents began to gain a stronger foothold, the United States began to increase the number of US troops in a more aggressive capacity. With the exception of a few indigenous soldiers, referred to as the Montagnard, the US troops were fighting the Viet Cong alone in spite of the complacency of the South Vietnam government. By the time I was deployed the US troops were fighting a full-blown war to defend an unappreciative nation.

***

We stepped off the Boeing 707 in Saigon at about midnight on March 15, 1967. The cabin door opened inviting in a cesspool-like stench. When we stepped onto the tarmac a furnace-like heat insulted our senses and our clothes seemed to melt onto our sweat soaked bodies.

Man! I had to take a leak! The Air Passenger Specialist pointed me to a bathroom and I ran to it as fast as possible before I peed my pants. Although my clothes were so drenched with sweat that no one would have noticed. I dashed towards my mark like an Olympic sprinter while holding my nose with one hand and my crotch with the other. Through my watery eyes, I spied an old Vietnamese woman cleaning the open urinal trough next to me. She flashed me a toothless grin but showed no interest in obliging me with privacy and I had no interest in waiting for her to leave.

With one hand occupied with holding my nose, I peed like a racehorse just as the rest of the hospitality committee arrived. A bug landed strategically on my person to inspect the steady yellow stream. The creature stayed long enough to convince me that I had already contracted my first bout of crabs, but to my relief the little fellow flew away leaving me to my business. I tried to ignore the local Welcome Wagon lady staring at me but she seemed determined to stay and enjoy my performance. When I completed my mission, I mustered as much dignity as possible under the circumstances and nodding my thanks I strolled back to the group.

Because of the late hour there was nowhere to check in to get to bed. We slept under the wings and tail of the B-707 while the rest of the base was being hit by a Viet Cong rocket and mortar attack. None of the incoming rockets and mortars fell near to us, but the piercing sound of exploding rockets rang in our combat-virgin ears and smoke filled the air, burning our eyes, lungs, and nose, starkly reminding us of where we were.

Most of us were sent to the 15th Aerial Port Squadron in Da Nang AB. Vietnam as Da Nang was still in the buildup stage. The squadron was responsible for providing facilities and service for the proper handling of passengers, mail, and cargo air transported to, from, and through Da Nang and its detachments—24 hours a day—7 days a week.

Almost everyone was assigned to live in 12-man field-style tents. A twelve-holer latrine had been set up and the public was invited. There was no privacy at all and those among us with bashful bowels learned to wait until dark to head to the latrine and drop off our daily deposits.

***

New arrivals to the base were put on Casual Status until they were fully processed into their units. This simply meant that they were assigned to basic unit duties such as area cleanup, janitorial tasks, kitchen services and other tasks no one else wanted to do. Casual Status usually lasted two weeks and in some cases were wasted days when no one accomplished anything worthwhile. During roll call one morning our squadron's First Sergeant, better known as Top, asked for a volunteer to clean the latrines and to paint the three Quonset Huts that served as our, storage buildings, showers, and bathrooms. Dad's advice to volunteer for anything that others were not willing to do prompted me to volunteer. After all, I had a lot of experience from basic training and it could not be worse than cleaning dog kennels or milk trucks. My plan was to make the

Air Force my career and cleaning latrines certainly met the criteria of starting at the bottom.

It was a vile job that appeared to have never been done before. It took over a week to clean the nasty building from top to bottom and then whitewash it all. I used a toothbrush to scrub between the cracks on the floor and behind and under the toilets. The effort paid off as I was the only Airman out of the group to be "Spot" promoted early. I am sure the other Airmen thought I got the promotion because I was a brown-noser, so to speak.

***

Mail Call was the prized event that everyone looked forward to every day. Everyone gathered near the squadron Orderly Room each day to wait for the Clerk to deliver our mail. It is impossible to adequately describe the excitement and competing tension and stress that hung over everyone each day as we waited for our letters and gift boxes from home. It was an especially bad time for me as the days, then weeks and months passed and I always walked away from Mail Call empty-handed. It would be six months before my name "WETZEL" was called. It was a letter from Mom. I had contacted the Red Cross representative on the base to ask if they could help me find out why I had not received mail from home. They contacted the Red Cross office that was located in New Brighton who in turn contacted Mom in Beaver. They strongly encouraged her to send me a letter to let me know that everyone and everything was OK.

One of the toughest things to witness was your buddy excitedly rip open that long anticipated envelope from that special someone back home only to find a Dear John letter. There was a derogatory term for the rogues who were lurking in the shadows waiting to console your lonely wife or girlfriend. This universally despised person may have been a friend who had not been deployed and had promised to look after your spouse or girlfriend or he may have finished his tour of duty overseas and returned home to replace you. But more than likely he was just a vulture that managed to avoid military service. They were referred to as Jody. While in the combat zone we learned many tricks on how to protect ourselves from the 24-hour attacks by snipers, bombs and mortar shells but being Jodied was the one attack you could not defend yourself from or be prepared for.

Some were so distraught that they committed suicide while some became careless and less cautious when facing dangerous combat situations and others like my two best buddies went into an inconsolable almost catatonic depression. They were loyal and decent men and husbands who loved their wives. One of them never recovered and it still affects him and his daughter over 50 years later.

***

We were a highly specialized mobility operations team but we all cross trained in different functions to ensure that we could handle any assignment. My first assignment was to the motor pool and I had a natural attraction to anything that needed a driver. The bigger, noisier, and more powerful the vehicle - the greater my desire to become qualified to drive it. I became certified for rough terrain forklifts, the tracked K-loader, the M-15 wrecker, and a variety of other combat vehicles. I even became certified to drive the "Blue Air Force" 58-passenger bus. These certifications served me well during my many challenging assignments to mobility operations. One certification led to some bad choices that justly hindered and jeopardized my career path.

My next on-the-job training assignment was in the air freight section. That is when I fell passionately and hopelessly in love. She was the most beautiful thing that I had ever seen. There were many others I had handled but this one was perfect. I will never forget my first love, the love of my life. She was equipped with everything, fresh off the show room floor, the Air Force C-141 Starlifter sleek jet engine powered cargo aircraft, easy to load and unload. Her brand-new tiedown chains and devices were unused hanging from their immaculate storage panels, and her pristine floor was what I would expect to see in a hospital surgical suite. What a sweetheart! I knew then that I wanted to be a loadmaster - I wanted to be and vowed to be *her* loadmaster.

***

The "Ranch Hands" were the C-123 aircrews that sprayed Agent Orange (AO) and other chemicals throughout Vietnam to kill jungle foliage and trees. We all received training on handling the toxic stew and were assured that it was not harmful. The instructor even demonstrated how safe it was by drinking a glass of the stuff in front of us during orientation class. Whether it was orange juice or AO we will never know.

There were no decontamination procedures that we were aware of if spills occurred when we handled the stuff and we were constantly exposed to the poisonous chemicals as we emptied the drums. During our rest periods between loading the C-123s we would sit on top of the empty 55-gallon Agent Orange saturated barrels that we had just emptied while the toxic chemicals soaked into our clothes and underwear.

On one occasion a forklift driver was unloading a drum filled with the chemical and during the process, his forks punctured the drum spraying several of us. Blissfully unaware of the dire consequences we did not stop to clean it up but offloaded the damaged container and proceeded to unload the others.

***

NEWS BULLETIN: On 23 March 1967, the worst ground aviation accident of the Vietnam War occurred at Da Nang Air Base, South Vietnam when a traffic controller cleared USMC A-6A Intruder for takeoff but also cleared USAF C-141A Starlifter, to cross the runway.

At about 2:30 AM on March 23, 1967 blurry eyed and exhausted, I received the cargo manifest for a C-141 cargo load that was inbound for offloading. I was standing with the offload crew near the edge of the cargo area prepared to inventory the cargo load. We were watching as the C-141 landed on the main runway and turned almost immediately onto the taxiway. During the taxiing process, the loadmaster opened the ramp and cargo loading doors in preparation for the unloading process. The aircraft stopped for a moment waiting for permission to cross the parallel runway, then continued to cross over to the parking ramp towards us.

We heard the high-pitched scream of a Navy A-6 fighter jet engine racing down the takeoff runway just before it impacted the C-141 between the number 2 engine and cockpit, instantly killing every crew member in its cockpit. The C-141 burst into flames upon impact of the A-6 and the acetylene tank cargo on the Starlifter soon exploded in the fire along with some of the ordnance on the A-6. Five Air Force crewmembers died in the fire. Only the loadmaster escaped out the aft section of the plane. The Navy jet pilot ejected and survived.

The flames were growing rapidly and we ducked as shrapnel flew past us. We watched in horror as the loadmaster jumped off the aircraft ramp, landed on his feet and ran away from the inferno.

Frozen with shock, I stood in an immobilized trance as shrapnel rained down all around us and flew past in every direction. The base Fire Chief happened to be standing nearby and, in a heroic-valiant effort to protect me he tackled me to the ground and covered my body with his until we could find safe cover in a nearby F4 bunker. He saved my life. Jolted back to reality we finally all grasped the gravity of the situation and if we did not get the Hell out of there, we were dead men.

The fire burned for several hours, consuming the plane, fuel, cargo, and mail onboard. After gathering our wits, we told the fire fighter responders that the loadmaster had jumped from the aircraft and run away towards the end of the runway. The search party located him, still running around in circles at the end of the taxiway.

Remains of the C-141A After the Fire Was Extinguished

Hundreds of body bags containing our military men and women were loaded and unloaded on a regular basis. Our training at Langley did not prepare us for the emotional effect it would have on us. We wondered in silence if that is how we were going home and every one of us felt the unspeakable pain and heartbreak that the war had caused so many loved ones.

Dealing with this day after day, to keep their sanity some the guys built up a layer of emotional callous while handling the deceased soldier's remains. A cargo plane loaded with body bags had just landed from a remote site and an empty Marine truck backed up to the ramp to receive the plane's cargo. Two Marines jumped onto the C-130 cargo plane and two Marines remained on the truck. In cadence, the well-muscled Marines that were unloading the plane would have one Marine at each end of a body bag and simply tossed each body onto the truck while the Marines on the truck stacked the body bags like cord wood.

Observing their irreverence for these fallen heroes, several airmen and I, lost our cool. We warned them that if they threw another body onto the truck that we would kick their asses. Upon sizing us up they knew we were not much of a threat and they laughed at the absurdity, but it jolted them back to the somberness of their assignment and they began to unload the bodies with respect and dignity.

***

Sometimes our responsibility was to transport living people. It could be military personnel or Viet Cong (VC) POWs. One day my friend Blain and I watched as a group of VC POWs disembarked a plane and shuffled across the tarmac with their heads covered by empty burlap sandbags and their hands tied or shackled behind their backs. Each VC was tied to the person in front or behind him as they dragged themselves from the aircraft to the holding area where they would squat in the typical Vietnamese fashion until someone came to pick them up. They were young men like us; sons, brothers, and husbands all sucked up in the ravages of war.

A single POW was squatting with his back against the fence out of sight of the person guiding a 40K-loader. As it was backing up someone yelled "STOP!" but it was too late. The flatbed of the K-loader struck the fence, shattering several of the fence posts. A fence post shard penetrated the prisoner's left ear and exited the right ear.

The K-loader driver was directed to pull away so that aid could be rendered to the prisoner. But only the squadron commander's Vietnamese secretary helped the dying prisoner as the rest of us all went about our business. He was someone's son and there was no choice but to emotionally block it out and I thought that I was getting particularly good at it. Death had become the norm and we had started to lose our humanness, our hearts, and our souls to the normality of war. It became hard not to hate someone. For us It was just another Cong.

One day while we were loading an aircraft a CBS news reporter approached me for a short interview. He asked me if I believed in what I was doing and our presence in Vietnam. At the time I had a real conviction that we were protecting the Vietnamese people from the North Vietnamese forces of evil and I was proudly serving my country. I answered without any sense of humanity. "Hell, yes and we need to bomb the shit out of these Cong so that we can go home!" Based on his immediate response I doubt that my interview ever appeared on the nightly TV news.

It was not long after that interview that there was a sudden shift in my attitude towards the general Vietnamese population. My abrupt change in attitude occurred during our only respite and return from swimming at a nearby beach.

We were all riding in the back of a flat-bed truck returning to the base. A group of children began chasing our ride. It was refreshing to witness children playing and hearing their laughter. We began handing out candy and C-ration snacks as they ran behind and along the side of our truck. I reached over the back of the truck tail gate to give a candy bar to one of the kids when he suddenly threw a rock at my head striking my glasses and shattering them. You little bastard!" I yelled, while wiping the blood from my forehead.

That was my instantaneous turning point, I no longer had the attitude that I was fighting for the justice and freedom for these *oppressed* people. I temporarily lost my sanity and I just wanted to get me some "Cong!" Where was CBS now when I really wanted to give him a new answer?

CHAPTER 18 – "QUAN CAHN - DI-DI MAU"

The sprawling and dangerous city of DaNang was off limits to all military personnel because much of the city was under the night control of the Viet Cong. There were a couple of small Army units downtown but other than them no one ventured there without official business and only accompanied by armed military police.

The workload was exhausting and death was everywhere and not always at the hands of our enemy. During just the first month we witnessed more than a half dozen fatal aircraft crashes and three accidental deaths because security police and others pulling guard duty were bored and had quick draw contests and we were loading hundreds of body bags containing Marines and Army soldiers from military trucks onto military cargo planes to send them home to Dover AFB, Delaware (DE).

***

This disclaimer is not an excuse, just an explanation for my bad judgement and my skewed decision to indulge in a thoughtless activity that was disrespectful to women, my position and character as an Airman. It displays the immaturity of young men who have left their sense of decency at home after being dumped into a world of war, death, and destruction. It is a world where life often has little meaning and the only goal is to stay alive and get home to loved ones in the *Real World*.

I am not proud of myself for participating in these events, but they are real. It is an important part of my story. It hurt my otherwise impeccable reputation as a decent God-fearing man and it deservedly hurt my Air Force career in the end. It was a blemish on my otherwise perfect record that prevented me from being nominated for the highest rank and honors that an Air Force Chief Master Sergeant (CMSgt) can achieve. To my peers and all the men and women I had the honor to serve with "I am sorry for the short-sighted and poor judgement I displayed in this event."

Prior to early 1967 the military had an approved whorehouse on Da Nang AB. Whether any official military spokesman will acknowledge it today or not does not matter. We all knew it existed and many of the guys frequented its mysterious rooms and sowed their teenage oats. Then one day one of the military members sent a letter home to his mother telling her of the house of ill repute on the base. Mom in turn notified her Congressman who immediately sent a Congressional Investigation team to the base. After confirming its existence, the establishment was closed permanently.

We had grueling 12-on and 24-hours off shifts and there was nowhere on base to get relief from the open binjo (sewer) ditches emanating the foul odor of human feces and urine. There was no escaping the searing Asian heat, monsoon downpours, and ever-reeking military uniforms. There was no avoiding diesel and aircraft fuel fumes or the never ceasing screams of aircraft engines or the frequent rocket and mortar attacks that were a constant threat to our sanity.

It was the middle of April and all of us who arrived in Vietnam together were still getting settled into the daily routines in the 15th APS. I was assigned to the motor pool as part of my on-the-job training program and scheduling the base transportation vehicles including the Blue buses. I was a horny virgin or "Cherry Boy" as referred to by the Vietnamese. My hormones were raging when the thought came to me that I could sign out a bus with the excuse of having to go to one of the Army posts in town. After all it would only take me about 5 minutes to do my business. That included two minutes to get undressed and two minutes to get dressed for my return.

Ben (his real name is not used here) was my assistant in the motor pool. It was his job to fuel and wash the vehicles. I broached the subject and my ideas with him and he thought it was a "great" idea. "Let's do it man!" he said. I signed the 58 passenger Blue Air Force bus out to myself and Ben signed on behalf of the Motor Pool Sergeant as authorization to leave the base. We put on our combat helmets and gathered our M-16s, got on the bus and drove to the main gate. The Security Policeman stopped us, inspected the paperwork, and let us through the gate. We had no inkling of where we were going.

We saw an Army Private First Class (PFC) walking down the road and he flagged us down. He asked for a ride, but we had no idea of how to get where he wanted to go. Now instead of two geniuses on the bus we had three. Ben told him all we wanted to do was find a cat house, make a short visit, and return to the base. Like any GI worth his salt, he knew exactly where to go and proceeded to get us there. Fear never crossed our minds. There was no hesitancy in doing what we were about to do. "Just get us there-Dude!" Within a few minutes the "Grunt" (a nickname Air Force guys gave to Army personnel) suggested that we park next to a warehouse type "U" shaped building that seemed to stretch out forever.

We entered the building and were immediately met by "Mama San.

"How long you stay GI? Wat chu want?" she asked.

"We want numbah' one quickie!" we responded.

"Ten dollah' each" she said.

The grunt and I reached into our pockets and quickly came up with the ten dollah' each and handed them to her. Ben reached into every pocket and turned them inside out. He opened his wallet and except for his military ID and Status of Forces (SOF) card it was as empty as our collective brains. Since we were only making $87 a month in military pay plus $55 a month in Combat Zone pay, $10 was a lot of money in "them there days." But I reached into my wallet and loaned Ben the $10.

Mama san took us to three separate cubicle type rooms separated only by curtains. Each room had a cot type bed, a wash bowl, and folded clean sheets. At least the sheets appeared to be clean – but by then who cared? The five-minute visit stretched to 15 minutes, then to an hour. We were having a ball - so to speak. It was party time and the "business girls" brought in some rice wine poured from a used 5-gallon GI gas can. We could still smell the odor of gasoline from the GI gas cans where the rice wine was fermented. It may have been aged at least a week. But then who cared? Two hours quickly passed and all of us had a good buzz going. We were too naive to know that guys had gone permanently blind from drinking this hooch.

Then it happened. The room lights started flashing and bells started ringing. Mama san was running down the narrow hall screaming "Quan Canh", "Quan Canh", and "Quan Canh" – "di-di mau" – "di-di mau! Loosely translated it means- "Military Police – Get the Hell out of here!"

It took a couple of minutes to sink in, but my new Vietnamese friend was shoving my clothes and boots at me and telling me "di-di mau"! Ben and I were now hastily donning our uniforms and trying to exit the building. The Army grunt grabbed his clothes, rifle and boots and rolled under the bunk. His girl used the blanket to hide him and left him alone in the room.

Ben and I parted ways looking for an exit. I ran from room to room until Mama San stopped me and pointed to an opening in the wall adjacent to and above one of the beds. I climbed up and she closed the panel door behind me while she continued to scream "di-di mau!" the entire time. The warning bells never stopped ringing. I was scared shitless when the panel door closed behind me putting me in complete darkness. Once my eyes adjusted to the darkness, I could see a sliver of light every 10 to 15 feet or so shine through the cracks in the wall.

I carefully felt my way along the endless, narrow, and twisting passageway. I found a partially opened panel and pushed it open and without looking jumped through it landing on a kitchen table where Mama and Papa San were eating lunch. After their initial surprise and my shock, they began to laugh and pointed me to another panel on the adjacent wall in their little kitchen. I exited the room and started my journey again. Apparently, this was a common occurrence.

It was lighter in this new corridor and in the distance, I could see what appeared to be a door. I ran to the door and stopped to catch my breath. The heat in the corridors took my breath away and the sweat poured from my brow burning my eyes. Gingerly pushing one of the exit panels I peeked outside to see if there were any military policemen in sight. Not seeing one I left the corridor and cautiously walked with my back along the building until I could see the back part of the bus at the corner. After waiting a few minutes and catching my breath I turned the corner just in time to see an Army MP come around from the front of the bus with Ben in handcuffs.

Exhausted and relieved it was one of our own guys. I slumped to the ground waiting for my own inevitable handcuffs. I laughed and determined that only God knew what was in store for us. Since I was the only person with a bus license, I had to drive the bus to the Army post for initial processing. Then I started to laugh hysterically and could not stop. Some irrational thought that this was a hilarious situation just took over any rational thoughts I had left.

Ben and I were put into a holding cell until our First Sergeant could be called to pick us up. He arrived after about two hours and just shook his head and said, "What were you two dipshits thinking?" We remained silent. "Wetzel – you drive the bus and follow me back to the base! Major Brown (our unit CO) wants to meet with you ASAP and you can kiss your asses and careers goodbye!" Major Brown was ticked off beyond description, but he was also short-handed. He gave us a choice between an Article 15 and a Court Martial. For the non-military reader, an Article 15 simply means nonjudicial punishment. A slap on the wrist that is meant to get your attention and a written warning to sin no more.

After a quick discussion with the First Shirt and following his strong recommendation we chose the Article 15. Besides the Article 15 I received a suspended bust from Airman Third Class to Airman and a $90 fine. The punishment went much further. This one blemish in my Air Force records would disqualify me for nomination to become Chief Master Sergeant of the Air Force. Ben received an Article 15, a $90 fine, and an immediate reassignment to Saigon. I never saw Ben or the $10 I loaned him again after that day. I had immediate regrets for my exploitations of others as well as the blemished record that followed me through my whole career.

And, by the way Ben, if you are reading this, you still owe me ten dollah' with interest.

CHAPTER 19 – BROTHERS IN COMBAT

Roy arrived in Vietnam two months after I arrived. By the time of his arrival the war had gone from a slow simmer to boiling over with casualties. I was grateful to be able to meet him at the passenger terminal when he arrived in Da Nang. He was on his way to the Dematerialized Zone (DMZ) where the life expectancy of a combat Marine was shortened considerably.

We only had a few hours together before he left for the DMZ and we were intensely aware of the fact this could be the last time we would see each other alive. But I promised him that I would get up north to visit him soon. He just laughed it off and said, "How do you think you're going to pull that off?" It was a lofty promise but I was determined to find a way.

Two months later, I had the opportunity to catch a ride on a C-130 to visit Roy at a location called the Rock Pile located close to the DMZ. When I arrived at Dong Ha AB, Vietnam I hitched a ride on a small convoy heading north to the Rock Pile. The driver of the jeep told me that he doubted that I would be able to see Roy because the unit he was assigned to was under heavy enemy fire and the forward operating base was surrounded. I was still determined to try.

The driver dropped me off near a small communication tent the size of about a 4-foot x 6-foot outhouse. A single radio operator manned the tent, with his back to me and preoccupied with his duties he pointed to a chair and motioned for me to have seat. After a few minutes he turned to me with a blink of shocked disbelief he said: "What the hell is an Airman doing here?"

"My brother Roy is with the "three/nine" and I am here to visit him and possibly help him get a pass to come to Da Nang for a few days." He searched my eyes looking for some way to tell me something. There was a long pause and his furrowed brow and pursed lips conveyed to me his concern for how to explain what was happening.

"I don't think that's possible Airman."

My stomach turned over, my head began to spin, and there was a buzzing in my ears as my body prepared for the jolt of the news. "Why?" I asked.

"Your brother's unit is in a fixed pitch battle and many of the Marines assigned to the unit are already dead." he said. He kept staring at me as if waiting for my response. I just sat staring back at him in disbelief and not sure what to do or say.

He broke the silence between us. "Ok, Airman. I will see what I can do. At least maybe you can talk to him on the field radio." There was doubt in his voice but it gave me hope. I waited while he tried to get through to find Roy. I paced back and forth for what seemed like hours. Suddenly he put down the transmitter and seemed to be talking to the wall in front of him, "I don't believe this." With that I fell into a chair and waited for him to relay the bad news.

When he turned to me his whole face had transformed from a contorted knot of tension to a beaming smile of relief and celebration. "The battle is over and your brother is on his way here. The survivors are pulled back and ordered to return to base."

Exhausted and relieved I slumped back in the chair and waited. About an hour later I heard the rustling of the tent door and turned around to see Roy leaning against the door frame with his M16 sling around his elbow and the end of the barrel resting on his boot. Blood was dripping down his right leg saturating his combat fatigue trousers and soaking his boot. I rushed over to him, put his arm around my neck, and helped him to a chair.

Trying to mask his pain he gave me a weak wincing grin. "You saved my life, Wim. Most of the guys are dead or wounded and your call came just in time. We won the fight and the Commanding Officer (CO) told me to go visit with you and that he would see us both later." The stench of death, blood, mud, and God knows what else was emanating from his clothes. The radio operator called for a medic to dress the wound on his right thigh while I did everything that I could think of to make him comfortable.

While the medic was dressing Roy's wound a Marine Captain came to the tent, introduced himself as Roy's CO and asked, "What the Hell are you doing here?"

I explained to him that I was based at Da Nang and was determined to see my brother. At that moment I thought, If you don't ask, you don't get. I spoke. "I would like to get permission for Roy to come back with me on a short pass."

"This is a bit unusual and I've never heard of such a situation before. But Corporal Wetzel has earned a few days off and he is cleared to go back with you for three days."

"Thank you, sir." I said unable to suppress a smile.

I called and contacted one of my buddies at the Dong Ha passenger terminal. He arranged for seats to be set aside for both of us on the next C-130 heading for Da Nang. When we were about to board the aircraft, we discovered that there was only one available seat. I looked for the loadmaster and found him in the snack bar and I explained the situation to him. He told me that if one of us would sit on an ammunition pallet then he would set up the seatbelts. I asked the loadmaster to assign the seat to Roy and to allow me to sit on the ammo pallet. The return flight to Da Nang was uneventful but if enemy ground fire penetrated the ammo pallet there would have been a whole different meaning to the term "get the lead out."

Roy fell dead asleep from pure exhaustion until we landed at Da Nang. During the next three days, he was treated like a celebrity. Any excuse to plan an event was a huge morale booster at Da Nang. The mobility team had planned a barbecue honoring Roy. He smelled like a cesspool and looked like he just crawled out of one and readily accepted the offer to use our shower facilities before the big barbecue event. He told me that he had not bathed in about three months.

Our shower consisted of a 12-man open-bay facility without privacy walls. I gave Roy shampoo, soap, and a clean white towel. After about 20 minutes, Roy came out of the shower drying off his back with the white towel. He had been in the filthy jungle field condition for so long that I do not think he even knew how badly he stunk. His back was still caked with black stinking mud and getting it wet in the shower only enhanced the stench. I retrieved another white towel and sent him back into the shower where I joined him and scrubbed his back for several minutes to get it clean. We had a good laugh later as we thought about the rumors that would start about two GIs bathing each other in the shower.

We had to throw Roy's boots and socks away. After wrapping him in a clean towel, we walked back to the 12-man tent. During our absence, the guys had barbecued several steaks. The beer cooler was filled, and the party lasted way past midnight.

Roy's wound began to bleed again. We treated it as best as we could and set him up with a clean cot with fresh sheets and a pillow. Within 5 minutes Roy fell sound asleep. During the night he had several nightmares and his thrashing opened the wound again. His sheets became soaked in blood and it dripped onto the floor. We rushed him to the base hospital, where the wound was properly treated and dressed.

For two days we savored the time we had together before it was eventually time for him to return to his unit. In our haste to get to Da Nang the Captain had not given Roy a written three-day pass. There was no way for him to obtain a seat on an aircraft headed north without a written pass. One of the guys came up with the brilliant idea, "Why not dress him in an Air Force uniform and let him use your ID card? Since we have open-ended mobility orders, no one in the passenger terminal is going to challenge his right to travel." I thought, "Why not, I've done worse things since arriving in this shit hole."

I told Roy what we were going to do. I gave him my ID card and one of my uniforms emblazoned with my name. Since it was the only ID card I had, I told him that he had to return it to me immediately after landing and gave him a pre-addressed envelope. As planned, Roy processed through the passenger terminal, boarded the aircraft, and returned to the DMZ. After the C-130 departed Da Nang, a horrible thought occurred to me. If for any reason the aircraft crashed, killing Roy, the casualty unit and the Red Cross would notify my mother that I had been killed in action. That thought stayed with me until I received the envelope containing my ID card.

CHAPTER 20 - DA NANG to DAK TO

The Viet Cong had been invading deeper and deeper into the country via the South China Sea from the west and the Ho Chi Minh Trail on the eastern border. The US Military Assistance Command for Vietnam had established a chain of Special Forces camps along the borders in an attempt to hold back the invaders. The Viet Cong's goal was to destroy those posts in order to infiltrate the country and the posts were being attacked relentlessly 24 hours a day.

US troops were also setting up those posts in the remote rural areas. Many of the South Vietnamese farmers and village dwellers hated Americans. They only understood that they were being displaced by Americans invading their homeland.

Da Nang was our home base but we knew we would not be there long. For the first few weeks our mobility team had been multitasking in almost every job capacity on the base. But ultimately the 15th APS was tasked to send us out on a moment's notice and we had to be ready to deploy to any fixed or mobile air terminal at any time.

The Army ground forces and Green Berets, Marine Corps and Navy units were all on the front line protecting the borders of Vietnam. Our mobility teams were their only source of food, ammunition and every essential supply needed for survival. Their lives depended us doing our job and our lives depended on them having our backs while we were unloading their supplies. We had to load and unload cargo from the aircrafts as quickly as possible, driving forklifts and K-loaders dodging enemy fire in order to get the planes back into the air and out of harm's way before the Cong could destroy the aircraft and cut off the unit's supply line.

We carried our own C-rations, ammunition, equipment and supplies necessary for any duration of a deployment. We lived, ate, and slept in the deadliest combat zones in Vietnam. The units that we were serving provided us with tents, latrines or outhouses, medical treatment, and hot meals in their field kitchens when they could.

Our team usually consisted of about five mobility specialists and we were often left alone to perform our duties free of adult supervision. Everyone was a participant regardless of rank or station.

The huge transport planes airdropped supplies and equipment into the remote outposts when the short or nonexistent runways made it too dangerous to land. These airdrops were the site defender's only lifelines so the missions were approached with the appropriate seriousness and accuracy required.

Over time and repeated deployments, we became very resourceful and sharpened our creativity skills. At two locations we re-used the heavy 463L cargo loading pallets and fashioned them into shelters by tying them together with chains. It was a five-star hotel compared to our musty WWII tents and we were immensely proud of our new living quarters.

Dak To was one of the hardest-fought and bloodiest battles of the Vietnam war. I was assigned there for 30 days, then 60, then 90, then 120 days. It was my home for a total of 210 days. The siege lasted for months and hundreds of our troops lost their lives and limbs. It became an integral part of the Vietnam War and of American history. We spent most of our time dodging rocket attacks, mortar shells, and sniper fire while handling innumerable aircraft that supported the Army during the battle.

On arrival at Dak To, we were billeted in an open pavilion type building with three of the four walls open to Mother Nature. We noticed a sweet putrid sickening odor emanating from every part of the building. The Army guys told us the building is also used as a temporary morgue to store dead bodies until they could be shipped out in one of the specially modified Killed in Action (KIA) aircraft.

Our first home at DakTo also served as a temporary morgue.

The bodies often laid in this building for days in the overwhelming, stupefying heat, causing them to decay rapidly. We could not escape the odor that penetrated all of our personal belongings and clothing. It is an unforgettable smell of death that penetrates to the core. I can still smell it today and it will awaken me from a dead sleep.

Technical Sergeant (TSgt) Lutz was our leader at Dak To and after a couple of days he was given a WWII tent by the Army Quartermaster so that we could escape the grossly unsanitary situation. Unfortunately moving into a tent brought us other misery. The monsoon rains came, and the floor of the tent would flood, soaking all our belongings. We unofficially confiscated several wooden cargo pallets and used them as a floor to get our belongings off the ground. For a false sense of protection, we surrounded the tent with concertina wire, as if that were going to stop anyone from throwing a hand grenade into it.

TSgt Glenn Lutz and Airman Wetzel in Front of Bunker Before Attack

A C-130 cargo plane landed unexpectedly in the middle of one night, and the Viet Cong rocketed our base immediately. Our robotic response was to grab our helmets, flack vests, and M-16s and run out of the tent to unload the aircraft.

During the turmoil, brain fog, and rush to get out to unload the aircraft we all had forgotten about the concertina wire surrounding the tent and were immediately wrapped up in it. The sharp spines shredded our clothes and ripped our bare skin to ribbons causing us to bleed everywhere. I became hopelessly tangled and the guys had to stop long enough to free me so we could complete our mission. There was no time to evaluate our injuries but no one seemed to have severed an artery. We knew it meant life or death to recover the ammunition supplies from the arriving cargo planes.

In July 1967, the attacks from the hills surrounding the base became more intense and frequent. None of us had combat training, but if it came down to it, we were not going to go down without a fight so we decided that we needed a bomb shelter. We dug one next to our tent and stocked it with all kinds of ammunition including hand grenades and flares but the bunker could barely accommodate two or three guys. There was one flaw in our plan. Our tent and our bomb shelter were located right next to the immense Dak To ammo dump-always a prime target for enemy attacks.

One day we were on the flight line unloading and loading the support aircraft. The Cong attacked us with a vengeance and the rocket and mortar shells hit their intended target, leveling the ammo dump, our tent, bunker, and everything surrounding it and we were back to sleeping in the horrid open-air morgue until we could get another tent.

Bai Sitting On the Remains of Our Tent

Our Bunker

We had just finished loading two C-130 aircraft that were parked nose-to-nose and I was walking from one to the other between them. A rocket slammed through the vertical stabilizer of one of the aircraft and impacted the ground in front of an Army officer and I watched in horror as he was blown apart and seemed to vaporize in a red fog only a few yards in front of me. The blast knocked me to the ground and killed several others nearby. That graphic image of the disappearing officer still haunts me every day and the inevitable survivor's question of "Why him and not me?" remains unanswered.

Over 200 Army soldiers were killed during that battle and we shipped them along with hundreds of palletized body parts on the outbound aircraft. A specifically selected C-130 morgue aircraft were used for transporting human remains and the odor of the decaying bodies became permanently imbedded in the airframe. The flight crews wore protective clothing and oxygen masks and these aircraft were ultimately destroyed due to the unbearable permanent stench of death.

I received word that my dear, loyal, and trusted childhood friend, Adolph Ellis, was killed by a Bouncing Betty land mine during a combat patrol a short distance from the base. There was no time to allow myself the luxury of mourning my friend but he took part of my youth with him to his grave. We received the Stars and Stripes newspaper every day. The issue delivered the day after the attack featured a colored picture of dozens of spit-shined boots lined up in perfect formation.

For a short time after the bombing, I was the only Air Force person physically assigned to Dak To and attached to the Special Forces A-Team. When the cargo planes came in, I was a fully exposed target for the enemy rocket and mortar attacks while unloading cargo as quickly as possible. The Special Forces A-Team commander and the Team members treated me as part of their family and I knew they always had my back.

Gate to the Special Forces Camp

Late one afternoon I was walking back to the safety of the A-team compound after working the flight-line when we came under a mortar attack. It was like being in the movies where the enemy was targeting a specific person or group and walked their mortar rounds towards the target. In this case the target was me. Rather than trying to outrun the mortars I dove for cover into the closest hole in the ground which fortunately for me was a foxhole manned by the A-Team medic.

"Have you ever fired a mortar round?" He asked.

"No – but this seems like a good time to learn!" I answered.

He showed me how to remove the appropriate number of sandbags from the base of the mortar and how to remove the safety pin. The pin was installed at the head of the mortar under a lot of tension and he warned me to be careful when removing it to avoid injury. He gave me instructions to remove four bags of ballast, remove the pin and hand the mortar to him. I nodded to signal him that I understood the directions then nervously removed the sandbags. While I was removing the pin, it went straight through my right thumb. The pain was unbelievable as the pin remained stuck in my thumb while I kept on handing new mortars to the medic.

The engagement only lasted a couple of minutes and I eventually ignored the pain until it was over. There was hardly any blood as the medic removed the pin and said, "You just got the Heart (Purple Heart)!"

"No, the wound was not bad enough to warrant it." I spoke. A decision I often regret.

***

One late afternoon, after an exhausting couple of days supporting the Army units, I was relaxing in the Green Beret compound, when a helicopter landed, bringing the famous comedian Martha Ray. Ms. Raye was a member of the Bob Hope tour group and was out visiting various Green Beret units throughout the war zone. She was so respected by the military that she was given the honorary title of Colonel Raye even though she actually was a Lt. Colonel in the Army Reserve Nurse Corps.

She was about to leave to visit another unit when she saw me sitting alone at a table. Colonel Raye came over, sat next to me, and said, "How are you doing Airman and why are you here?" Then she put her arm around my shoulders and gave me a fantastic, never-to-be-forgotten big hug. We spoke about ten minutes before she hugged me again, kissed my cheek and said goodbye. My spirits soared, and all my tired aching bones and muscles felt rejuvenated and I was ready to get back to work. What a phenomenal experience that was.

Lt. Colonel Martha Raye

With the Troops In the Field

Raye had entertained troops during World War II and the Korean War as well, but she developed her close relationship with the Special Forces during the Vietnam War.

The recall order was made to send most of the mobility guys back to Da Nang but someone had to stay behind to guard our K-Loader and forklifts. I volunteered to stay, along with Staff Sergeant (SSgt) Hampton. As we settled down for the night, sleeping on the forklifts, we were hit hard by the Cong. The word came that the base was going to be overrun that night and we were warned to expect the worst.

The survival of the men on base depended on securing their mobility lifeline so a handful of infantry soldiers were assigned to protect us. The Viet Cong made one failed attempt after another to overrun us while a C-47 aircraft gunship, affectionately referred to as "Puff the Magic Dragon", flew circles overhead all-night firing down at the VC that surrounded us and the base.

The following day a fresh mobility team led by TSgt Lutz was rushed back to Dak To on a support aircraft containing ammunition. Numerous aircraft containing fresh troops, supplies and new combat equipment were landing one after another and lining up like railroad cars. Engine Running Offloading (ERO) procedures were in place to speed up offloading the cargo and to expedite their departure to make space on the parking ramps for the next aircraft. The heat from the idling engines caused our watches, jewelry, and the brass bracelets to burn our hands, arms, and necks.

TSgt Lutz asked me if I could help marshal and guide the Army Huey gunships landing all over the tarmac. With some quick training from a helicopter crew chief, I had no choice but to accomplish my new skill very quickly. Many of the helicopters were arriving with dead or wounded soldiers which we helped unload. We then loaded fresh rockets onto those helicopters so they could return to battle. It was an exciting blood-pumping and dangerous job. During one of the landings as I was marshalling an armed helicopter and directing him to turn towards the de-arming site, he accidentally pickled (pulled the trigger) causing the rocket to launch past me and exploding on the parallel taxiway. I pissed my pants but continued to work. The pilot landed the chopper and came over to apologize.

For more than three days we supported our cargo aircraft, moving our dead and wounded, fortifying helicopters, and returning mortar fire. When we became too exhausted to work, we caught 5 to 10 minute "combat naps". This continued until the attacks ended. There were massive casualties but by the grace of God the entire mobility team survived the ordeal without injuries and the essential equipment was unscathed.

During the heat and chaos of the enemy attack I had forgotten to roll up my bed roll. Exhausted and a little absent-minded, I took off my clothes and boots and jammed my body into the sleeping bag. Feeling a sudden excruciating pain in my right big toe I let out a blood curdling scream. I reached down and wrapped both my hands around my ankle trapping whatever had latched around my toe. A couple of the guys helped by using their boots to beat whatever it was until it stopped moving. Then I pulled my foot out of the sleeping bag dragging the critter still attached to my foot. The huge rat attached to my toe had been enjoying my sleeping bag when I was not using it. We had to pry its teeth off my toe with a combat knife. The medic treated my toe and told me to be more careful in the future, as if I would not. For a fleeting moment I considered that my rodent friend could have been rabid, but I hoped for the best and passed out from exhaustion.

A few days after the battle ended, TSgt Lutz and I were ordered to report to the 173rd Airborne Brigade commander's tent. Upon arrival, we came upon a surreal scene as numerous brigade officers and senior NCOs came to attention. Without knowing why, we were told to stand at a specific location and directed to stand at attention, Brigadier General Schweider awarded Sgt. Lutz with the Bronze Star and me with the Army Commendation Medal for Meritorious service because of our actions during the battle at Dak To. At that time, no accomplishment in my short career meant more to me than receiving that Army Commendation Medal.

Army Commendation Medal

Early in September I was asked to fly back to Da Nang to collect all our team members' payroll even though there was no place to spend money in the field. I approached it as another new adventure and being a hopeless opportunist, it gave me a chance to get a hot shower, clean clothes and visit to the BX for groceries.

After collecting our pay, I tried to catch a flight back to Dak To. The only available flight was to Pleiku which is on the way but short of Dak To by several miles. Upon arrival at Pleiku I was concerned about carrying all the payroll around with me until a flight to Dak To would become available. I asked around for possible alternative transportation and discovered that an Army supply convoy was leaving for Dak To within the hour. I immediately asked the convoy commander for a ride and he told me that the only available seat was in the lead vehicle, but I was welcomed to take the seat. I accepted and introduced myself to the driver. The positive side was that the driver was a guy who graduated from Beaver High School with me but I soon discovered that there is a reason the lead vehicle in a convoy has vacant seats.

We were about half-way back to Dak To when the convoy came under ground attack. Following instructions, I bailed out and into a roadside ditch. It was the only actual firefight that I participated in during the war. Because this was their first firefight the new Infantry soldiers qualified for the Combat Infantry Badge (CIB). The Noncommissioned Officer (NCO)in charge of the convoy suggested that I should also qualify for the CIB, but another NCO told him that only Infantrymen are qualified for it by Army regulations. My badge was the gift of just being given the intense opportunity to actually fire my M-16 in a firefight and one more day to live.

***

One day we all watched as a C-130 landed and taxied to the terminal. A noticeably young cocky loadmaster disembarked from the aircraft and looked around as if he were expecting a brass band to welcome him. He headed in my direction checking his watch as if he had something more important to do. I understood the urgency to get the aircraft back in the air but his obvious disrespect for all of us was palpable and disgusting. He graced me with an impatient nod.

"What do you have for me Airman?"

"We have a wrecker, its driver and shotgun rider to load for urgent redeployment. The total weight is just over 35,000 pounds."

"Load them then, let's go." He ordered.

After loading the vehicle and drivers, the loadmaster said "We have room on the ramp for more cargo. Do you have anything else that we can haul out of here?"

"You are already at gross weight with what you have. We have a jeep and its driver, but you are already close to being overloaded and I can't give you more."

"Who's the loadmaster here? What do you know about what I can load or not load? I have room for more."

"No" I said

I looked up and saw another charm school graduate disembark and start swaggering toward me. He was also looking at his watch. I thought to myself, *they must be cloning assholes in that aircraft.* He was obviously the AC (aircraft commander).

"What's the holdup here? Let us get her closed up and get out of here." He asked.

"Captain we have room on the ramp for more cargo, but this Airman will not give us anymore. He has a jeep and driver going to the same place as the wrecker and we can take them."

"Are we good for the extra cargo load weight?" the pilot asked.

"Yes sir!" Replied the loadmaster who turned to me and ordered - "Load it up Airman!"

The Form F is a document that is required to be completed for every cargo aircraft, and it certifies that the aircraft is within weight and balance standards for flight. Exasperated I answered, "Okay Sir, but only if he will sign the Form F, stating that he was briefed about the overload condition."

"Just sign the form and let's get out of here." The pilot said to the loadmaster.

Against my better judgement we loaded the jeep and driver and the loadmaster gave me a copy of the completed Form. "Wait a minute Load." I spoke. Then I wrote a statement on the back of my copy stating that he had been briefed by me that the extra jeep and driver put the aircraft over gross for the takeoff and runway at Dak To on this date. Then I insisted he sign and print his name before departure. He did and walked away.

By this time several of our Army buddies and all the Airmen gathered along the flight line to watch the departure of the aircraft because we all knew it was not going to get airborne. It taxied to the end of the runway, revved up its engines and rolled slowly down the runway. It became obvious that they were running out of runway and might not be able to get airborne. She labored to get into the air, near the end of the runway, but rose only a few feet before striking a bulldozer, killing the driver, and throwing the shot gun rider unconscious to the ground.

The aircraft disappeared into the valley at the end of the runway and we watched and waited for the plane to explode into a fireball. It seemed like an eternity before seeing it slowly climb up and away from disaster. The crew declared an emergency and was diverted to Saigon where it landed gear up. The damage was significant, but no one on the aircraft was killed or injured. The nose landing gear was ripped off as the aircraft hit the bulldozer and a significant part of the bottom of the aircraft was ripped away during the impact.

Bulldozer Struck By C-130 and the Aircraft Nose Gear From Impact

A few days later, an Air Force investigation team arrived, ordered me to testify about what had happened. They accused me of lying to the crew about the actual cargo vehicle weight and threatened me with court martial actions. I presented them with my copy of the signed Form F and showed them the statement on the back. Several Army and Air Force guys testified on my behalf and the investigation was concluded. I assume that the pilot and loadmaster were both disciplined but I never knew what happened. But for me, it was the end of that story.

***

The Cong were relentlessly slaughtering civilians around the base to make their way into the interior of the country. One day a group of five children came by our tent begging for food. They had become orphaned as a result of one of those brutal killings. Innocent victims of a senseless war, they were starving and left alone to rely on their own resourcefulness. The ages ranged from 4 to 9. Their names were Bai, Minh, Siu, Nam and Nee. Bai was the oldest and Nee was the youngest, but they were far more mature than any typical American kid at the age of 10.

I was hesitant at first, vividly remembering the kid that had thrown a rock into my face at China Beach. But as I watched the guys start to feed them, my softer side started to melt, and I proceeded to help also. We could not get rid of them after that. For the remainder of our tour at Dak To, they slept nearby, ate our food, shined our shoes, and guarded us when we slept.

They lacked the most basic hygiene skills. Like mongrel dogs, the boys stunk from a lack of soap and water and their teeth had never seen a toothbrush. Their hair was filthy, their feet were crusted with jungle rot and mud and their breath was horrendous. We taught them how to remain clean and even how to brush their teeth regularly.

On slow days they would take us down to the Dak To river to swim and bathe in the red, fast moving waters. Bai, and a couple of the older kids, would stand guard on the shoreline with our M-16s. We had no doubt that they would be able to use them if needed, to protect us and the other children.

Nee and Minh Lifeguards on the DakTo River

I contacted a dear friend, Mrs. Charlotte Vento, in Beaver and asked if she could obtain any clothing for children from her church. Her sons, Mike, and Bob were high school friends and fellow scouts for many years. Mr. and Mrs. Vento were my adjunct parents. They took the role knowing that I was lacking proper parenting at home. Mrs. Vento took on the challenge with a passion. She gathered the women at the church and collected boxes full of clothing, hygiene supplies, toys, and food to send to us. We finally had to ask her to stop because we had no place to store the stuff and all the local kids were now adequately clothed.

" Thank you, Mom, - for your letters and support during my tour in Nam and for being there and keeping me grounded throughout my teen years, when I needed you so much."

Almost seven months had passed at Dak To and it was time to return to Da Nang for a well-deserved rest. It was tough to leave the kids behind. They had become an extended family. There is a belief in Vietnam that if you depart and leave friends behind, they will cut off a lock of your hair as a keepsake. We were unaware of this ritual until the kids all came to us with a pair of scissors and asked us to let them cut our hair. We gave our permission and they all took their mementos, hugged each one of us and walked away, never to be seen again. I cannot help but believe, if for nothing else but my sanity, that after all these years these boys survived the war, married, had children, and told stories about their American friends.

Clipping Hair for Memories

CHAPTER 21 – RETURN TO DA NANG

After almost seven months of Dak To I was ready for a change of scenery and fortunately we were recalled to DaNang. It was a major change of pace for us as we returned to the relative calm of DaNang. There were continued attacks on the base but its sheer size and scope provided us with some needed calm and protection.

At Da Nang cargo terminal several of us were waiting to offload C-130s and C-7s delivering ammunition and other high explosives. Like clockwork the two C-130 aircraft taxied in on schedule and Marine Corps trucks backed up to each aircraft. The ramp doors opened immediately releasing the recognizable stench of death.

Both aircraft were filled to capacity with body bags. Several of us began to vomit uncontrollably. We turned away attempting to breathe fresh air while still retching but finally managed to take a few deep breaths before we began the task that had become all too familiar.

I was on the aircraft ramp helping the Marines offload one of the body bags. My offloading partner was standing on the ground. As I raised my end of the bag the drain plug came loose, and body fluids poured down onto the face and body of my partner causing him to drop his end of the bag. He convulsed into a heaving vomiting attack that triggered a chain reaction causing all of us to begin retching violently. We finished the offload in record time but my partner was taken to the hospital for treatment. He had swallowed some body fluids and was too sick to continue his duties.

We all tried hard to suppress the human aspect that each bag represented with their human contents of brothers, sisters, parents, spouses, children, and hopeful fiancés whose lives were forever changed. The Marine in charge of the trucks informed us that everyone that was killed was about our age, barely out of their teens.

***

Flaps are critical to landing any aircraft, and especially the massive and ungainly B-52. A B-52 had just returned from a bombing mission over Hanoi, North Vietnam. Enemy rockets had severely damaged it. Blain and I watched as it circled overhead several times before it limped in on final approach attempting an emergency landing.

The aircraft's hydraulic system had been critically damaged disabling its ability to lower the landing gear and flaps for landing. The crew could manually lower the landing gear but was unable to do anything to manipulate the flaps for landing.

Blain and I held our breath while praying for the best. We watched in horror as the aircraft touched down past the runway's halfway point and bounced several times. The aircraft bounced one last time right over a guard shack at the end of the runway barely missing the shack and the Marine guard in it. It landed in the base's perimeter mine field and exploded in a huge ball of fire.

We knew there was no way anyone could have survived the inferno. The gallant and heroic firefighters could not get to the crew because of the exploding mines surrounding it. At some point they heard a banging and someone screaming near the tail of the aircraft. It was the tail gunner who was trapped in his gun turret just outside the minefield. They were able to extricate the lone survivor and rush him to the base hospital.

***

On December 25, 1967 several of us were loading and offloading C-7 Caribou aircraft. As an F-4 fighter jet was taking off in full afterburner his engine quit in flight. Both pilots ejected safely but they were too low for the parachutes to open. To our horror, both crew members impacted the ground in front of us killing them instantly. We stared in shock as we watched the debris from the exploding aircraft rain down after them. I have no idea how we avoided injury or death from the debris but one more time we were direct witnesses to the brutal death and destruction of war.

It was a Christmas nightmare none of us will ever forget and for the families of our fellow fallen Airman, Christmas will never be the same. In an attempt to keep our sanity, we were all determined to block out the scene and think about the Christmas celebrations beginning in a few hours.

A small artificial Christmas tree adorned with bulbs and lights was put on the refrigerator in the corner of the tent and a Santa Claus doll was hanging by the neck nearby. We were celebrating being alive and being back together. We were ready to party and forget the horrors of the day. Libations were flowing freely and personal countdown calendars were displayed on everyone's lockers for the world to see.

Gary and Blain

In a feeble attempt to mentally block out the flash backs of the exploding inferno, flying shrapnel, and the two young pilots lying on the ground like discarded rag dolls, we got shit-faced drunk. I had reached my limit of seeing our dead and dying brothers in arms. My last memory of that drunken night was falling asleep with uncontrolled tears soaking my clean white pillow.

CHAPTER 22 – THE KHE SANH SIEGE

Khe Sahn, Vietnam was a prime target for the Cong to push through, penetrate and infiltrate South Vietnam. The battle to hold the Cong back had been fierce for several months but on January 21, 1968 the Viet Cong carried out a massive attack on the U.S. Marine garrison and for the next 71 days, U.S. Marines and a handful of their South Vietnamese allies fought off the intense siege of the garrison.

The actual body count for the North Vietnamese Army forces will never be known but the official estimates exceed 150,000 enemy killed. Waves of American B-52 bombers routinely carpet bombed the enemy with devastating accuracy. The enemy remains disappeared in red clouds of blood and guts under these bombing runs making it impossible to conduct official body counts.

Khe Sahn Memorial

On February 1, 1968 I crossed off one more day on my personal "Return-To-the-World" count-down calendar, leaving me 45-days until March 15, 1968, the second anniversary of my citizenship and last day of serving my country in combat. I was satisfied that I had fulfilled my duty to serve my new country with honor and fidelity. The day to return home and sanity was so close now that I could smell and taste the hot dogs and steaming French fries at the Brighton Hot Dog Shoppe.

The curse of being one of a hand full of experienced mobility team members in Vietnam made us prime targets for emergency orders to report to Khe Sanh. We were being deployed within 24 hours. The first-hand information coming back from Khe Sanh was not good. Our odds of going home in body bags had just increased significantly.

Four of us were selected from the 15th APS at Da Nang along with numerous other unfortunate mobility experts from sites throughout Vietnam. The 24-hour a day enemy assault was so intense that mobility experts were deployed on the basis of a one to two-week rotational tours. The Marines did not have that option and were posted there for the duration of the battle.

Dad's voice once more echoed through my mind, "just buck it up, go forward without second guessing and don't look over your shoulder." I put my fears aside, packed my duffle bag with extra clean underwear and reported to the squadron.

We had no time to wait, discuss or think about the departing C-130 because it was waiting for us with engines running in front of the passenger terminal. We boarded the fully loaded aircraft and buckled-up in the only remaining seats. The aircraft was fully loaded with about 30 Marines and pallets of supplies including Class A ammunition and rations. The Marines were all fresh and it was obvious that they were new to Vietnam and combat. No one spoke a word as the aircraft taxied to the runway and conducted a full power rolling take-off.

The flight time to Khe Sanh was less than an hour and no one spoke or even looked at one another. I could smell the tension and hear the labored breathing of my comrades but I sensed no real fear. It was more of a zombie like acceptance of an inevitable fate.

The horror began before anyone even put boots on the ground. As we approached the outpost for landing several of the Marines stood up and disregarded the loadmaster's instructions to remain seated with their seat belts buckled. Sympathetic to their fear the loadmaster did not challenge them. Many Marines refused to sit because of nightmare stories about bullets coming through the aircraft floor and striking their genitals while they were sitting. Several Marines took their flak vests off and sat on them to prevent such a horrible thing from happening to them. It was rather comical to think about. Their fear of dying was negligible compared to their fear of losing their manhood but I must confess that it was a fear that I shared with them all.

If that were not enough to scare the shit out of us, the high-altitude combat landing procedure did the trick. The aircraft initially approached from a high level above the runway and executed a steep spiraling combat landing to avoid ground fire. Even though we were aware of the procedure, the sensation that we were about to crash was still palpable.

As any GI who ever landed in a hot combat zone will attest, the adrenalin rush is so intense that you do not notice that your asshole puckers up so tightly that it sucks the aircraft's combat seat halfway into the colon.

When my boots touched the tarmac, I realized the horror stories that I had heard about the place were grossly understated. Bile caught in my throat and my eyes teared up as I breathed in air that reeked of gun powder, jet fuel, unbathed exhausted soldiers and thousands of decaying enemy bodies lying outside the outpost's perimeter.

When the mobility team leader whom we were replacing approached me, I knew we were in trouble. There is a phenomenon common to combat fatigued men called the "1000-mile stare." I had seen it on hundreds of faces of Army and Marine Corps veterans at other outposts but this was the first time I had ever seen it on an Air Force member. He started to give me some cursory instructions on what to expect but then stopped and said: "Shit – you'll figure it out. Just get us out of here now!" The other new team members from the other bases were already unloading and loading cargo and passengers from engine-running aircraft. I wanted to quickly introduce myself to the other new guys and then briefly acknowledge the outgoing team but they had already boarded the aircraft and disappeared from sight. We finished off-loading the aircraft, loaded the dead and wounded and it departed the base.

***

Immediately after the aircraft left another C-130 was already taxiing in to replace it. But this aircraft had been shot up badly and JP-4 fuel was pouring out of its right wing. The ramp and rear cargo door were opened during the taxi-in to the offloading area. The fire department, a term I use loosely, sprayed foam on the wing to prevent a fire. The engines were never shut down as we finished offloading the aircraft and the fuel continued to pour out of the wing. Eventually they were able to stop the fuel leak and we onloaded several Marines and KIAs and the aircraft took off for Da Nang. The entire event lasted less than 10 minutes and we had only been on the base for less than 30 minutes.

***

My first assignment was to offload a heavy pallet of Class A ammunition with a forklift and transport it to the holding area. An enemy rocket hit the ground near my forklift and exploded. The percussion blew me off the forklift rendering me unconscious and badly bruised next to the still running forklift. The Marines that were nearby assumed I was dead and stayed in their bunkers while I laid on the tarmac with mortars and rockets continuing to rain in on us.

The Marines must have thought I was Lazarus raised from the dead because at some point I regained consciousness and got back on the forklift, robotically continued to transport the ammo, and finished the offload. During the heat and excitement of battle there was no time to seek medical attention and I did not report the incident. The common theme was that if you were able to walk, talk and do your job, you soldiered on. I did not need a doctor to tell me that I had suffered a concussion. The severe debilitating headaches that have become a way of life after the incident is proof enough. It was a purple heart incident that I never had time to pursue.

The next C-130 that landed had been shot up badly during its landing approach. The cargo ramp was already opened during the taxi in so that the aircraft could be evacuated. As we jumped on the ramp to help evacuate the wounded passengers I slipped and fell on a pile of intestines, body parts, and blood of what was left of a Marine who was gutted from the groin through his head by a 50-caliber round that came through the cargo floor. He had been standing during the landing to prevent the loss of his manhood during the enemy fire. We carried the human remains out while two Marines used a water hose to wash the residual body parts off the aircraft onto the tarmac.

***

It would be another nine hours before we were able to check into our new bunker home in the middle of an active enemy rocket target. My bunk was in the Air Force's command bunker, near the center of the base. A 105 Millimeter (MM) Howitzer was positioned directly on top of the bunker and it was fired constantly. It was odd to find that someone had posted a photograph of Anne Margaret on the refrigerator. Yes! - A refrigerator. Only the Air Force would arrange for a standard sized refrigerator to be taken into combat.

While living and barely surviving the two weeks in Hell there were only two states of mind; adrenaline overload or complete exhaustion from the life-threatening events that had caused the first state. The sound of the Howitzer became a soothing lullaby instead of a distraction because it signaled that we could reduce our body's alert system a few notches and melt into our bunks.

A few days after landing at Khe Sahn we were in the middle of conducting an ERO of five ammunition pallets weighing about 25,000 pounds. There were two sets of roller conveyors required for this operation and it took two guys to connect them. During the process of hooking up the roller conveyors one of the "Cherries" (new guy) was experiencing difficulty hooking the roller conveyor onto the end of the cargo ramp. Three of the four guys had completed their task and moved to safety while the "cherry" was still having difficulty with his connections. The loadmaster during EROs is required to wait for a signal from the offload team before releasing the restraining locks from the pallets and notifying the pilot to add power so that the pallets can roll off the aircraft. He did not wait and seeing that the mobility guys from his side of the aircraft had moved to the safe holding area he released the 463L pallet locks and directed the pilot to taxi.

Engine Running (Taxiing) Offload

The new guy saw the first pallet rolling off the main cargo floor towards him and tried to stop it with his arms. The first pallet hit him just above the knees and pinned him to the ground landing on his chest. The second pallet struck the first, then the third, fourth and finally the fifth. As each pallet hit the offloading train the guy's body slid a few feet because of the impact of 25,000 pounds of ammo. He remained conscious waving his arms in the air and screaming. Screams clearly heard above the din of the running engines. Screams that still ring in my ears today.

I was pre-positioned with my Jolly Green Giant forklift and moved immediately to pick up the edge of the pallet sitting on his chest. The guys pulled him out from under the pallet and the medics took him away and loaded him on the next departing aircraft never to be seen by us again. The loadmaster and the aircraft that caused the accident apparently never knew what happened because they taxied to the end of the runway and conducted a combat takeoff and departed the scene.

Accidents at Khe Sahn happened every day. Some were just plain stupid like the Airman who was playing with a pistol that a Marine had captured from a Viet Cong. He was unfamiliar with the weapon and somehow shot another airman in the left side of his face blowing out all of his teeth through a huge hole on the other side.

***

Every day was more intense than the previous one but the day before I left Khe Sahn the base was hit harder than most. The Air Force Forward Air Controller (FAC) was sitting in his jeep controlling traffic. He had us arrange three stacks of 25-each – 463L cargo pallets around his jeep in the shape of a large "U". An enemy rocket landed on the tarmac's pressed steel plating (PSP) and skidded along the length of it and imbedded itself under one stack of the pallets before blowing up and scattering 463L pallet shrapnel everywhere. The FAC escaped uninjured.

With less than 24 hours left in Khe Sanh I was moving a cargo pallet from an aircraft to the cargo holding area. One of our F4 fighters came in low from behind me and dropped a huge bomb, targeting something outside of the perimeter, but it landed short just outside of the fence line. The shock wave blew me off the forklift and this time I was not knocked unconscious but went completely deaf for about an hour. My ears rang and I could see people talking to me but could not hear a word.

***

It was time to rotate back to Da Nang, pack up and get the Hell out of Hell. While our replacements were exiting the aircraft, I walked towards the aircraft with a 1,000-mile stare, stopped briefly to give the leader some instructions and finally I said "Shit-you'll figure it out. Just get us out of here." We boarded the aircraft, sat down, buckled our seat belts, and departed for the relative peace and safety of Da Nang.

The siege of Khe Sanh is considered one of the longest and bloodiest battles in the history of the Vietnam War. My best memory from serving at Khe Sahn is that it is one of my proudest achievements. We were awarded the Navy Marine Corps Presidential Unit Citation with a "V" for valor.

I may have told you more stories than you wanted to learn about Khe Sanh but many young men lost their lives, many lived through it, and many still relive it every day of their lives unable to talk about it. So, in my own small way I owe it to them to be their voice.

Learn more about the siege and battle for Khe Sanh at:

https://www.pinterest.com/w_sonnenberg/khe-sanh-vietnam-67-68-usmc-semper-fi/

Khe Sanh Runway and Base Destruction

CHAPTER 23 - GOING HOME

Blain, Sheppard, Gary Torres, and Jack Hiles were the first to leave Da Nang for home. I left with the rest of our troops on March 15, 1968. The impact the war had on my body, mind and soul were suppressed and forgotten for many years however one day the horror snuck in the back door with a vengeance that I never expected and for which I was not prepared. One of the guys told me that I looked too much like a VC and that the Air Force would never let me get on a plane to "The World."

My Last Night in Vietnam

Going Back Home to the "World"

We boarded the Boeing 707 Freedom Bird that would take us "to the world." Every seat was occupied by a man that only twelve months ago was a boy. The air in the cabin was thick with silence and everyone seem to be holding their breath as the plane taxied down the runway. We felt the plane begin to lift into the air and heard the landing gear retract. As the plane climbed free from the massive runway the silence was broken and exploded into one single roar of cheers and clapping hands. Tears flowed like champagne as everyone realized that they had actually survived this indescribable nightmare.

It was a grueling thirty hours of flying to get back to the United States and by the time we touched down on American soil in San Francisco, CA we were exhausted but grateful to be alive. Some of the guys got on their knees and kissed the tarmac at the bottom of the aircraft stairway.

We were advised to change into civilian clothes before landing in the USA but I chose to wear my uniform. Those who opted to wear civilian clothes were easily recognizable by their short military haircuts and disciplined posture. We were greeted by a group of hippies and anti-war radicals waiting in the terminal for us as we stepped off the plane. They shouted insults and slurs while spitting at us and hurling feces and garbage.

On my flight from San Francisco to Pittsburgh, I slept on both legs of the trip, but when we approached the Pittsburgh International Airport for landing, I was instantly awake and alert. I had no fear that I would be attacked by flying garbage in Pittsburgh. When I stepped off the aircraft it was like walking out of a time machine and into the future. Awestruck, I wandered aimlessly through the newly renovated modern terminal and basked in the reality that I was truly and safely home.

I did not tell anyone that I was coming home and did not want to put anyone out by having them drive to the airport to pick me up. Mostly I needed some time alone to ease back into normal life. Broke as usual, I hitchhiked home from the airport and because I was wearing my uniform, I quickly got a ride.

It was 10 AM when I arrived at Dad's house and I was greeted by the Red Star flag hanging on the door displaying three stars. Each star represented one of his sons who was serving in combat. Dad answered and immediately greeted me with welcoming hugs and kisses on both cheeks before letting me in the house. I did not offer any information about Vietnam and he did not ask any questions. He did not have to. At the risk of using a cliché, he had been there, done that and now I understood. The flag still hangs proudly in my office.

Three Star Flag Flown By Dad While We Served In Nam

Peggy offered me breakfast but all I wanted was a hot shower so that I could unwind after the long trip. Dad then told me sit down for a minute and he shared the news that Roy had sustained serious injuries on the battlefield some months before and had been in the Yokota AB, Japan hospital since then. The good news was that he was getting intensive physical therapy and was expected to be discharged to come home soon.

After my long hot shower, I laid on the living room couch and fell asleep immediately. I was jolted awake by a long loud fire department siren blast signaling the community that it was noon. Without thinking I immediately rolled off the couch, lifted the couch from the floor and partially rolled under it. Dad was sitting in his chair watching TV and ran over to pull the couch off me and guided me back onto the sofa. I was shaking violently and he spoke to me in a calming voice until I settled down and fell asleep again. When I awakened, he was still sitting in the chair asleep. He never left me alone that night and his actions told me more than his words have ever been able to speak. He loved me deeply and he understood but more importantly: "I understood!"

A few days later I attempted to pick up the couch but it was too heavy to move by myself. That was the beginning of a life that has been saturated with moments of terror that would strike any time there was an unexpected loud noise.

I took another long shower, put on my uniform, donned all my medals, ate a big breakfast, and borrowed one of Dad's cars to make my rounds of the Valley. I had served my country in combat and had no hesitation to show and tell everyone about it.

***

I was saving my visit with Mom and my baby sister Cindy for last. I knew that it would be a long intense emotional visit but I had to deal with my own raging emotions and calm down first.

***

My first visit was to Mrs. Vento to thank her for supporting me and getting all the donations for the kids at Dak To. She told me to sit down in the kitchen and she proceeded to make me my favorite meal of "southern-fried" chicken with all the fixns'. It still melts my heart when I think of all her love and kindness. I made it a point to stop at her home every time I returned to Beaver County until she passed-away many years later.

Later that day I visited Mr. and Mrs. Wildman. The news that I was home safe had spread like wildfire and several of the Explorers and Rovers showed up at their home to welcome me back. I answered all of their questions about Vietnam and relayed the sad news of Adolf Ellis' untimely death. He had been a selfless and loyal friend to all of us and the news brought a river of tears and hugs as we comforted each other.

To celebrate my homecoming Mr. Wildman ordered Mazzio's pizza from Rochester and we had a huge welcome home party. I fell asleep on their couch until the next morning and we enjoyed a nice breakfast and time of reflection together before I returned to Dad's to shower and get cleaned up for my next visit to see Mom and Cindy.

I called Mom before leaving Dad's house to tell her that I was on my way because I knew if I showed up unannounced, she would pass out from the surprise. She had moved from the hood to a second-floor apartment that could only be accessed from the outside. I pulled up to the house and parked across the street and saw her standing on the landing outside the apartment. It was my turn to be surprised. Roy was standing next to her.

He had a cast on his right leg going all the way up to his underarm. His left arm was in a cast that extended 90 degrees from his body at the shoulder. My first thought was "What the Hell?"

Mom came flying down the stairs, ran across the street and gave me the biggest hug I had ever received from her. She was sobbing and laughing and I could not hold back my own tears. I could see Roy was watching from the top of the stairs grinning so big that he could have been auditioning for a toothpaste commercial. I knew what he was getting ready to do and I tried to head him off. "Stay where you are, I'll be right there, Buddy…" It was too late.

He hobbled down the stairs and we all met in the middle of the street and hugged, cried, and laughed. It must have been a sight to see as the vehicles swerved around us to avoid hitting the crazy trio hugging in the street.

We spent the rest of the day catching up as if it were just another ordinary day. Roy explained the reason for his body cast and why and how he was evacuated to Da Nang and then to Yokota AB.

"So, what happened to your arm?" I finally ask. Mom chimed in to give Roy time to catch his breath. "Well, your brother came to visit me just as you did today. When he left the apartment, he had some trouble maneuvering back down the stairs with that heavy body cast. The next thing I know he is tumbling down the stairs, ass over tin cup landing at the bottom and breaking his arm and collar bone.

I sat there speechless for a few seconds picturing the event. I could not help myself. I finally retorted "You dumb ass!" As tragic as it was, my comment brought all of us a moment of uncontrolled laughter that rudely awakened our infant sister Cindy. Mom picked her up from her tiny bed to calm her down before handing her over to me. As I cradled her in my arms, I was awestruck by witnessing this beautiful miracle of life after seeing so much death.

***

Trouble seemed to be attracted to Roy like bees are to honey. He decided to take a ride down to our old stomping ground, the Roller Rena, where we had been bouncers. Roy, Duke, the lead Karate instructor, and a few other guys from the Karate school went to catch up with our old boss and owner of the business. Roy asked if I wanted to join them and I begged off because I had other plans.

When Roy appeared at the Roller Rena remnants of the football jocks were still hanging out there and spotted Roy. Roy's casts were a great opportunity for them to exact some revenge. They waited for the right opening and it came when Roy had to go to the bathroom. Roy chose a stall because he needed support while going to the restroom and he could lean against the wall while taking care of business. Someone struck him from behind knocking him down causing him to rotate during the fall and sit on the toilet.

The attacker came in for a second hit and Roy kicked him in the balls with his good leg then pulled himself up off the toilet. With his good arm he reached up to the door frame above him and kicked the second attacker in the chest knocking him to the ground. The guy recovered and got off the floor and ran out of the restroom.

Duke was standing just outside the bathroom waiting for Roy to finish. Roy called out "Duke – Help – get him!" A third attacker had been waiting for his opportunity to get to Roy and he ran out at the same time as the second guy. Duke held on to the second guy as the third ran past him out the door into the parking lot and locked himself in his car.

In the meantime, Roy had recovered and was determined to go after the punk. He hobbled out to the car and banged furiously on the car window before grabbing one of the instructors by the shoulder and used his good leg to kick in the driver's window. He reached in to drag the guy out when the police arrived. The guy in the car was lucky to be saved by the arriving police. You just did not screw with Roy.

***

I had visited everyone I cared about and mended broken family relationships. Jim was in Vietnam and I prayed he would make it home and we would have a chance to talk things out and put the past behind us.

I had purchased a sword in Vietnam from a Montagnard tribesman and a set of three authentic Samurai swords while I was in Japan. Without intending to do so my gifts were the bridge that healed the open wounds that Dad created between Roy and me and we moved forward in our relationship never looking back at our past painful disputes.

Dad's mystery sword had been missing for several years and I was amazed to find out that Roy had found and purchased Dad's sword from an antique store in New Brighton.

When he settled into his civilian life, he displayed all the swords proudly on an elaborate steel and glass etagere in his living room near his front door along with Dad's mystery sword. As his friends and visitors left Roy's home, they often stopped to admire and comment about the swords and asked questions about them. Roy proudly described how I gave them to him and the history of the swords as related to the martial arts.

***

Near the end of my time at home I was anxious to move on to my new assignment but Dad told me that there was a student at the school who wanted to see me before I left.

Since Dad had opened two new schools, I wanted to stop by anyway just to see the changes that occurred while I was away. A wiry-chiseled young man walked up to greet me. He reached out shook my hand and hugged me while flashing me a winsome grin. "It's good to see you again Mas Wim." Mas is the term used to refer to one's martial art instructor. Welcome home."

Mas William "Bill" Dobich with Wim

I was looking up at him studying his face and embarrassed that I did not have a clue who he was. Suddenly his smile gave me a flash of recognition. "Butch?" *Was this the insecure chunky little boy that sat in the corner wrapped in his mother's arms?*

I stood there gawking at him like a kid that just saw Superman. He snapped me out of my trance by challenging me to a match. All the students and instructors were staring and expecting nothing less from me; the teacher being challenged by the student. Dad recommended that I should go home, and rest first and then come back another day but for the sake of my "honor" I accepted his bold but friendly challenge. I won the short-intense match but the thought crossed my mind, *"Did I win or did Bill let me win?"* I understood then why Dad suggested that I rest first. Bill was good.

I left home for my next assignment at Dover AFB, DE with a lightened heart after reconnecting with friends and loved ones and knowing family wounds had begun to heal.

CHAPTER 24 – DOVER AFB

Dover AFB is the home for the largest military mortuary in the Department of Defense. It is used for processing military and government personnel killed in both war and peacetime. The remains of those killed overseas are traditionally brought to Dover AFB before being transferred to their grieving families. During the Vietnam war more than 50,000 dead American soldiers were brought back to the United States via Dover. The Vietnam War dead comprised over 90% of all the remains processed at Dover before 1988.

I doubt there is another country in the world that treats their returning fallen heroes with as much dignity as the United States Military. I highly recommend the movie TAKING CHANCE if you have not seen it.

My first assignment after returning from Vietnam was to the Aerial Delivery (AD) shop at Dover. The hangar used as the morgue for all returning KIAs from Nam was co-located with our AD parachute packing room.

We packed parachutes four feet from the KIA human remains processing line. The remains were treated with reverence and respect but the morgue workers had become so accustomed to the smell of death and formaldehyde that they ate their lunches standing or sitting next to the bodies they were processing. It was a grotesque sight.

About a month after reporting to the Aerial Delivery shop our rigging team was sent on a temporary duty (TDY) assignment to Fort Campbell, KY to support the Airborne Brigade's equipment airdrop training to learn to rig the equipment and vehicle (jeep) airdrop loads. We shipped ten WWII surplus jeeps and assorted supplies and equipment for airdrop rigging as well as for the actual scheduled airdrop exercises.

We were only there for a couple of days when our unit was recalled to Dover AFB. Our boss CMSgt John (Shaky John) Tapley asked for a volunteer to stay behind for two weeks to guard all our equipment and cargo parachutes. Contrary to the general consensus NEVER to volunteer, I raised my hand and stepped forward from the group formation.

Chief Tapley gave me specific instructions and one of the NCOs showed me the duties and responsibilities that I would be required to accomplish during their absence. Within an hour after my briefing, I was left alone. On the second day of sheer boredom from just walking around the building and "guarding" the equipment I became extremely restless. Out of curiosity I opened the jeep rigging manual and studied the procedures for rigging a jeep for airdrop.

It was not a difficult procedure but it is quite laborious and normally required two or three certified riggers. It also required paramount precision to avoid any chance of malfunction during the airdrops. To pass the time I decided to become a self-appointed rigger. Hey! I had 13 days left to screw up and fix what I screwed up and remember that I only had a barely average 109 IQ.

Since I was already certified to pack parachutes, I started with the easiest task. Following the instructions in the manual I packed thirty 125-pound G-12 cargo parachutes for ten jeeps. Check.

Next, I assembled the cargo airdrop-pallets that the jeep sits on. Check.

Then I made the honeycomb cushioning that is placed between the Jeep and the pallet. Then I used the 10K forklift to lift and put the Jeep on the honeycomb and air-drop pallet and then secured it with tie downs. Check.

Using the 10K forklift to save my back I lifted the three each 125-pound parachutes on top of the jeeps and secured them according to the manual. Check.

Next, I built the parachute extraction system and connected it to the jeep and the final completely rigged airdrop jeep package had to be placed on roller conveyors. Check.

Half-way through the entire process I decided that I should have just guarded the damn stuff. But after a day-off and getting a lot of rest I once again took up the challenge to complete my goal to rig the 10 jeeps. Twelve days after its inception the self-assigned on-the- job (OJT) project was complete with two days to spare.

I used the two days to recover from my ordeal and I was fresh and well rested before Chief Tapley and the team returned. Perplexed and confused, the Chief scanned the finished job and stared at the neatly rigged Jeeps. "Damn, did the Army riggers come over to rig the equipment and to pack the parachutes?"

"No sir. I did it myself!" I answered proudly.

His head snapped around and he flashed me a mocking grin. "What? You're full of shit Airman – No way!" After finally convincing him that I had indeed accomplished the task at hand he assigned two of his certified rigger NCOs to inspect my work.

Other than a couple of non-critical errors, the completely rigged jeeps passed inspection. None of the riggers trusted the parachute packing jobs and random parachutes were pulled from the jeeps and inspected. No errors were discovered, and all the jeeps were airdropped from C-141 Starlifters a few days later without a single malfunction.

Soon after my self-directed two-week on-the-job airdrop rigging and parachute packing program, Chief Tapley sent me back to Fort Lee, VA to train and become a certified rigging inspector. It was then that I learned about all the rigging mistakes I had made. It is safe to say that I dodged 10 bullets when all my airdrop loads deployed safely during the airdrop.

My rank at the time was Airman Second Class (E-2) or 2 stripes. I was honored to have Chief Tapley nominate me for a Spot promotion to Airman First Class (E-4) or 3 stripes and it was quickly approved.

CHAPTER 25 - KOREA

While the rest of the country was burning the flag and protesting, my hometown in Pennsylvania was still proudly holding on to the values of God, country and family and I went home frequently and still wore my uniform everywhere.

At twenty-one I had not dated anyone seriously since Penny. My military life left little time to meet someone and nurture any serious relationship. During the fall football season, a friend invited me to watch him play for his hometown high school football team in Beaver Falls. While I was waiting for the game to start, I walked around the high school stadium that launched Joe Namath's career. The game had not started yet and I was enjoying watching the cheerleaders practicing before the game. One girl in particular caught my eye and I was smitten. I asked my buddy who she was and asked him to introduce us. Her name was Gerry and she seemed to have the same immediate attraction towards me. It had to be the uniform.

I received Permanent Change of Station (PCS) orders for Kwang Ju South, Korea soon after meeting Gerry and until I left for my new assignment, we spent every available moment together. I broke down and bought an old used rusty Fiat 124 convertible and every possible weekend, holiday, and official military leave opportunity I drove home from the base to be with Gerry.

Before leaving for Korea, I decided to ask Gerry to marry me. I asked her father for permission in the old-fashioned way and he and his wife gave me the blessing to ask her. Gerry accepted, and we planned to be married upon my return on midtour leave from Korea. I left for Korea full of anticipation for building a promising future together.

On May 1, 1969, the day I arrived in Korea for my thirteen-month tour it was 20 degrees below zero. It is not possible to adequately describe the bitter wind and cold. It was even more impossible to believe what I was seeing as the Korean soldiers were doing Physical Training (PT) in their white underwear obviously oblivious of the bone numbing cold. They were the toughest foreign national soldiers I ever had the honor to serve with. Their quarters were extremely sparse as they contained one small dresser, a steel framed bed, mattress, a thin thing meant to be a pillow and a standard green army blanket.

I was focused on my career track so my first order of business after I reported to my new assignment was to take a new examination for promotion called the Skill Knowledge Test or SKT. There were six participants taking the exam at the same time in an exceedingly small, confined room and it was almost impossible NOT to see the answer sheet of the guy sitting next to you. I was sitting alone at the back of the room near the exit door. The proctor was a SSgt who handed out the exams and a sheet of white paper for mathematical calculations and other exam-related purposes. The proctor reminded us that the exam was not an open-book and warned us that sharing questions and answers was prohibited and violations would result in military disciplinary actions.

About 15 minutes into the exam the proctor left the room to smoke a cigarette. We were left alone for at least a half hour when four of the test takers started to show each other their answers. Finally, the fifth test taker gave in to the temptation and joined in.

The Proctor eventually returned and walked around the room looking over all our shoulders before returning to his seat for another 10 or 15 minutes. He once again left the room for a smoke and to go to the head (bathroom). He was gone for most of the exam completion time and all of the cheaters shared answers to their tests. Near the end of the allocated exam time the proctor returned until the clock alarm sounded. He collected all of the exams and note sheets and dismissed us.

The scene bothered me but I was not involved in the cheating and I quickly put the incident behind me. I scored a 95 on the test and along with good performance evaluations I was soon promoted to Staff Sergeant or E-5. I was euphoric since I was going to marry a wonderful girl and I would sew on my stripes exactly 2 years and 10 months after joining the Air Force.

Five days after completing the SKT I was ordered to report immediately to the Office of Special Investigations (OSI). I was puzzled. Why would the OSI want to talk to me?

When I met with them, I felt like they had just thrown a bucket of ice water in my face. I was under investigation for cheating on the SKT along with the others taking the test that day. The investigators added that if found guilty I would be dishonorably discharged and possibly sentenced to the Leavenworth military prison.

The two investigators advised me that they were aware that I may not have been a participant in the cheating and offered to give me immunity from prosecution if I cooperated with them. I had no reason not to cooperate since I was merely a captive observer but did not understand why I needed immunity for something I did not participate in. I testified under oath and in writing about what occurred and had to sign a non-disclosure document not to discuss my meeting with the OSI with anyone.

I left their office shaking and fearing for my freedom and the loss of my beloved Air Force career. Although I did not believe that I would be found guilty, just being interrogated by the infamous OSI would throw suspicion on my otherwise impeccable reputation. It was obvious that I would have to watch my back moving on because the recriminations and retributions for being identified as a "Rat" by the other men on the base could become hazardous to my health.

The fifth Airman told the OSI that I did not participate in the sharing of answers. That statement turned out to be the justification used to offer me immunity.

The five perpetrators were sentenced to dishonorable discharges and fines in pay and allowances. I was exonerated because the cheaters' answer sheets were almost exactly the same. The clincher was that all of them had the same incorrect answers. My high score raised suspicion but after interviewing my Chief they decided that I indeed had the technical knowledge to excel on the exam.

***

About four months into my tour in Korea I received a care package from Gerry's mother. It was a pleasant surprise initially until I opened it and found Gerry's engagement ring and a short "Dear John" letter from her breaking off the engagement. I had been "Jodied". I walked off the job and went to the NCO club and got shit-faced drunk. My boss followed me to the club to find out what happened. We talked for a long time and got drunk together.

Martial arts and consuming alcohol just do not mix and I do not tolerate alcohol very well. At some point I pushed my chair back from the table. I bumped into the chair at the table behind me which angered the guy sitting in it. He got up, turned around and grabbed me by the collar and jerked me out of my seat. My self-defense instincts kicked into gear and I turned around and grabbed his wrist and twisted it over causing him to bend over and exposing his elbow which allowed me to forcefully strike and break it. My boss grabbed me and dragged me out of the bar. Security Police arrived and after hearing the explanation from my Non-Communized Officer in Charge (NCOIC) and other witnesses that I was defending myself, they released me to return to work.

I was given an Emergency Leave to go home and settle my affairs. This typically would not have been considered a justification for an Emergency Leave but I was facing the possibility of military disciplinary action and the Chief wanted me off the base until things calmed down. Working as a supervisor in the Air Freight and Transportation unit made it an easier process for me to obtain an Emergency Leave flight back to the states.

When I arrived home, I discovered that while Gerry and I were dating, she had been dating another guy whenever I returned to Dover AFB. I had been "Jodied" even before leaving the states. When I reported to duty my immediate supervisor informed me that the guy who I had hurt in the bar had dropped the charges against me because he started the fight. To my relief, I fell into an, almost, uneventful routine for the rest of my 13-month tour in Kwang Ju, Korea.

My passion was working in Aerial Delivery and I could not imagine doing anything else. I had soaked up everything I could learn about Aerial Delivery and had my sights set squarely on becoming a loadmaster.

However, I received my PCS orders for my new assignment to McGuire AFB, New Jersey and I became enraged by the orders. Rumor had it that McGuire was one of the worst bases in the Air Force and adding insult to injury my orders assigned me to the Base Supply Squadron to be cross trained to work in Supply. Supply is a critical and important job. Nothing in the Air Force functions without it but I knew I was not suited for working in an enclosed warehouse.

After reading the PCS orders I swore, made a fist, and punched the wall. Unfortunately, there was a nail sticking out of the wall and head had imbedded in my fist between my index and middle finger. Remember, I had an IQ of 109.

My first four-year enlistment was coming to an end in another year and I decided to leave the Air Force after finishing my tour at McGuire.

CHAPTER 26 - MCGUIRE AFB

As a hail Mary while en route back to the states and McGuire I formulated a drastic plan. Immediately after arriving at McGuire, I went to see Captain Johnson, the Aerial Delivery Unit commander, and knocked on his office door. A deep authoritative voice called out from behind the door.

"Enter!"

My heart was pounding wildly and I knew this was my only chance to get this right. I took a deep breath, opened the door, and walked in with as much confidence as I could muster. I stood ramrod at attention, saluted, and introduced myself.

"SSgt Wetzel requesting to meet with you Sir." I wondered if he noticed my eyepopping expression as I stood there dumbstruck in awe of one of the most professional, massive, and imposing officers that I have ever had the pleasure and honor to meet - Captain Johnson.

Apparently enjoying my nervousness, he furrowed his brow and flashed me a knowing but puzzled half smirk. I remained at attention and waited for permission to speak. Trying to hide his amusement at my bold intrusion he returned my salute and said,

"At ease SSgt Wetzel. What can I do for you?"

I took in a deep breath then all in one breath I blurted out my rehearsed speech.

"Sir, I just returned from Korea with orders to report to Supply here. However, I am experienced and highly qualified to work in AD. I served in Vietnam and was involved in the siege at Dak To and Khe Shan. I have extensive experience and am certified to operate every vehicle in your unit, inspecting and packing cargo and personnel parachutes and rigging every type of cargo and vehicle for airdrop. And frankly Sir, my skills and expertise would be wasted in Supply and I want to work for you, Sir."

He opened his mouth but nothing came out for a few seconds. He shook his head and chuckled in amazement. I swallowed hard thinking I had just lost my last chance at working in AD. I handed him my personnel file for review and nervously waited for a response.

I watched him flip through the pages while slightly shifting my weight from side to side. I became aware that I was holding my breath and slowly let it out through my slightly parted lips while letting my eyes scan the room looking for something to focus on. My eyes landed on a clock on the wall and I watched the second-hand sweep slowly from one minute to the next.

He finally closed my file, handed it back to me and with steely eyes and said:

"You've got balls SSgt Wetzel. I think you will fit nicely in my unit. Report to me in the morning. I will make some calls and see what I can do to arrange for you to work in Aerial Delivery but I cannot promise you anything so be prepared to go to Supply if things do not work out as I expect. You are dismissed."

I snapped to attention, saluted again, and said:

"Thank you, Sir, I promise you will never regret your decision." He returned my salute and I did an about face, held back the urge to do a happy dance and left his office. I was in. Somehow, I knew that Captain Johnson would be successful in getting approval for my transfer. I reported to him the following morning, he shook my hand, handed me a red rigger's hat, and welcomed me aboard the team. I was ecstatic and once again I reminded him that he would never regret going to bat for me.

Captain Johnson introduced me to his Admin Assistant Sergeant "Bunny" Chris. A highly professional Airman from Pittsburgh. We became lifelong close friends. He gave me a tour and orientation of the AD shop and introduced me to all the guys assigned to the unit.

My first introduction was to a loadmaster named SSgt John Burkhardt. John became my mentor and another life-long friend. He took me under his wings – so to speak - and trained me on every aspect of my new assignment. When he realized that my goal was to become a loadmaster, he a made a point to introduce me to every Loadmaster in the unit and provided me with additional airdrop training that I would need to become one. We went on to serve together several times, our careers closely paralleled each other and we both retired as Chief Master Sergeants.

***

In 1896 dyslexia was referred to as "congenital word blindness". It is a learning difficulty that primarily affects the skills involved in accurate and fluent word reading and spelling. It affects a range of people from those with high intelligence to the intellectually challenged. Adult dyslectics frequently make bad decisions and do not learn quickly from those mistakes or they may have problems remembering or recognizing colors. The most known characteristic features of dyslexia are difficulties in phonological awareness, verbal memory, and verbal processing speed. Phonics instruction for those with dyslexia is still the general approach recommended today. Whether I have high intelligence or am intellectually challenged is a matter of debate, probably a level of both.

About the time I was preparing to apply for loadmaster school I realized that I had a real problem with reading. No matter what I did or how hard I worked to improve my reading skills they were at best - extremely poor. A friend of mine and I were conversing and she was complimenting me on how quickly I was moving up through the ranks. I confided in her that I was really struggling to comprehend what I was reading in my job-related technical manuals and feared that my dream of becoming a loadmaster might be in jeopardy.

I described to her what I was experiencing and her face lit up. "I had that problem too, but I got help." Now she piqued my interest.

"What kind of help, what did you do?" I asked in desperation.

"Well, some psychologists are beginning to work with people like us with reading struggles."

My heart jumped. I had no idea anyone else had that problem. This was new hope for me. "What do you mean like us?" I asked.

She said, "They call it dyslexia. We don't see things on the page the same way most people do."

With a little convincing my friend referred me to a psychotherapist who specialized in helping people with dyslexia. I wasted no time making an appointment.

After some testing the therapist worked out a sensory based learning program for me that focused on my verbal skills to improve reading. Wow! I had already learned that process by sheer luck at Brady's Run Park where I used to do my homework. All I had to do was build on to the skills that I had already taught myself. She gave me some additional homework to improve those skills and scheduled follow-up testing over a six-month period.

Slowly my confidence in reading improved and I was less nervous about moving forward with my Air Force career. Since I was receiving my dyslexia therapy from a civilian doctor, none of it was recorded in my military medical records. If I had not reached out for help my goal to become a loadmaster would never have come to fruition. Over time I took control of dyslexia instead of dyslexia controlling my life.

About 6 months into my McGuire AFB assignment, I asked John and Captain Johnson for help in getting me into Loadmaster School. Captain Johnson made some phone calls and arranged for me to get accepted into the next available class. My application was accepted to attend the very next class instead of waiting in a long line of candidates.

***

Basic Loadmaster School was a two-month course at Sheppard AFB, TX. I was frustrated and bored with how slow and redundant the technical part of the training seemed to me. I already knew most of the training material and flew through each phase of training. Just short of completing the first month I decided to ask the school superintendent if I could somehow take a bypass test to avoid going through another month of training. At this point I had passed every exam with high scores. Frustrated and bored I asked the school superintendent if there was a by-pass exam. He advised me that there was but no one had ever passed it. With some powerful persuasion and convincing he gave me the chance to take it.

I passed the exam and graduated with honors at the halfway point of the course. To my knowledge no one else has ever completed the course through a by-pass exam, however I would strongly recommend against allowing it to ever happen again. There are many intricacies about any career field that cannot be learned without classroom training and I was about to find out how unprepared I was.

Upon reporting back to McGuire AFB, I was selected to fly the C-133 Cargomaster, sometimes nicknamed the Flying Silo. It had a history of self-destructing in flight and crashing. Still young and feeling immortal, I was excited to start my new assignment and reported to the 18th Military Airlift Squadron (MAS) Chief Loadmaster. He advised me that my assignment was changed and I would be flying the C-141A Starlifter.

C-133 Cargomaster

C-141A (Top) and C-141B (Bottom) Starlifters

The Air Force had just lost another C-133 and its entire aircrew over the Atlantic Ocean. All that remained at the scene of the crash were seat cushions and other floating debris. All of the remaining C-133s were permanently grounded.

As tragic as it was, I could hardly contain my excitement that I would be flying all over the world delivering and air dropping supplies and equipment as a Loadmaster on the most beautiful cargo jet in the nation. I was informed that there was one restriction. Because my last name was Wetzel I could not travel to Indonesia. My family was still blacklisted there and my safety, even as an American citizen could not be guaranteed.

My instructor loadmaster was TSgt George (Clutch Cargo) McCluskey. Clutch was a huge guy with a heart that matched. He was very outspoken and definitely "one of a kind." He was a great teacher and became a good friend very quickly.

During in-processing at the 18th Military Airlift Squadron (MAS) I was presented with a disorganized pile of manuals along with changes to them that could have filled a wheelbarrow. I was told to organize them into proper order. I gathered the stack of unorganized documents and went to the barracks. I sat on my bunk bed and stared at the small mountain of manuals and began the process of trying to make sense of it all. Every manual had a series of changes that had to be inserted in some sort of organized order. I immediately noticed a pattern that indicted that Change 1 was followed by Change 2, then Change 3, etc. This was going to be a piece of cake after all. Proud of myself that I had easily figured it out I simply found the most current change and threw the other previous changes in the trash - thirty minutes later - DONE!

The first duty for a newbie in every airlift squadron is to go through orientation and inspection of your manuals. When it came time to present my brand new impeccably organized manuals to Clutch for inspection, he opened my book bag and began the process of inspecting my technical orders and Air Force regulations and manuals. I noticed that he looked puzzled and it took him a few minutes to finally give me an incredulous look.

"What the Hell is this? Where are all the changes?" He asked.

"They are all in there, Sir!" I answered proudly.

His response, "The Hell they are! You are missing all the consecutive changes. Did you not get them?

"Of course, I did Sir. I threw them away." I said, quite satisfied with myself.

His mouth flew open in surprise and he stared at me speechless for a few seconds. "Don't they teach manual maintenance and management at Loadmaster school anymore?"

Now I was speechless. I was about to learn why no one should be allowed to graduate from technical schools through by-pass tests. Oh shit!

"Well Sir, I guess it was probably part of the second month of training. The first month was very boring and redundant so I took the by-pass test and aced it and was not required to attend the second month. I guess I should have."

I knew he was about to blast me for my arrogance but instead he laughed uproariously and then escorted me to the manuals NCO and together we rebuilt every improperly organized manual one by one per regulations.

We were scheduled to fly my first training mission the next morning at 0500 hours (5 AM). Clutch told me to get to bed early and expect to be alerted by Base Operations at 0200 hours. Because of my excitement at fulfilling a long-term dream I did not sleep at all.

After being alerted by Base Operations I reported to Clutch and we boarded the crew bus to begin preparation for the mission. Mission preparation included getting briefed about our destination, the length of the flight, the en route weather forecast and finally the cargo load and number of passengers.

To my amazement when we pulled up to the aircraft, the C-141 tail number was 133. I took it as a message that flying on the C-141A instead of the C-133 was a blessing from above. I said a short prayer to thank God for it.

***

Clutch was a great instructor and had an answer for all my challenges no matter what the circumstance were. Some of his solutions were unorthodox but he always had one. During my training for airdrop qualification, I could not control the queasiness of the low-level terrain following flights and constantly threw up. Clutch got tired of my running to the latrine to vomit so he tied a large blue garbage bag around my neck. From then on until I became used to the rough and turbulent flights, I wore the trash bag around my neck. Sort of a backwards blue superman cape.

The Army paratroopers thought it was the funniest thing they had ever seen on their paratroop airdrop missions. Regardless of my embarrassment during these missions, I owe a great deal of my success as a Loadmaster directly to Clutch.

***

Clutch was my instructor for my first over water mission to our Pacific bases that included Elmendorf AFB, Alaska; Yokota AB, Japan; Kadena AB, Okinawa; Clark AB, Philippines; Anderson AFB, Guam; and Hickman AFB, Hawaii (HI) with a return home to McGuire AFB.

During our trip through Clark AFB, I turned 22. Clutch and the enlisted crew decided to celebrate my birthday in style. It was a hotel pool-side celebration and the details will be left to the readers imagination. I passed out by the swimming pool and Clutch hoisted me up and carried me over his shoulder back to my hotel room. The crew laid me on my side in the bed so that I would not aspirate if I threw up. Clutch and one of the engineers slept in the chairs in my room to ensure that I was going to be OK. Eight hours from "Bottle to Throttle" was the rule and every one of us violated it. It was to all our benefit to ensure that we covered each other's back.

When the alert call came from Base Operations I was passed out. It was not my proudest moment, but I was unfit for flight duty. Clutch and the engineer cleaned me up and helped me get my flight suit on and carried me out to the crew bus. We arrived at the aircraft before the pilot and co-pilot and Clutch was able to carry me over his shoulder up to the crew entry door and up the cockpit ladder. He put me in the crew rest bunk and covered me with a blanket. Somehow, he found a way to keep me out of the pilot's view.

He conducted the preflight and cargo on-load and when the pilots tried to contact me Clutch responded on my behalf. We took off from Clark AB and I finally regained consciousness when we arrived at Anderson AFB. As far as I know, only the enlisted crew was aware of my fitness to fly the mission.

John had taken the time to teach and mentor me to be on the Airlift Control Element (ALCE) team. I was able to join the team because of John's personal recommendation. The ALCE is a specially trained team of aircrew members and mission planners that train and prepare combat support members from every branch of our military to deploy anywhere in the world.

The ALCE assignment significantly limited my flying missions and duties but gave me a wealth of experience in supporting combat and other missions across the globe. A key side-benefit was the real-world mobility experience it provided me. It was a goldmine of opportunities to accumulate the experience and knowledge that I needed to ace every Skill Knowledge Test (SKT) for promotion. Combined with my high-performance evaluation scores I was promoted to TSgt on the first attempt at the sixth year point of service. This usually takes and average of up to twelve years. There is nothing like teaching to force you to excel in your field of expertise.

CHAPTER 27 - THE PILOT

Because my additional flight pay improved my financial status significantly, I could afford to pursue my lifelong dream of being a pilot. I promptly joined the McGuire AFB Aero Club and bought my very first new car– a green Dodge Challenger. Blue is my favorite color but I picked green for my first fully financed car. The green one was on sale because no one apparently wanted their pretty cool sports car to be green.

Becoming a pilot took on a slow start and I even considered quitting the training program. I did not solo until the 15th hour of training instead of the normal 7 to10 hours.

On November 10, 1971, the 17th hour of my flight training, I was cleared to go on my first solo short cross-country flight to Millville, NJ. The weather was awful. Lots of humidity and cloud cover with the dew point spread of 2 degrees. I had a bad premonition telling me not to fly and expressed my concern to the chief flight instructor. He insisted that I would be fine and that he had full confidence in my ability to make the 100-mile round trip. With deep trepidation, I drove to Base Operations and filed my flight plan.

My takeoff was smooth, and I leveled off at 3,500 feet. Clouds were well above me but there was a great deal of visible moisture with rivulets of rain striking the wind screen. Twenty minutes into the flight I looked behind me and McGuire AFB was no longer in view. Forward visibility was limited and getting worse. Suddenly the aircraft started to rattle and vibrate, and the propeller turned slower and slower. It did not stop but I sensed that it would if something were not done quickly. I pumped the throttle several times thinking that the engine was not getting fuel. The engine revved up and the propeller sped up causing the Revolutions Per Minute (RPMs) to return to normal. I breathed deeply and began to relax.

Then suddenly the engine vibrated badly, sputtered and the propeller stopped turning. Nothing happened after pumping the throttle and trying to restart the engine. I freaked out but had the sense to put the aircraft into its best glide speed. I remember clearly saying three times: "God help me, God help me, God help me!"

I picked up the microphone and transmitted "Mayday – Mayday – Mayday – Cessna 23414 over southern New Jersey with total engine failure.

The tower at the Millville, NJ airport responded, "Cessna 23414 what is your location?"

"I do not know. Visibility is almost zero and my engine quit – Over!"

The tower directed me to follow specific microphone keying procedures so that they could determine my location. But by then I had dead-engine-glided to about 2,000 feet. I was looking out and below at scrub trees and brush that are common in southern coastal New Jersey. I repeated "Dear God please help me!" and He did.

I looked out the pilot door window and down again. I saw a small house with a pasture behind it and I continued my emergency landing procedures. Descending with the best glide speed I flew downwind, base, and final with flaps down for a soft field landing.

On final approach, I rigidly and robotically followed standard landing procedures and even though I had no power I pulled the carburetor heat knob and powered down for the landing. The main landing gear touched down and the engine screamed to life - startling me. There was enough room to take off, but I said; "Hell with it!" and came to a full stop.

I sat there in shock for quite a while until I heard someone banging on the passenger door and cussing at me. As I reached across and opened the door, the red-faced enraged farmer continued to cuss me out. His wife told him to calm down.

"What are you doing here?" She asked me.

Badly shaken I opened the door and got out and the couple stared me down waiting for an answer. Unable to speak for a few minutes I finally recovered my wits and explained what happened. Then they invited me to come into their house. I asked them to let me call the airport tower to let them know I was OK.

The local area Federal Aviation Administration (FAA) flight examiner answered the phone and I told him who I was and that I landed safely and was OK. He asked me to tell him exactly what had happened. I explained the incident and he responded, "You had carburetor icing."

"What is carburetor icing?" I asked.

"Who is your flight instructor?" he asked.

Seventeen hours of flight time in my logbook and my instructor never told me about carburetor icing. He had taught me the landing preparation procedures but did not teach me why a pilot had to use the carburetor heat lever for landing. To be clear – I do not blame the flight instructor for failing to teach me about carburetor icing. That information should have been clearly understood through the training manuals I used to pass the FAA written test.

The FAA inspector sent a mechanic to my location that was only 15 minutes away from the Millville airport. The mechanic cleared the airplane for flight after doing an engine test run.

"Wim, do you feel confident enough to take off using a soft field take off procedure?"

"Sure, no problem." I confidently told him.

"Alright. The airport is due west of here and you should be able to see it from an altitude about 1,000 feet."

"Thanks. I appreciate your help."

I turned to the farmer and his wife and thanked them profusely.

I made a quick call to the tower and spoke with the FAA inspector and was cleared to take off. My 15-minute flight was uneventful. The FAA inspector met me on the tarmac and helped me refuel while teaching me about carburetor icing. The weather had cleared, and he gave me specific instructions on how to return to McGuire AFB located due north of the airport. After thanking him he entered his clearance into my logbook and I continued my flight to McGuire.

I landed at McGuire without any further incidents and received a call from Ground Control directing me to report to Base Operations immediately. I put the Cessna in the hanger and reported to the civilian Base Operations officer. There was no mistaking his mood. He was livid.

My flight instructor was standing there with a confused look on his face and asked me: "What happened?"

"Never mind that Wetzel! Why did you depart without approval and not filing a flight plan?" The Base Operations officer said.

"I had approval from my flight instructor and I did file a flight plan with the Sergeant."

"We do not have a flight plan for your flight on file, so you took off without filing." he stated.

I looked at the Sergeant and reminded her of our earlier discussion and about handing her my flight plan. She remembered the discussion and confirmed that I had filed a flight plan with her. She removed the vertical folder from the top of the file cabinet looking for my flight plan. It was not in the folder. We looked everywhere and finally found it behind the file cabinet. The Operations officer apologized but I went home and decided my flight career was over.

It took me two months to recover from the calamitous flight experience and regain my courage to continue with flight training. I met with my new flight instructor who convinced me to start again. After 76 hours of flight training, which is close to double the minimum requirement, I finally obtained my private pilot's license.

Regardless of the extended time to achieve my goal I did it and was not disappointed that it took so long. Eventually I obtained my commercial pilot's license and instrument ratings culminating in my single and multi-engine instrument flight instructor ratings.

***

Roy was my first passenger after I received my Private Pilot's license. I rented a Cessna 150 from the McGuire AFB Aero Club and flew cross country to Beaver County Airport, PA. Roy met me at the airport to drive me home, but I asked him to give me the honor of him being my first passenger. He just flat out refused but would not tell me why.

Roy drove me back to the airport when it was time to return to McGuire AFB. En route to the airport I was able to convince him to take a short ride around the Valley with me. He was obviously not overjoyed but accepted my invitation.

As we walked up to the aircraft, he seemed anxious and visibly shaken. I was puzzled by this response because Roy was fearless and this behavior was completely out of character. We buckled in, taxied out and took off. Roy was shaking and sweating profusely as we took off.

Not even 200 feet above the ground he said "Get me down! Get me down! Can't you see the tracers? Get me down now!" and he reached for the door handle to open the door. I grabbed his hand and yelled that I would land immediately but he had to calm down or we could crash. He closed his eyes and refused to open them as we climbed to the pattern altitude and started to fly downwind for landing.

As we turned to base and final, he said "I'm going to throw up."

"Not in my airplane you're not!" I yelled as I reached across and unlocked the window and shoved his head out. He lost his cookies outside the window just in time.

We made the final approach and landed. Soon after and while still taxiing he jumped out of the door and ran to his car. He did not fly again for several years. Only the lure of going hunting and fishing with friends in Canada got him through the memories, trauma, and fear of falling out of the helicopter in Nam. Eventually the hesitancy and fear of flying disappeared and he routinely accepted offers from his friends to fly to Canada on fishing trips.

I had an uneventful flight back to McGuire but I was heartbroken that my fearless, confident, and brilliant brother was brought down by a senseless war and we would never be able to enjoy flying together.

My next trip home was to visit Roy in the hospital. Along with Roy's emotional challenges he suffered extensive medical issues after leaving Vietnam. He started having debilitating grand mal seizures that required him to take medications in an attempt to control the events. The seizures continued to strike without warning.

One day while working out at his Karate school, he suffered a major seizure event. He landed on his chin when he fell to the floor mat and bit off half of his tongue. The separated tongue flopped on the mat as he writhed on the floor. His instructors called for an ambulance and did what they could to keep him alive. Someone recovered the severed tongue and wrapped it in a cloth and covered it with ice to save it. The doctors were able to reattach his tongue and save his life.

When I saw him in the hospital, he was still unable to talk while the wound was healing. He communicated with me on a note pad and explained that his worst experience was not being able to breathe as the part of the tongue that did not get severed retracted into his throat cutting off his airway. Roy was again "one tough Dude."

CHAPTER 28 - MY FRIEND KEN AND SKYDIVING

My previously dreaded three-year tour at McGuire AFB turned out to be one of the best assignments of my Air Force career. My roommate was a Combat Controller (CCT) by the name of Ken Ritter. We became friends immediately. He was a monster of a man who could do unbelievable numbers of sit-ups, pushups, and chin-ups. He could outrun anyone within the CCT community. But the quintessence of Ken was his universal reputation as an unwavering, trustworthy loyal friend who was also a crazy kind of guy who never shied away from challenges. Did I mention that he was a chick magnet?

Our antics would fill another book but there is one classic story that screams out to be shared. Combat Controllers are required to jump from the C-141 and other combat aircraft regularly to maintain currency. For Ken, these jumps were as routine to him as it would be for most of us to drive to the grocery store. He was always striving to spice up his routine.

On one scheduled jump he asked the Aircraft Commander (AC) if it was OK if he jumped from the aircraft buck-naked. The pilot was hesitant but finally conceded. Ken dressed down to only his helmet, socks, boots, and parachutes. Then before the 10-minute warning Ken walked up to the cockpit, tapped the navigator on the shoulder and asked for the winds on the ground (speed and direction). Unaware that the AC had approved the unusual request the Nav turned around shocked to see Ken standing there in his birthday suit and parachute. He provided the winds information and wanted to be sure someone took pictures.

Ken returned to the troop door and the student Navigator took several pictures. On "Green Light" Ken exited the aircraft.

We were on the DZ to recover airdrop equipment when Ken appeared under his parachute buck naked in front of us and his waiting girlfriend. She handed him a change of clothing and both disappeared under the deflating parachute. Pictures of Ken standing at the jump platform before leaving the aircraft and the event were sent to Playboy Magazine for publishing. Playboy contacted the Air Force about the pictures but were denied publishing opportunities.

***

Ken encouraged me to learn to skydive so that we could go into competitions. He took my buddy Tom Householder and me out to the local sky diving center to become certified. On my first static line jump from the Cessna 172 I was so excited to jump that before the jumpmaster told me to jump, I had already done so. Fear never entered my thoughts. My first landing was in a 5-foot-high pile of manure in a farmer's pasture. A parachute landing fall (PLF) was unnecessary. The jump school owner made me ride in the back of the school's pickup truck on the way back to his training center.

Wiser on my second jump, I exited the aircraft and stood on the aircraft tire and strut and held on for dear life waiting for the pilot to cut the engine power and for the instructor to tell me to jump. The engine went to idle and the jump order came. I was paralyzed with white knuckled fear, gripping the strut so tight that it took the instructor several attempts to break my hands free so that I could fall free before the aircraft stalled. When free and away from the aircraft I was able to relax and enjoy the drop. We all jumped three more times to obtain our certifications. During my remaining time at McGuire, I recorded 35 parachute jumps.

Ken signed us up to compete in the annual Combat Control skydiving competition at Hurlburt Field near Panama City, Florida. With Captain Johnson's blessing the Air Force provided us with TDY orders to attend the competition. We jumped out of Huey Helicopters and a C-130 and ultimately won first place in our division and received a nice write up in the base newspaper. Tom had landed five inches from the target and I had landed four feet from the it and clinching "First Place.".

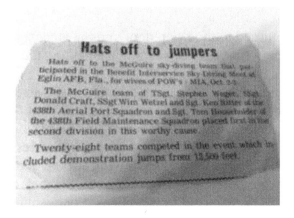

McGuire AFB Newspaper Article

Tom Householder Hit the Target Clinching First Place

My lust for skydiving was hampered by disaster. We were skydiving over the Perris drop zone near the Salton Sea, CA. The jump plane climbed to 17,500 feet with six jumpers. I was the fourth jumper leaving the aircraft and free-fell to 2,500 feet where I opened my chute. The person who jumped after me continued to freefall. I expected that he would open his parachute at about 2,000 feet but he did not. I watched in horror as he impacted the ground at 120 miles per hour. The accident investigation determined that he committed suicide since neither of his parachute handles had been pulled. It was enough for me and after this 49th jump I sold my parachute and never jumped again.

***

Unfortunately, and painfully for me, Ken decided not to re-enlist and received his discharge from the Air Force. That was a tough day for all of us who knew and loved Ken. He was unconventional and lived life to the fullest. Before leaving for home, he asked me if I would like to have his parasail with one stipulation - to get professional training before using it.

"Of course. I will!"

It was a cold, windy November Sunday, and several of us were watching the Pittsburgh Steelers game. We had been drinking Boone's Farm Apple Wine for most of the afternoon and were feeling bored, drunk, and feisty.

Tom Householder said, "Hey Wim – why don't we check out the parasail that Ken gave you?" In a less than sober retort I quickly said "Hell yeah! – Let's Go!"

The wind speed for Parasailing should be steady and from no more than 3 – 5 knots. The November winds were 15 to 25 knots and variable, constantly changing direction and velocity.

I was wearing street clothes and a pair of black loafers. no boots, no helmet or other body protection. Did I mention my IQ? We went to the aerial delivery airdrop rigging shop and borrowed 350 feet of 1,000-pound tensile strength nylon rope and a set of C-130 seat belts for the quick release system. We drove my brand-new Green Dodge Charger out to the city park located right next to the Interstate highway. Apart from some trees there was no barrier separating the park from the Interstate.

One of the guys got in my car and waited for the word to start and pull forward to tow me into the air. I donned the parasail harness and tied my end of the tow rope to the seat belt quick release system. Tom connected the other end of the nylon tow line to the axel and I stretched the tow rope to its full extended length while holding the bundled-up parasail in my folded arms. When I reached the end of the tow line, I turned to hand the parasail over to my two assistants who were charged with stretching the parasail out to its full deployment width.

I tripped over the tow rope and dropped the parasail. The variable winds inflated the parasail to its full deployment width and dragged me back as far as the tow rope could stretch. The winds shifted to the left and dragged me across the ground and partially into the air. The winds shifted again and swung me to the right again bouncing the parasail and me off the ground. I was told later that they lost count of how many times this recurred. But finally, as I was rapidly ascending into the cool November sky, I heard one of the guys say out-loud – "Wim's DEAD!"

At some point the winds stayed steady and the car was being pulled backwards by the fully inflated parasail even though the driver floored the gas pedal and was attempting to drive it full power forward. The rear wheels lifted off the ground pulling the car backward. I distinctly recall looking straight down at my car when I reached for the seat belt quick release. It was the last thing that I remember as the Dodge bumper cut the fully stretched nylon tow rope. The rope reacted like a rubber band with the steel seat belt hitting my chin and forehead with full force. I still have the scar on my chin and the lump on my forehead as proof. Part of the released nylon rope wrapped itself around the parasail suspension lines and partially deflated it. I fell from an estimated height of 250 feet to the ground under a collapsed parachute like a sack of stupid dumb-ass crap. I faintly remember regaining partial consciousness just before hitting the ground and saying "Ohhhhhh Shit!"

If the parasail had fully deflated, I would not be writing this after-action report. Upon impacting the ground, the tow rope partially unraveled from the suspension lines and the parasail fully re-inflated and dragged me at high speed on my back across the park towards the interstate. The guys regained their sensibilities and chased me across the park to try to deflate the parasail. No such luck this day! In desperation, I rolled over onto my stomach to try to collapse the chute or anything to stop the violent, furious, and painful drag - losing my shoes and tearing my new trousers in the process.

Just before seeing and hitting the Interstate highway I heard car horns blaring and screeching tires. While rolling over onto my back I closed my eyes expecting the worst. I hit the median strip concrete barrier hard as the parasail continued to drag me across the grass. Cars going North slammed their brakes hard as I was dragged across their path. After clearing the highway with the guys and other witnesses chasing me, the parasail hit a barrier fence and collapsed as did I. Everyone knew that I would be dead. I thank God and Boone's Farm Apple Wine that I did not die that day. Parasail training would also have taught me that there is a quick release system on the harness that I should have pulled to stop the dragging.

I do not recall how I returned to the car, but my parasail stayed behind collapsed against the fence never to-be-seen again. Tom drove me to the Fort Dix hospital at a high rate of speed without stopping at the main gate. The Military Police (MP) did not stop him but followed us since my car's emergency flashers were going. Upon reaching the hospital I was put in a wheelchair and treated in the ER. The doctor asked my partners in stupidity "What happened to him and where are his shoes?"

Someone answered: "He slipped and fell down the barrack's stairs!" The doctor shook his head and asked me what happened. I answered that I fell and knocked my head on the ground and do not remember anything. My medical record entry simply reflects "Airman fell while descending a stairwell in the barracks and was knocked unconscious."

CHAPTER 29 – HICKAM AFB, HAWAII

McGuire holds many great memories for me and a lot of experiences that helped me to grow in character and to gain knowledge of the job I loved. The friends I made there will also be part of who I am. One of them was a former Air Force Recruiter named Cricket. She was part of our group that met frequently at the Airman's Club, went to the beach, and took excursions to New York City.

In August 1972 I received PCS orders to the 61st Military Airlift Wing (MAW) ALCE team at Hickam AFB, HI. I decided to drive across the country to San Francisco, California to catch my flight to Honolulu, HI. Cricket was from Decatur, Illinois, (IL) where she was on leave visiting her parents. She had invited me to stop in Decatur on my way through and stay with her family for a couple of days. When I arrived in Decatur Cricket told me she had arranged for a blind date with her best friend. Generally, I had not had good experiences with blind dates but after much convincing by Cricket I accepted her offer. We drove to her friend's home in my new Challenger to meet her. When we drove up to the house her friend Debbie was standing on her porch. She was drop dead beautiful and I was immediately attracted to her.

We only had three days together but we enjoyed every minute we had and I knew that I wanted to see her again even though we never discussed any further contact. Unknown to me at the time that I met Debbie she was in the Army but had been Absent Without Leave (AWOL) for over a month and the Army was looking for her.

I continued on my trek to my new assignment at Hickam AFB through San Francisco International Airport where I shipped my Challenger to Hawaii.

The Hickam ALCE team's mission was to support all contingencies in the Pacific region. One of my key assignments was to conduct mobility and contingency training for the Marines at Kaneohe Marine Corp Air Station (MCAS) and the Army Transportation soldiers at the 173rd Airborne Brigade at Wheeler Army Airfield. The day after arriving at Hickam AFB I reported to my new boss SMSgt Howard Berg.

My immediate supervisor was a good old boy, redneck racist from Mississippi. I will refer to him as Jimmy-John. Jimmy-John was an equal opportunity bully that hated all Asians and referred to them as zipper heads. He asked me where I came from and I responded, "from Pennsylvania." "No, where are you from?"

"Well, I was born in Indonesia." I answered, still unsure where he was going with his line of questioning.

He turned away in a huff muttering. "Now I have to work with a damn zipper head."

For the next nine months Jimmy-John made it his lot in life to create new and better ways to bully me and make me as miserable as possible before he rotated back to the mainland.

His departing shot before leaving was to write me a career-damaging negative performance evaluation. SMSgt Berg rewrote the evaluation that reflected my actual performance and Jimmy-John signed it under the threat of repercussions that he might have to face as a result of filing a false performance evaluation.

***

Debbie and I stayed in touch by phone and letters and I learned through these communications that Debbie was actually in the Army. It appeared on the surface that we had a lot in common and I assumed that we would enjoy building a life together especially since we both understood what military life was all about.

She became special to me so when I received orders to go to Norton AFB, CA to attend the NCO Leadership School I asked her to come to the graduation ceremony and banquet. I bought her the airline ticket and picked her up at the Los Angeles Airport (LAX) the day before graduation. I was so proud that I graduated with honors and was really happy she wanted to be there with me and see me graduate. We celebrated with my peers, their wives, and girlfriends all night.

During the celebrations I noticed that a couple of my fellow graduates were pretty handy and friendly with Debbie on the dance floor and Debbie did not discourage the extra attention. I was uncomfortable with the situation but I shrugged it off as a natural response to the graduation celebrations. I proposed to her that evening and we set a date for the wedding to take place in Hawaii. Since Debbie was still in the Army she would need to arrange for a transfer once we were married.

Then Cricket called me to let me know that she had just found out that Debbie was AWOL from the Army. Her NCO and a couple of the women in her unit were lesbians and sexually harassing her. When Debbie reported it to higher ups, they refused to believe her. The bullying became so aggressive that she felt she had no other recourse but to get away so she went AWOL.

I was upset by the deception but I gave her the benefit of the doubt. It did seem like she could have been in danger and no one knows better than me that we all make bad decisions. I called her and talked her into turning herself in and to get her record straightened out. Hesitant at first, she finally agreed to face her punishment. Several other soldiers came to her defense at the court martial and let the board know that they had also been sexually harassed. The charges were dismissed, and her record was cleared. Debbie returned to active service and was promoted to E-4 at Fort Bliss, TX. Looking back, I should have been alerted by all the red flags for this relationship but infatuation can severely blind a naïve dyslexic.

About two months later in May 1974 Debbie arrived at Hickam for the wedding. The base chaplain officiated the wedding and the reception was held at the squadron. The reception room was packed with my peers and civilian friends. There was no normal honeymoon since I was scheduled to be sent on a thirty-day mission just two days after the wedding.

Our short two-day honeymoon was held at the military resort on the north shore of Oahu. We were rudely awakened early in the morning of our first day of the honeymoon by the loud sounds of tank treads and explosions. We looked out the cabin window and watched a Marine Corps unit practice an invasion of the beach and resort. A tank gun barrel was pointed directly at our cabin window. Not exactly a romantic Hawaiian honeymoon but the practice invasion was an ominous warning of things to come.

After the honeymoon I saw Debbie about seven days over the next three months. Because she was now married to an Air Force NCO Debbie applied for her reassignment to Hawaii. Her reassignment orders arrived, and she was assigned to the Fort

Derussy Army post in Honolulu. We started planning and working on having a baby, but it did not go well. Debbie had an ectopic pregnancy and lost the baby. Doctors determined that her ability to have children was improbable without special medical assistance that would be expensive. She applied for a discharge from the Army and it was approved. My ALCE job required me to travel about 23 days a month and the constant time away from home caused a tremendous amount of distress between us and the marriage began to rapidly disintegrate.

***

I proved to be a lousy husband. My dedication and devotion to my Air Force duties were my first priorities instead of my responsibilities to our marriage. I was oblivious to Debbie's needs.

We decided to take a leave to visit my family in Pennsylvania and hers in Decatur. The time at home seemed to be a calming effect on our troubled marriage but the loss of our first child had a devastating effect on both of us and Debbie went into a deep depression that she never seemed to overcome.

My family seemed to have gone to its prospective corners, reconciled their differences and made peace with the past so I was looking forward to Debbie meeting my family. Mom hosted a party at her home in Vanport but things were not as I had hoped. Dad showed up uninvited and he arrogantly walked in the door and behaved as if he owned Mom's home.

Expecting a welcome matching my return from Vietnam, I tried to introduce Dad to my new wife but he simply looked at her and turned to me and said, "Get in my car, I need to talk to you!" I was shocked at his rude response but by looking into his crazed dark eyes and seeing his threatening formidable scowl I did not dare ignore his instructions and have him make a scene in front of Debbie. I followed him out to his white Corvette.

Before I could even close the door, he floored the Vet and spun-out leaving Debbie standing there stunned. He drove across the bridge that accessed the new high-speed four-lane highway from Vanport to the Pittsburg International Airport. I was paralyzed with fear by his reckless and erratic driving and had no idea what speed we had reached.

His expression was foreboding and ominous as he rambled on and on about how my stepmother was divorcing him and that he was broke. Things were going south in his life and he wanted to end it. His hands gripped the steering wheel staring straight ahead and the muscles in his lower jaw tightened. I looked down to see the gas pedal pushed all the way to the floor. The car weaved all over the highway until it suddenly swerved right and onto the freshly seeded roadside. Not even my worst life-threatening experience in Vietnam struck that much terror into me. I was sure that we were dead men before he suddenly returned the car to the highway.

If I wanted to survive this I had to think fast. Hiding my fear, regaining my senses, and trying desperately to appear calm I finally spoke. "Dad! Let me show you how to really drive this car if "this" is really what you want to do." To my amazement his features softened and he turned to me with a wry grin, pulled over to the side of the road, opened the door, got out and started walking over to the passenger side of the car. He had a self-satisfied swagger as if he were pleased to have an accomplice in his endeavor. I opened my door and slid out of the passenger seat. I gave it my best shot to appear confident, relaxed and in agreement with his insane decision. I got in the driver's side and before he could close the door, I rammed the gas pedal to the floor and shoved him back in his seat as his door slammed closed and I peeled tires as we resumed our high-speed adventure towards the airport. He began to take on a relaxed demeanor. He smiled, exhaled softly, and rested back in his seat as if his anxiety drug had just taken affect. His voice quieted and I felt confident that whatever crisis Dad was experiencing had been reduced for the moment.

I exited the highway at the next turnout and reentered the freeway on our way back to Vanport. When we arrived at Mom's home, I turned off the ignition, reached over and put my arm across Dad's shoulder and kissed him on his cheek. I left the car and went back into the house as Dad got into the driver's seat and drove off. It was the last time that I would ever see Dad alive again.

***

On that same visit home, I discovered how financially destitute Mom had become. Mom and Debbie seemed to enjoy each other's company and got along well. So, with Debbie's blessing I offered to pay for Mom and my 5-year-old sister to move to Hawaii to live with us. Mom accepted our invitation and we arranged for them to become my Air Force dependents so that Mom could get a military ID card and all the privileges that came with it. We were even successful in getting Mom her Social Security Card and early financial benefits.

Mom regained her health and seemed happy with the arrangement at first. She even dated one of my older NCO buddies. I was naïve enough to think that two women could actually coexist in the same house, manage the household and be compatible. Mom and Debbie turned out to be completely different personalities but they did have a few things in common. They were both head strong, prideful, and uncompromising.

Mom was an organized, immaculate housekeeper but the best part for me was that she was a phenomenal cook and regularly cooked my favorite fantastic Indonesian meals. She prided herself in keeping the laundry bright, clean and wrinkle free. Debbie on the other hand had no interest in domestic responsibilities, cooking or doing laundry, nor did she accept advice about how she might become more proficient at it.

I was gone on TDY deployments much of the time and when I was not, I had my boss send me out again in order to not have to deal with the situation at home. The relationship between Mom and Debbie continued to go south and out of control. Then one day I got home just in time to witness them screaming at each other and my little sister Cindy was crying uncontrollably. When Mom referred to Debbie in very unflattering terms, I had to decide quickly about what to do next to end this family crisis.

I was at work at Kaneohe teaching Marines how to load plan cargo loads for the C-141 when I received an urgent call from my office. The Administration Clerk told me that there was a problem at my apartment and that my Commander told me to go home to tend to it immediately. He and Howard had enough of the constant interruptions caused by the two women in my life.

Mom and Cindy's stay lasted for six months until we mutually agreed that they should return to Pennsylvania. Mom was homesick for her grandchildren anyway and she admitted that was what caused her to be so short tempered and anxious. She apologized sincerely to Debbie for her behavior and both of them agreed that returning home was best for all concerned. I bought Mom and Cindy one-way tickets to Pittsburgh and drove them to the Honolulu International Airport.

Neither Mom nor I was angry about the situation but rather resolved to the facts that staying with me in Hawaii was not appropriate for anyone at the time. We were just sad that things did not turn out the way we had hoped.

About 18 months after our wedding day, I was on an assignment for a month at Clark AFB to train the Philippine Air Freight team members on load planning. The classroom telephone rang while I was conducting a class and since it was an alert phone, I had to answer the call. I responded as SSgt Wetzel. The caller did not identify himself but said "I need to speak with TSgt Wetzel." I responded twice more as SSgt Wetzel. The caller finally identified himself as my First Sergeant and stated "No I'm talking to TSgt Wetzel. You just got promoted to Technical Sergeant. Congratulations!" I was ecstatic by the unexpected news and told the students what just happened, and they congratulated me. I was in celebratory mode, and on such a natural high that I did not think anything could break the spell when the First Sergeant said; "Just a minute. Your wife is here and wants to talk to you." I was expecting a "congratulations," which she did.

Then she followed up with "I hope you are happy with your promotion since that is all you care about. Goodbye! I am leaving you!" She hung up, leaving me flatfooted and shocked. I was learning a hard lesson that my career path and a stable relationship were probably not compatible.

I tried to continue the class without much success and released the students for the remainder of the day. Someone in the class told his supervisor what had happened and that I was not handling it well. The supervisor contacted my First Sergeant at Hickam and suggested that I be recalled for humanitarian reasons. The First Sergeant called me back and advised me to return to Hickam on the first available flight.

Newly promoted CMSgt Berg supported that order and I returned to Hickam immediately. When I arrived at our on-base housing unit I opened the door to an empty house. Even the dog was gone. The telephone was disconnected, and I could not call Debbie. The next day I went to the base credit union to get some cash only to find out the accounts had zero balances. I tried to get cash through the three credit cards we had only to find out that they were maxed out. Debbie had purchased First Class tickets to return to Decatur and she left me bankrupt and financially helpless.

Howard asked me to move into his house since I had to vacate base housing and was too broke to rent an apartment or house. He was worried about me and wanted to help. While staying with Howard I suffered a complete mental breakdown and overdosed on sleeping pills that were taken with a half a bottle of Vodka. I remember lying down on the bed not caring to wake up before falling into a coma.

Howard told me later Debbie called him and asked to speak to me and he told her that I was in bed asleep. Debbie yelled at him in a panic "Go into his room and wake him up. Make sure he is OK." Her abruptness jolted him into action and he found me unconscious. He called for an ambulance and I was transported to the Tripler Army Hospital. I remained in a coma for three days and awakened to see Roy sitting next to my hospital bed. My First Sergeant was standing at the foot of the bed and said he was glad to see me alive and recovering. He also said, "We are processing you for medical discharge and red-lining your TSgt promotion orders for the misuse of prescription drugs." My Air Force career was essentially over.

I refused to accept the news and told him that I did not accept that action. Not only would I stay in the Air Force, but I will get my promotion because one of the major reasons I was in this predicament was his failure to take care of his men. He like everyone around me had known about Debbie's infidelity and failed to tell me about it. She had been seen with other men at the NCO club and at the Pearl Harbor enlisted club.

I was assigned to a mental health specialist at Tripler Army Hospital for thirty days. She did a complete mental evaluation that included my entire family history and how I was raised at home. Her report to my commander was conclusive that I had not been trying to commit suicide but attempting to reach out for help and to dull the pain.

My commander permitted a delay in any disciplinary action based on the initial report but I was ordered to vacate base housing and to move off the base since there was no available room in the barracks. I was too ashamed and embarrassed to ask Howard to let me move back into his home. I looked for an apartment around the base but everything was too expensive and I was broke.

A friend told me about a Mormon family that lived in Aiea and that they had a room in their garage that they rented for $400 per month including meals, access to a guest bathroom and phone for privileges for calling the base and to receive Base Operations alert calls. I contacted them and made an appointment to check out the room.

It was a spartan walled-off 8-foot deep by 30-foot-wide space at the back of their garage. There was room for a sink with running cold water, a single bed, a small refrigerator, a chair, small table, and television. My thought was that based on one to five stars it was a negative five-star accommodation but at least I did not have to sleep in an alley or on the sidewalk with the other unfortunate Honolulu homeless. Even at $400 a month, it was more than I had in my personal housing budget but I had to take it.

CHAPTER 30 - DEATH BY A 1000 CUTS

Debbie had been gone for six months and I was still recovering from the emotional tsunami when I received a call from Roy who had returned to Pennsylvania. It was Sunday March 16, 1975 around 6:20PM Honolulu Time and the phone rang as I was leaving the garage apartment. I picked up the phone "TSgt Wetzel speaking."

"Are you sitting down?" Roy asked.

"No."

"Sit down! I have something to tell you. You need to sit down for what I have to tell you - so sit down!" he commanded.

"OK! I'm sitting." I lied.

"Dad is dead, and I killed him."

I sat down. "What did you say?"

"Dad is dead, and I killed him Wim!"

Before I could respond a stranger answered the phone and said, "Who is this?"

"I'm Wim. Roy's oldest brother. Who are you?"

"I'm Chief Colaluca, the Center Township Chief of Police and, yes, your father is dead, and it appears that Roy did take his life. From what I can see it appears to be self-defense. Wherever you are - you better get home quickly." The phone went dead, Chief Colaluca had hung up before I could respond.

Our lifelong fears about Dad's death threats finally came to fruition. While still in a zombie like trance I called my First Sergeant and told him what had just transpired. The "Top" said he would confirm the emergency with the local Red Cross but for me to pack my bags and to get ready to go home. The next two hours passed agonizingly slow and my brain waves shot into overdrive.

Our family had been sitting on this powder keg for at more than a decade. We all knew that someday we would have to face this reality but I had always thought it would be at least one of us being killed by him, not one of us killing him. My mind was racing, What the hell happened? I waited for the First Sergeant to call back.

My head was flashing through all the threats, the beatings, the fleeting moments of caring and love dad had shown and then back again into unprovoked rages. What the hell happened?

When the phone finally rang, I was startled back to the present and grabbed the phone. "This is TSgt Wetzel."

"Sergeant Wetzel - this is Base Operations. Are you packed and ready to travel? We have a C-141 ready for take-off from Honolulu International for Travis AFB and ordered it to return to the holding area and prepare for an ERO (engine running on load). Base Transportation is on the way to your quarters to pick you up."

"I'm packed and will be waiting outside. Thank you very much Sir".

I was overwhelmed by the response of my First Sergeant and I would never forget it nor adequately repay the Air Force for this huge show of support. I recognized several of the C-141 aircrew members when I boarded the aircraft. They had been ordered to return from the main runway at Honolulu and they were shocked to see that it was for me.

They assumed that I had a high priority mission to support and never questioned the reason for the urgent departure abort and return to base. Upon arrival at Travis AFB, I was immediately whisked off to a waiting taxi heading for San Francisco International. Airline reservations to Pittsburgh were already made and paid for. I do not know who made the arrangements or who paid for the ticket and taxi. All I know is that "The Air Force takes care of its own!" was no longer just a casual comment.

As my flight descended for landing at Pittsburgh International the aircraft flew over Dad's house next to the Ohio River in Vanport. As I looked down at the house, I felt a sense of relief as if a heavy load was lifted off my back. For the very first time in my life coming home was not filled with fear and dread. I did not have to wonder any longer if my demise would one day come at the hands of my own father. A sense of peace fell on me that I never thought was possible. God help me for feeling that relief!

My flight landed at about eleven AM and a Karate student friend was waiting for me. We shoved my bags into the trunk and immediately headed home. I asked him to take me to the police station first so that I could see Roy. Words cannot adequately describe the terrible condition Roy was in. His jail cell reeked of smoke and other unidentifiable odors. The top of the mattress on his cot was burned to a crisp. Apparently, another prisoner had lit the mattress on fire the previous day and the jail staff had yet to replace it.

Roy's right arm from the wrist to almost his elbow was red, swollen with portions of his skin peeling off. The jail guard had brought Roy a pot of boiling hot coffee during the night and while handing it to Roy through the bars he spilled it on his right arm. The skin literally boiled off part of his forearm. When I looked at his face through my tears Roy was in obvious shock and terrible pain but true to his nature, he just gritted his teeth and soldiered on.

He was shirtless and hardly recognizable as human let alone my brother. His chest, arms, neck, back and face were so bloody and flayed that it was hard to tell where one cut started and another began. As he turned his back to me, I counted 56 slash wounds. In Karate this knife slicing technique is referred to as "Death by a Thousand Cuts." This is a martial arts technique used induce a slow bleeding death to one's opponent through endless slices that cannot be treated in time to prevent significant blood loss and painful death.

His jaw appeared to be dislocated and his cheeks were horribly swollen. "He tried to rip my jaw off Wim!" He opened his mouth wide and showed me what appeared to be four long scratch marks at the back of his tongue and down his throat.

During his medical exam after the ambulance arrived the medics found fingernail marks deep in Roy's throat and along his tongue. His right thigh was bleeding and there was a slash type hole in his pant leg at the site of the wound. It was the place where Dad stabbed his pen knife deeply into Roy's thigh. I would find out later it was the last action Dad took before expiring during the fight. A feeling of helplessness overwhelmed me as tears welled up in my eyes. His body was so scourged that I could not even hug him without inflicting more pain. I fought back my failing emotions and gathered myself enough to give Roy the confidence that I would help him through this.

He gazed at me through swollen eyes and an expression of defeat and hopelessness. "Wim, Judge Beryl Klein set my bail at $15,000 and wants the cash before I can go home. Where am I going to get that kind of money Wim?"

"I don't know Roy, but I will get every cent and get you out of here as soon as possible. I promise. What do you need now?"

"They would not let me take any of my grand-mal seizure medications the Veterans Administration (VA) provides me."

"I'll take care of that before I leave. We will get through this Roy so try to get some rest. I'll get you a new mattress and clean sheets." After calming him down, getting his medications and a new rack, I left with the promise that the next time I saw him would be to get him out of jail.

The final irony was Dad's advice. "If you don't ask, you don't get!" The remainder of the day and most of Tuesday I knocked on every door of every friend or acquaintance to beg, plead and grovel for assistance in getting bail money. On March 18th, my stepmother put up most of the bail because, as she told me then, Roy was not guilty of murder. She knew that dad had a history of violence towards his first family, even though he was gentle and kind with his two new children.

After gathering enough bail money to satisfy the court Roy was released into my custody. For some reason only known to my stepmother, on June 23rd she pulled his bail. She had changed her mind about Roy's innocence.

I had recently received a re-enlistment bonus of $7,500 and I used it to make the initial down payment for getting Roy quality legal counsel and Roy had many friends who also came to help keep him get out on bail. On June 24th loyal friends and followers of Roy's career in martial arts, Mildred Gatty and Ted and Virginia Laszlo pledged their personal homes and property to meet the bail requirements. Ted Laszlo, the son of Ted and Virginia was a Karate student and good friend and shared with me in later years that his parents had made a huge sacrifice by doing this but it was a testament to their family's belief that Roy was innocent and would be exonerated.

Dad had grown accustomed to a comfortable income from the Karate schools, and a two-income family. He had been enjoying prestige, respect from the local community and fame in the international martial arts community. Now his lifestyle, his marriage and his financial situation were about to unravel. The Internal Revenue Service (IRS) was closing in on him for failing to pay income taxes and he was in the midst of a divorce from my stepmother.

This would be an international humiliation for this immensely proud man and he had depleted all his options to save face. Roy had a degree in accounting and financing from Robert Morris University and had been advising Dad against some of his bad financial choices. Roy's advice fell on deaf ears.

My sister, brothers and mom were all getting nervous about Dad's erratic behavior and emotional instability. Even for Dad the behavior was over the top. He was drinking more and becoming more aggressive than he had been in the past. He seemed to be tormented by demons and had become impossible to reason with. The day we took on our suicide joy ride was just the tip of the iceberg.

Roy's martial arts expertise had far surpassed Dad's and Roy's teaching methods were more progressive and yielding positive results at the school. In Dad's deranged and troubled Post Traumatic Stress Disorder (PTSD) mind, Roy was a worthy opponent and a conduit to die honorably and save face.

We think he may have had a plan to die by the hands of one of his sons and I was not completely surprised that this tragedy had happened but I still wanted to know the sequence of events and how Roy managed to survive the March 16, 1975 ordeal.

"What the hell happened, Roy?" I asked.

The sequence of events leading to the attack on Roy that night was gathered from information provided by Mom, Jane and other friends and family.

Dad first went to Mom's house and pounded on the door but she refused to let him in. Then he went to Jim's house but he was not home, which probably saved his life. Mom called to warn Jane that Dad was on a rampage and was probably on his way to her house.

Mom was right. He showed up at Jane's house and she and her husband did not allow him to come in. She instructed her children not to answer the door, and amazingly Dad gave up and left.

He then drove to Roy's home, arriving about 6PM. He let himself in without knocking and Roy's Doberman, Blade, went into an aggressive attack mode baring his teeth, barking, growling, and lunging at Dad. Meanwhile Roy's two-year-old daughter, Rochelle, slept peacefully in the next room. Roy grabbed Blade by the collar and put him in the room with Rochelle. Sensing the danger, Blade viciously clawed and chewed at the bedroom door. Rochelle woke up and began crying and screaming.

Ignoring the chaos that he had created Dad asked Roy "Are you done with my income taxes?"

"Yes. You owe Uncle Sam some money, but you can review and sign the tax forms now if you want to."

Dad started to review the tax forms and suddenly stopped. He grumbled some unintelligible words and yelled "I hate this country! I am losing everything, my house, my car, the Karate school and Peggy and the kids! It is over!" He crumpled the tax forms into a ball and threw them against the wall, then turned around to leave.

As he approached the door, he spotted the Montagnard sword displayed on the étagère by the door. Seeing the ancient artifact triggered something deep within his troubled and angry soul. He snapped! It was as if he saw every Indonesian rebel that murdered his mother and every Japanese prison guard that had controlled his life.

He grabbed the sword and walked towards Roy while unsheathing it and started to rant and rave yelling "It is time for you to die!" Seeing the demonic look in Dad's eyes Roy knew at least one of them would die that night. Roy met him halfway to the front door and grabbed the sheath in one hand and Dad's right elbow to keep him from completely unsheathing the weapon. During the struggle, the sword was bent but still useable to strike a fatal blow to Roy's body. Dad lost control of the bent and unbalanced weapon as it fell to the floor. He rushed Roy, and both tumbled to the floor in a fist pounding and kicking mass. They wrestled and fought in this deadly match until Roy managed to free himself. Now they were two Karate masters fighting to the death.

As they both stood up Dad completed a round house kick making hard contact to Roy's abdomen. Roy countered with a kick to Dad's head temporarily knocking him to the floor where he hit his head on the floor heating grate. The blow to the head opened a large gash that exposed Dad's brain. Brain matter started oozing from the horrible gash into the floor heating vent. This blow to the head would have immediately ended any further hostile action from anyone else but the demon that consumed Dad had taken complete control as he continued his relentless pursuit to kill Roy.

Dad could no longer control the demons that haunted him. Roy had become Dad's cruel father, every Indonesian rebel that slaughtered his mother and every prison guard that ever beat and belittled him. He snatched the worn and damaged Japanese Samurai mystery sword from Roy's display case and swung it wildly at Roy trying to decapitate him. Seeing Dad coming at him and winding up to make a final fatal slash to his head, Roy reached just behind him and grabbed one of the supporting beams of his étagère and pulled it across his chest. The Samurai sword struck the étagère bending the sword in half. The étagère slammed to the floor scattering and breaking all its glass and collectable contents.

Hearing Rochelle crying hysterically and Blade still barking furiously just inches away, Roy briefly turned his head towards the baby's bedroom door and lost sight of Dad. The loss of focus was a lethal mistake as Dad grabbed Roy from behind with his left arm while reaching around with is free hand to grab Roy's lower jaw with four fingers of his hand in his mouth.

Roy was now the victim of what he had taught so many of his karate students to do. Get your opponent to turn away for just a second so that you can counterattack him in any way possible. In this case Dad grabbed Roy's lower jaw attempting to break it and possibly even ripping it from his face.

The fighting continued for over twenty minutes with both men achieving direct and potentially deadly blows to each other. Dad managed to maneuver his pocketknife from his pocket and proceeded to slash and cut at Roy's torso each time they wrestled. Since Roy was not wearing a shirt it made his body a perfect target for the slash wounds. Roy's body was covered with blood oozing cuts.

Dad had made the mistake, knowingly or unknowingly, of exposing less than the required eighth inch of blade in his slashing attempts. Roy broke away and delivered a near fatal kick to Dad's head causing him to fall again. Dad rose on all fours and growled like a Tiger before attacking again. Roy reached for a set of Nunchucks and quickly struck Dad with two successive blows to the head knocking him down. The forceful momentum caused Roy to fall to the floor next to Dad. He slung the Nunchucks across the back of Dad's neck, rolled over on top of him pinning him to the floor. One of the Nunchuck sticks was lying across Dad's throat and under Roy's upper body.

Roy explained to me that he only wanted to subdue Dad and to stop him from fighting. The fighting caused the adrenalin to flow uncontrollably as it coursed through Roy's body. His own heavy breathing caused him to believe Dad was still breathing heavily as he was trying to get up to continue to fight. At first his own heaving from his heavy breathing caused him to believe that Dad was still alive, but the fight was over, and Dad was dead.

Roy lay that way for quite a while before finally getting up and calling his fiancé Tatha. Roy realized that Blade had stopped barking as if he knew Roy and Rochelle were now safe. After telling Tatha what happened he asked her to call the police. Immediately after hanging up he called me in Hawaii to tell me that: "Dad is dead, and I killed him."

After the police cleared the crime scene Mom cleaned Roy's house and meticulously removed the blood that stained everything in the room. She carefully collected the remnants of Dad's brain matter and put them into a small container. Mom never told me what happened to those remains. Regardless of what Dad had done to her and the family during his life, she remembered the man she fell in love with at the Air Force dance in Indonesia after the war and even now she loved him.

CHAPTER 31-THE TRIAL

The odds were not in Roy's favor since it was no secret that Dad and Roy had been clashing for a long time about the philosophical teaching style the Karate school should be using. The chasm grew wider as the students became divided as well. Dad's prize students eventually became his head instructors and he referred to them as the "Golden Boys." They were the elite, cult-like loyal followers of Dad and probably would have fought to be first in line to drink the Kool-Aid if Dad had instructed them to do so. They had deemed Roy the enemy to be reckoned with, while Roy had his own passionate followers. Now the students on both sides of this position became witnesses at Roy's trial, complicating an already difficult situation.

Dad was highly respected in the community for his efforts to train law-enforcement personnel. During the trial, a rumor was circulating that if Roy were found not guilty there would be a riot and he would not leave the Beaver County Court House alive. But if Roy were found guilty Roy's supporters would surround him and find a way to escape the courthouse to get Roy to safety. Beaver police, state police and other police agencies were on alert and prepared for the worse.

The circumstances surrounding Dad's untimely death attracted public attention locally, nationally, and internationally. My Uncle Hank, Mom's brother, heard about it on a national news report in Perth, Australia. The news media there was calling it the "fight to the death between father and son." Uncle Hank was not surprised it happened but he called me to find out how it happened.

The opportunity to be the prosecuting attorney at Roy's trial was highly coveted. The two assistant district attorneys were Frank S. Kelker and Charles M. Marshall. For them, the trial was a political opportunity with lots of media exposure. Getting a guilty verdict would be a prestigious accomplishment in their careers. A Beaver County Times bias reporter assigned to the story used sensationalized reporting to put a pitifully few feathers in his own cap by embellishing on this front-page headline news story.

God was with us because Roy already had a long-term trusting relationship, with a highly competent African American attorney - George "Tooky" E. James and his assistant Rex Downey. They had represented Roy in his business affairs for years and observed our family's instability over a long period of time. They had witnessed Dad's volatile and sometimes dangerous behavior in contrast to Roy's integrity and character. They were confident that Roy had no choice but to defend himself.

Thanks to the Chief of Police's initial observation at the death scene our legal team had a firm basis from which to build Roy's defense position. It was clear that Roy was fighting for his life and the life of his two-year-old daughter. The jury leaned forward in their seats riveted as Tooky addressed them with passionate animation as he delivered his emotional discourse. He had to pause periodically to rein in his emotions as he replayed the events leading up to Dad's demise. The jury members were mesmerized and visibly struggling to suppress their tears.

The presiding Judge, H. Beryl Klein, disallowed our mother's testimony about Dad's lifetime pattern of inflicting abuse on her and the children. We all had grave concerns that this would reduce the chances of a positive outcome. Fortunately, the testimonies of Roy's siblings and Roy's own personal testimony and description of that night were permitted and the painfully descriptive expositions from each member of our family left no doubt about Dad's lifetime history of physical and mental abuse and his untethered bursts of anger towards all of us. These testimonies would be just one of many times jury members would shed tears during the trial.

One of Dad's mislead students, a police deputy, took the stand and stated that "If Willy Wetzel wanted to kill anyone, including his family, then he had the right to do so." The jury and the audience gasped at this horrendous suggestion and our attorneys strenuously objected immediately. Many of his statements under oath were just as bizarre and misleading. I suspect that his many contradictory statements invalidated his entire testimony. The deputy's sister took the stand as a key defense witness and her testimony discredited every one of her brother's statements.

It sickened all of us to hear the prosecuting attorney pointedly trying to convince the jury of Roy's lack of character and making ridiculous claims that Roy's injuries to his tongue and throat were self-inflicted and even describing in detail a ludicrous theory of how Roy self-inflicted 56 knife slash wounds on his own back. To me these claims were an insult to the jury's intelligence.

It was a painful sight to see Roy sit in silence listening to lies about himself and being forced to repeatedly relive that night of horror and have his character and integrity destroyed in the most public of settings imaginable.

At the end of each day during the course of the trial we all stayed together with Mom and met with the lawyers before and after the daily trial sessions. Contrary to the advice of his attorneys Roy asked to testify on his own behalf. Whether the world believed him or not he wanted to tell the truth about the fight. Since he was the only eyewitness, who could better explain what actually happened? We unanimously supported his request to speak on his own defense. It turned out to be the right decision.

What made Roy a great teacher also made him an excellent witness. He was unwavering and exceptionally articulate throughout the questioning by both sides. He carefully detailed every moment of the vicious 25-minute fight causing an eerie tense silence that was occasionally broken by gasps of horror that frequently interrupted Roy's testimony prompting the judge to admonish them.

After an exhausting tortuous five days all the testimonies and closing statements from both sides had been presented. Prior to adjourning for the week end the jury was cautioned about the penalties for talking about the case with anyone outside the courtroom and told not to read newspapers, watch television, or listen to a radio until after the case was closed. The court was adjourned and we would all return on Monday to wait for the jury to deliberate and decide Roy's fate.

Our family remained together the entire weekend meeting with our legal team discussing what we would do next if Roy is found guilty. It was an agonizing time as our emotions teetered back and forth from being confident that Roy would be acquitted to despair should the unthinkable happen and he had to spend the next 20 years to life in prison.

On Monday, the jury deliberated for several hours. We waited anxiously and every time the bailiff appeared; we were sure a verdict had been decided but he would just go about his business keeping us on edge guessing what Roy's fate would be.

When the jury finally filed in and took their assigned places in the jury box, we all tried to read their faces to no avail. I do not think anyone in the room was even breathing. The jury foreman was asked to announce the verdict and she could barely contain her emotions. In her nervous excitement she had forgotten to use courtroom decorum.

She was supposed to say, Not Guilty but the words she used were even sweeter and more appropriate to us. "The jury finds the defendant Roy Eduard Wetzel "Innocent of the charges of Murder and Involuntary Manslaughter." The word innocent seemed to bounce off the walls.

Immediately upon hearing the verdict Mom fainted and fell in a heap to the floor. Most of the jury members wept and the people attending as spectators cheered loudly. The judge dismissed the jury and released Roy immediately. The news was wonderful but now we were all on edge as we knew we would be walking into a hornet's nest as we exited the courthouse to freedom and safety. Several police officers walked in close proximity to us as we left the court room to the court house's main entrance. There was a large police presence in and around the courthouse in anticipation of the impending threatened violence. But it turned out to be an uneventful exit.

I had an opportunity to ask three of the jury members why they voted not guilty and why they broke down in tears at the reading of the verdict. Still filled with emotion all three had the same answer. The abuse that all the family members had endured for so long at the hands of their father left no doubt in their mind that the death was due to self-defense. One jury member said to me. "I would have killed the guy a long time ago."

***

Roy and I went to the Karate school the day after he was released only to find graffiti covering the front door. As soon as we went inside, we separated to different areas of the school to make sure there was no additional damage to the inside of the building. Roy called out from his office "Wim, come here and look at this!"

Roy pulled the chair from under his desk and pointed to the back of the head rest which faced the second-floor window. He turned the chair around towards me to show me what appeared to be a hole in the leather. We looked at each other puzzled about how it got there. Roy poked his finger in the hole and felt a hard object inside the headrest. He used his pocketknife to dig out the fully intact spent bullet prompting both of us to turn towards the window behind the chair and as expected, there was a bullet entry hole in the window. We got the message loud and clear that someone was going to ensure that even though the trial was over, the goal to kill or seriously hurt my brother was just beginning.

Soon after the trial was over Roy started a Karate magazine and asked me to be his international correspondent. Since I traveled all over the world, he wanted me to take that opportunity to write articles for Karate and self-defense schools from worldwide locations. My first article was entitled "The Masters of Old Were Wary!" It was a great article if I do say so myself. The magazine was titled "Kung Fu International". Twenty-five thousand copies were in the Karate School ready to be distributed. The night before its release, all 25,000 copies of the magazine and the Karate school were burned to the ground. My first published article went up in smoke.

Honor among thieves prevented us from proving who the terrorist was in those vicious retributions but a police deputy, one of Dad's dedicated followers, had given a hostile testimony at the trial with conflicting irrational statements and he made no attempt to hide his disdain for Roy. He was the maestro of a string of witnesses with similar discreditable testimonies falling in line like sheep.

Still seeking revenge and attempting to further destroy Roy's reputation his co-conspirators started a rumor in the community that Roy had burned down his own school and destroyed his first and only magazine publication.

The incident happened long before the internet but Dad's followers are so obsessed with Dad's untimely death that today they continue to be convinced of Roy's guilt. To the extent that some of them have brainwashed their children into a new generation of deceit. Since the inception of internet, these same radicals seized the opportunity to use the internet as a source to continue their false claims regarding the trial and contemptuous rhetoric concerning the Wetzel family. Karate web sites still share sensationalized bogus comments and stories about the death, trial, and aftermath.

***

The trial was over. The Wetzel family members had all gone back to their separate corners of the world to heal and recover from the many months of public pain and misery. But I was not sure I had a corner to go to. The reality that Dad was gone had not yet sunk in for any of us but we had to move on, pretending life was back to normal.

Roy and I mended all our past misunderstandings that had been initiated by our dysfunctional family life. The trial had done nothing to ease Jimmy's hurt and mindset of being deserted. He was cordial toward me during the trial, but the brotherly love we had once evaporated almost ten years before when I left home to join the military.

Our sister Jane rallied in the midst of the family crisis but after the trial she returned back to the protective shell she had created for herself as a mother and wife. Our seven-year-old half-sister, Cindy, had her innocent childhood snatched away in the wake of her first encounter with a death in the family. The senseless family violence surrounding the tragedy at her young age was too much for her to fully comprehend. This event would continue to have a painful and lasting effect on all of us.

My emotions were frayed as I had to return to my Air Force duties but leaving Roy brought on overwhelming feelings of guilt about abandoning him while he was still recovering from the aftermath of trial. I had not yet come to grips with Debbie leaving so abruptly and still did not know what my fate was with my Air Force career. The bright spot was that Dad was gone giving me a sense of peace that I never felt before in my life.

I felt completely drained and empty inside except for the exhausting remnants of the two-month adrenaline rush that had kept me moving forward as I supported Roy. My next hurdle was yet to come, returning to my Air Force career; that is - if I still had one.

CHAPTER 32 – RETURN TO HAWAII

I returned to Hickam AFB and my empty garage living quarters. I threw my duffle bag into the corner and collapsed onto my quickly made bed and stared at the garage ceiling as if it held all the answers. I was breathing and still had a pulse but felt like a robot, dead and empty inside as I began to process what had transpired.

The war-torn Samurai sword had maimed, tortured, and killed countless prisoners of war, saved my family from certain death, and followed us from Indonesia to Holland and America. It was displayed in every home we ever knew and served as a constant reminder to Mom of times she desperately wanted to forget. I could not help thinking how it mysteriously disappeared, turned up in a second- hand store and as if it had not finished its deadly mission made its way back to us, saving our lives one more time. Now, after Roy's acquittal, it vanished from our lives permanently. If only it could talk, it would have quite a story to tell.

My head felt as if it were being squeezed in a vice and tears began to well up and flow down my face and onto my pillow. The reality that my Air Force career might be over after reporting to my commander in the morning sent an overwhelming feeling of pain and grief to my soul. The possibility of being discharged from the Air Force and returning to Beaver County was just too incomprehensible. What else could I do that gave me as much satisfaction and pride more than serving my country? By the grace of God, I finally fell asleep from sheer exhaustion.

Immediately after awakening the next day I visited my base mental health counselor and shared the events of the past few weeks with her. She had been following the trial with the help of a friend who lived in Pennsylvania. She gave my Commander and the First Sergeant daily updates about my progress and continuing recovery. She was able to get copies of the Beaver County Times stories about the trial through her Air Force channels and now she could finally see the tapestry from the inside and untangle the Wetzel family puzzle. Now she got it and determined that I really did have reasons for being so screwed up.

She compiled a final mental health progress report based on our discussions and the supporting evidence provided by the Times stories to justify her report recommending that the Air Force retain me. With her recommendation and God's grace the mental health department's commanding officer cleared me to return to work and strongly recommended that my discharge actions were to be terminated.

My Commander asked me to report to his office where he promoted me to Technical Sergeant with full back pay dating back to the first day the promotion became effective. With a congratulatory handshake and reassuring pat on the back he advised me that the individual who admitted having the affair with Debbie was discharged under less than honorable conditions. My self-destructive reaction to Debbie's behavior and sudden departure could have been the end of my Air Force career. God was definitely watching over me considering what could have happened.

With the trial behind him, Roy continued running the schools and began pursuing his dream of helping underprivileged at-risk youth, offering them free martial classes, and offering a counseling program for parents to teach them how to break the cycle of family abuse - two subjects close to his heart.

I spent the summer engaged in becoming the best I could be at my responsibilities as a Technical Sergeant. I was determined to make the best of the opportunity the Air Force had given me. Roy was never far from my thoughts. I missed him and our childhood comradery. In some ways I even missed our juvenile spats.

One day at the end of the summer I got a phone call. "Hey, what are you doing next week?" "Well, I don't know Roy. What are you doing?"

"I think I'll go fishing at our favorite spot. Want to join me?"

"I'd love to but I don't know if I can get permission to take leave on such short notice but I'll be there as soon as I can?"

"Great, I'll wait for you. Just let me know when."

Roy met me with a huge hug when I stepped off the plane in Pittsburgh and rushed me off to the baggage area to grab my duffle bag. "We have to hurry Wim. We need to get to the golf course. It is getting close to dark and the night crawlers will be waiting for us." He wasted no time on trivial matters and went straight to the important stuff – getting ready to go fishing in the morning. When we got in the car, I noticed two flashlights and two large tin cans containing dirt on the floor by my feet.

He drove straight to the golf course and we quietly walked around on the damp grass with flashlights snatching up worms and dropping them in our cans as if they were gold nuggets. It was a cool fall night with a full moon so bright that we barely needed flashlights to see. Both of us were quietly entrenched in our quest for the best juicy night crawlers that we could harvest. Suddenly I heard Roy's panicked voice "Wim, come here quick!" I ran towards his urgent declaration expecting to find him in some kind of trouble. "What's wrong Roy?"

Roy was holding a spotlight in one hand shining it on his other hand that held the plumpest specimen of fish bait I had ever seen "What do you think Wim?"

I shrugged "I don't think I can beat that find Roy."

"No! I mean do you think we should save this one for Jane for her breakfast?" Giggling like the two Dutch boys from long ago, we were taken back to happier times and I almost expected Mom to show up and scold us for our mischievous behavior.

With a healthy dose of juvenile-level of excitement, we were both up before the sun the next morning and on our way to conquer the King. The King was a legend, a huge bass that Roy and I had been stalking for as long as we had been frequenting our favorite fishing hole. While riding to our secret fishing spot the conversation was focused on wondering if the King was still lurking below the water's surface, under the rotted tree trunk.

When we arrived at our destination, we had to park the car, grab our gear, and walk the rest of the way. The anticipation of the adventure was as important as catching the King. The morning light was starting to break through, the air was crisp and clean and the meandering trail was covered with a carpet of decaying foliage. The amber and crimson leaves were fluttering down from the blazing canopy of oaks and maples and swirled about like butterflies in the gentle autumn breeze. There was an earthy aroma of autumn and I was catching whiffs of someone burning leaves nearby.

We drew closer to our destination and began to hear the sound of the water rushing over the rocks. The music of chirping birds and the humming of insects surrounded us as we encroached on their peaceful habitat, but they seemed unfazed by our intrusion. When we reached the banks of the rushing stream, we stood transfixed by the tranquility and peace that God had provided to sooth our weary souls.

Roy effortlessly cast his line and with focused determination hit his intended target near the King's last-known hiding place. Then he sat down and leaned casually back against the rough-hewn bark of an aged Oak tree. He looked peaceful and satisfied as he settled back and watched his fishing line go slack across the surface of the water.

It was time for the competition to begin. Two brothers and one of nature's greatest fresh water fighting fish were about to have a battle of wills. King Bass suddenly stole the tempting and juicy bait from my hook and I had to re-bait my hook. Anxious to get my baited hook back in the water before the King lost interest, I struggled to get the slick shiny worm on the hook as it stretched and contracted, refusing to yield to my will; but I finally succeeded in impaling the luckless critter. Roy sat on the bank grinning in amusement knowing I was determined to keep up with him and save face. He could no longer contain his laughter towards my antics and could not pass up the opportunity to throw a few barbs in my direction. "Looks like the worm almost won that fight Wim. I hope you did not find that too strenuous bro?"

The King had no mercy on either of us over the next few days. I could imagine him laughing at us as we went home in defeat each day. Then one day my luck had turned. My cast was straight and true as the baited hook glided lightly through the air and lazily sank to a watery splashdown within inches of my predetermined target. The King was lying in wait at the base of that old, rotted tree trunk and my hook slowly settled to the bottom where it came to rest on the silt and mud. The frantic squirming of the worm attracted the attention of King Bass.

The King nudged and prodded at the bait in a vain attempt to dislodge the worm and he finally clamped down on the worm's loose and flailing tail and ran with it until the tense line prevented him from running any further. The line became even more taut and a large portion of the worm was viciously ripped loose from its body providing an appetizer for the big boy. The free sample enticed him to come back for more and he engulfed the entire baited hook. He ran again, impaling the hook deeper into his jaw.

Roy ran over excitedly to give me instructions and to state the obvious "You got him! Do not fight him! Keep the rod tip up but do not fight him. Let him wear himself out."

Always the teacher. Dear God, I have missed him! Roy stood beside me with an excited face splitting grin, encouraging me as the King ran and ran with the line. My reel screamed in protest and the rod bent in agonizing contortions in a valiant effort to hold its own against the furious fight of the King. The shrieking reel came to an abrupt halt—the King could run no further. Cautiously I rewound what seemed to be miles and miles of outstretched nylon while constantly maintaining a light tension. I knew that Roy was as engrossed in the action as I was but I did not dare turn to look at him and lose my focus. Roy began to instruct again. "Don't let up on the tension Wim or he'll be gone leaving you in his wake."

King Bass was fighting for his life. I was fighting for my pride. Once again, he ran in every direction and broke the surface of the water with all the grace of a trapeze artist, then he leaped into the air spinning and twisting and arching his body as he dove back into the water, now determined to head for the rocks, weeds and tree stumps. Roy was pacing up and down the stream bank trying to get a better look at the contorting fish. "Don't let him head for the rocks Wim or he'll be gone."

From the waning resistance of my rod and reel I could feel the fight going out of him as he weakened. It was getting easier to reel him in closer and most of the never-ending nylon line was back on my reel. Now we could see that he was spent from the battle but making a feeble attempt to escape. I felt a twinge of guilt when I saw him losing strength and watched the fight going out of him.

Roy quickly handed me the net and I triumphantly scooped him up. After I freed him from the entanglement of the net, he laid listlessly battle weary and exhausted. We proudly surveyed the prize that we had waited so long to attain. I gently removed the hook from his mouth and his black bulging eyes seemed to plead with us to have mercy on him.

Gently holding him in both hands Roy slowly lowered the massive fish into the streaming water allowing King to breathe again. I gently smoothed my hand over his glistening scales as if I were petting a puppy. We basked in his massiveness for a fleeting moment and then Roy let him slowly slip from his hands into the cool flowing stream allowing the water to wash through his gaping jaws and over his gills. Revitalized and re-energized the King returned to his tree stump and we watched in awe as our friend disappeared from sight.

The King had returned to his castle but we were glad for his brief visit with us. He was meant to swim freely surrounded by Mother Nature and her beautiful world. The King belonged to no one.

We lounged on the creek bank and gazed at the clear fall sky reflecting on what just happened. Roy's demeanor showed a sense of peace that I had not seen for years.

"Wim, we both know Dad tried to kill me."

"Yes, of course?" I said in a questioning tone and thinking it was an odd remark.

"We know better than most how he planned to do it."
"What do you mean? Death by A Thousand Cuts?"

"Yeah. Did you ever think about how that correlates with how our family fell apart?"

"What do you mean Roy?"

"Think about it. We started out as a unified family where we were all loyal to each other. We had each other's back and loved each other unconditionally. We were an unstoppable team, fighting together to survive and thrive in our newly adopted country. It was not just one thing that killed that. We fragmented slowly, cut by cut - like a slow death by a thousand cuts."

I sat up and gazed pensively over the water watching it detour around the moss-covered rocks and letting Roy's words sink in. "You know Roy, you are right. There was not any one thing that destroyed us, it was an accumulation of a lot of different things. Our family was hemorrhaging one cut at a time."

"Life is so short Wim; we never know what is in store for us or why things happen. We just must let go and let it take us where we are meant to be. I need to get on with my life and let go of these horrible memories."

I reclined back on the grass again pondering Roy's wisdom and listening to the quiet sounds of nature. "Roy."

"Yeah Wim?"

"I want you to know that you are not just my brother, you are my best and dearest friend and I will always be here for you.

CHAPTER 33 - STUPID IS AS STUPID DOES

I was married on paper but living a bachelor existence at Hickam for almost a year when I received a call from Cricket. She told me that Debbie was a "changed" person who had finally settled down and wanted to give our marriage another chance. She wanted to call and talk with me about the possibilities but was ashamed for all that she did and was afraid that I would reject her. Always the fool – I told Cricket that Debbie could call me anytime.

The next day Debbie called me and we spoke at length about her miraculous change. She apologized for what she did and asked if I could give her a second chance. After all that transpired since our separation I was finally recovering from her abrupt departure and I had a gut feeling this was not good. To me marriage is sacred and I was deeply committed to my vows: "Until death do us part." But now I was gun shy and I did not want to get burned again. I told her "No."

She recruited another couple who were our mutual best friends at the time to plead her case. I received some very convincing calls from them assuring me that Debbie had turned her life around. She was no longer bar hopping, drinking, or smoking marijuana. I was very reluctant but just could not turn my back on our marriage. She sounded sincerely sorry and I wanted to forgive and move forward. After many phone calls we agreed to patch things up and to prove her commitment to make it work she bought her own plane ticket to return to Hawaii. I found out the hard way that forgiving is one thing but going back for more abuse is outright stupid. I still did not understand that Debbie was a master of deception and if she opened her mouth-she was lying.

We were on a long waiting list to move into base housing so we rented a high-rise apartment in Honolulu. It was expensive and really stretched the limited budget and it would be our home for the remainder of my tour at Hickam AFB.

Things were going well and Debbie showed me that she was sincere about making the marriage work and we talked about starting a family. We both wanted children but Debbie seemed to be especially anxious to have a baby. We had difficulty getting pregnant and after a disappointing start with her prior life-threatening ectopic pregnancy, Debbie got pregnant again.

She was in labor for a grueling 38 hours and we saw it through together until finally Wim Kenneth Wetzel decided to face the world seven weeks early. As a preemie he was significantly underweight and his limp fragile body actually fit into the palm of my hand. His tiny right foot was awkwardly turned inward and on its side. The doctor called it a club foot. Little Wim was confined to an incubator for six weeks getting oxygen treatments several times a day until his lungs were fully developed. I did not realize how profound love could be until our beautiful son entered my world. In an instant my world had expanded by light years.

It was agonizing and painful to watch him struggle to survive but he was my son, and he was perfect. The doctor assured us that Wim's foot alignment could be corrected with special shoes and a brace but we would have to be diligent about making sure he wore them over the next couple of years.

It was an incredible miracle for us to finally bring our son home. He became "WK" and we were the typical new doting parents. Nervous and inexperienced but excited all at once. It was a new beginning for the three of us and I was basking in the possibilities for Debbie and me and vowed to put the past behind us and do everything possible to finally be a normal happy family.

Debbie developed extreme post-partum depression and began to neglect Wim to the extent that she became jealous of the attention that Wim was getting instead of her. She was in denial that he was not perfect and needed to wear the corrective shoes. I tried to overlook a lot of her apathy about being a wife and mother but I could not ignore her noncompliance of the doctor's orders. Whenever I tried to address the foot issue with her, she became enraged and defensive, even with the evidence clearly visible she denied that Wim had a problem. I continued to put his special shoes on his feet each day but find him shoeless when I returned home from work.

When I came home from work Debbie was almost always very agitated and would rudely hand Wim over to me, saying "Here, take care of your kid." Then she would shrink into her own world excluding both of us.

I loved caring for Wim and developing a father and son bond but I knew that he could sense his mother's rejection and when I was not home, I feared that he was receiving no nurturing. He would only sleep if I would rock him and even then, he would wake up several times in the course of a night. I had grave concerns about leaving WK while working and traveling in my Air Force aircrew job. When I was at work, I had a sense of overwhelming guilt that Wim might not even be getting his most rudimentary needs met.

Our son was the center of my universe but it was exhausting taking care of him and going to work while Debbie became more and more distant from both of us. I knew that taking care of Wim would eventually get easier and I prayed my relationship with Debbie would too.

Four months after Wim's birth I received orders to report to Wright Patterson AFB, Ohio where I was assigned to the Air Force Flight Test Center (AFTC). The day before departing Hickam for my new assignment to Wright Patterson I received a call from my supervisor who asked me to help load several C-141A aircraft for the Marine Corps monthly mobility exercises to Hilo, HI. The operational Loadmaster became suddenly extremely sick and was grounded by the flight surgeon and no one else was available to manage the deployment operation. I had no obligation to honor the request because I was already processing out but I knew that he was in a bind.

I geared up and went to the flight line one last time. We were shipping Marines from Kaneohe NAS to Hilo through Hickam AFB. While directing the second outbound load on a C-141, I briefed the driver of a fully loaded 5-ton Marine Corps truck how to properly back his vehicle up the aircraft ramp. My last words of instruction to him were "DO NOT RIDE THE CLUTCH!"

Riding the clutch while backing up the inclined aircraft ramp causes the vehicle to jerk and jump or bounce up and down as it progresses up the ramp. I was apprehensive because a newly trained or untrained driver will often lose control of the vehicle in this situation but the driver confidently acknowledged all my instructions.

I took my position at the front left of the vehicle and in line of sight with the aircraft Loadmaster and the driver as I proceeded to guide him in backing up the ramp. As he reached the half-way point in backing up the incline, he started to ride the clutch. The vehicle started to stutter and bounce up and down. The driver panicked and pushed the clutch to the floor but did not use the brake.

The fully loaded monster truck barreled down the ramp and hit me sending me spinning 15 feet through the air. My body slammed down on the tarmac. I saw the uncontrolled vehicle continuing to pursue me and I unsuccessfully attempted to get up to get out of the path. It was too late as the front left tire rolled across my left foot crushing my steel toed boot. He slammed on the brakes and stopped the truck on my foot. I screamed in pain, "Stop, do not move!" He did not hear me and put the vehicle in reverse and back over my foot. I could feel the steel toe of my boot digging into my toes and I was terrified that my toes had been amputated.

Three of my Marine friends witnessed the incident in horror and dragged the driver out of the truck and beat the crap out of him. Another Loadmaster witnessed the accident and called for a vehicle to take me to the hospital. When they cut off my boot, they found only minor bruising to my toes, but the steel toe was almost completely collapsed around them.

I was evaluated by a doctor and x-rayed for broken bones. Since there were no Computer Axial Tomography (CAT) scan or Magnetic Resonance Imaging (MRI) machines in those days the final diagnosis was based on the limited imaging capabilities of the era. The primitive conventional x-rays showed some injury to my back but no apparent bone damage or breaks in the vertebral bodies. I have been told since then that my back injuries would not have been detectable on conventional x-rays. The physician on duty carelessly entered the accident in my medical records and failed to record that the accident had occurred on base by a Marine Corps vehicle while conducting a military deployment exercise. Because of my failure to properly record the scene and specifics of the accident, my last day at Hickam would have an adverse effect on the rest of my military career and life.

For the rest of my active-duty career, I suffered debilitating back and hip pain but reporting the pain would have most likely ended my Loadmaster career for medical reasons and I loved my job more than I hated the pain.

CHAPTER 34 - EDWARDS AFB

We were at the Honolulu International airport waiting for our flight to Travis AFB, in route to Dayton, OH and Wright Patterson AFB. Debbie was eagerly anticipating the move to Dayton because it was only a few hours away from her "real" family and I was excited at the opportunity to be a primary Loadmaster on the flight test team.

I was paged over the terminal speakers to pick up a phone at the check-in desk. The operator told me to meet a representative from Hickam who had an important message for me. The runner from the base personnel office met me and handed me amendments to my PCS orders. Instead of going to Wright Patterson AFB I was going to report to Edwards AFB, CA. The home of the AFFTC, Air Force Test Pilot school, and National Aeronautics and Space Administration (NASA's)'s Armstrong Research Center Flight Test Center.

Debbie's mood escalated from euphoric anticipation to explosive red-faced inconsolable screaming rage and anger with no regard to how she was upsetting little Wim or anyone else nearby.

When we arrived at Edwards AFB she seemed to rebound from her initial anger and appeared to have recovered from her depression. Debbie was a bright woman and an articulate speaker. Soon after we reported to Edwards she was hired at NASA as a Communications Specialist in the Public Affairs Office where she was quickly promoted to the spokesperson for their events and space shuttle program. It was a prestigious high-paid position and she had a promising career going forward.

The director of the base's child-care center was the wife of a pilot who I often flew with and WK now had safe, loving care while Debbie and I were working. Debbie and I became close friends with both the pilot and his wife. His wife often ensured that our son was taken care of if I could not get to the child-care center before it closed each day.

The child-care director expressed serious concerns about WK as he was showing evidence of developing learning disabilities. She feared that Attention Deficit Disorder (ADD) was a part of our future and counseled both of us on how to prepare for that eventuality. I was panic stricken but Debbie again was in denial about any imperfections in our son and ignored the advice.

Dyslexia was still not a commonly understood learning disorder and there was extraordinarily little awareness or published material on the subject. I believe that he had inherited this terrible malady from me and I knew firsthand that it was something that could be managed over time but the ADD and dyslexia proved to become a major life-altering-problem for our son and us.

Except for this bump in the road things were going smoothly and I was encouraged that Debbie seemed to be well recovered from her depression. But she still had significant uncontrolled anger issues and did not have the strength of character to accept constructive criticism. She was suddenly terminated from the high-paying and influential job after throwing a heavy stapler at her boss's head during a very public argument.

Our family income was greatly reduced when Debbie was fired and she was still not engaged as a mother or wife. We could no longer afford the costly base child-care center services and Debbie was not tolerating the High Desert sonic booms and test flights roaring above our heads every day. Inside our home Debbie was creating unpredictable explosive fits of anger that competed with the sonic booms above our heads.

The increased tensions at home made for several rocky months at Edwards. Using the pretext that she needed to get away Debbie took WK home to Illinois for a couple of months. When she returned to Edwards her anger and frustration about living on the base escalated and she became increasingly colder and more apathetic than I thought was humanly possible. Her sharp tongue and rude behavior made it impossible for her to hold a civil conversation. I was deeply concerned about how her temper tantrums were affecting WK.

Then one day I came home for lunch and found her loading our son in his car seat and the station wagon was filled with baggage. Taken aback by the scene I just stood there in silence and disbelief watching her throw things in the car. She noticed my puzzled expression and answered my unspoken question. "I am leaving you!"

I finally managed to speak. "Why?"

"I met another man who is a better man than you. Don't try to stop me - Goodbye!" She replied coldly.

Stunned, I stood speechless as she pealed out of the driveway in our only vehicle leaving me in a cloud of desert dust. For a few minutes I just stared after her in shock and then went into our house and proceeded to destroy every piece of furniture in a frenzy of frustration and rage. *How could I let her do this to me a second time? This time was much worse. She had taken my son, the very center of my being.*

After allowing myself some time to gain control of my emotions I called my boss Lieutenant Colonel (Lt Col). George Prewitt and told him what happened. He was understanding and encouraged me with a soothing voice. "Wim, I am so sorry to hear that. I will support you regardless of what you need to do."

Left with no form of transportation I walked everywhere in the High Desert heat, including to work. Eventually a friend and co-worker became my ride to work until I was able to buy a used Yamaha motorcycle. It was a convenient solution but not a practical one considering my mental state of anxiety and anger. The pain of losing my son was limitless and so was my travel speed when I hopped on my bike.

The office secretary had noticed my high-speed travels and told Colonel Prewitt that she was concerned for my safety. He pulled me aside and asked me to slow down and calm down. It was what I needed desperately – someone to let me know that people cared.

I needed another form of transportation but could not afford even a clunker. The base was conducting an auction of surplus equipment. The auction included all types of furniture, equipment, trucks, cars, and many other items. Out of curiosity I attended the event and decided to bid on one of the blue-used Air Force staff cars. Most of the Air Force logos on the doors, hood and bumpers were still visible. The paint was badly faded but the engine was sound and all the tires were in fair shape. When it was put up for bid, I submitted mine for $20.00. No one competed for my bid and I walked, rather drove away with my brand-new car. I probably should have been embarrassed to drive away with it but "No" I was happier than a pig feasting on slop to have a safe and hopefully reliable ride. I sold my cycle for $350.

My marriage vows were still important to me but what I really wanted was my son. I made several telephonic attempts to reconcile and save the marriage but Debbie finally sealed our fate. "Wim, I want a divorce. You can file for it and I will not challenge it. I am engaged and want to remarry and will not ask for child support or alimony. Just get it done!"

I was silent for a moment as I processed what she had just said and I realized this was my opportunity. "OK, I will file for a divorce using your infidelity as justification but I want permanent custody of Wim."

I was only mildly surprised with her answer. "OK, just do it and I will not contest it except that I will not give up custody of Wim."

For her it was all about having someone to pay the bills so that she could continue her free-spirited lifestyle. I actually felt sorry for her "better" man. He was in for quite a roller coaster ride. She was not budging on the custody issue and I knew the law would be on her side if I pursued the issue. I was worried about Wim's future if Debbie raised him but the legal system is very biased towards mothers in these battles and California was the absolute worse place for a husband to win custody.

I gave up and filed for an uncontested divorce in "Pro-Per" (without the assistant of a lawyer) at the Kern County courthouse. The divorce decree was approved including no child support or alimony. Although I had no legal obligation to provide child support, Wim was my son. I made out a monthly child support allotment through the Air Force Pay section. She never missed a child support allotment check and I made sure to keep copies of all my alimony and military pay records. Debbie's vindictive nature had no bounds and my gut instinct told me that this would not be the end of the subject.

About three months after Debbie left me, I drove to Illinois to see WK. Debbie was living in a cheap dilapidated trailer. Her new love and "better man" had left her for another woman and Debbie was working in a bar as a waitress/bar tender. She took Wim to work every day and his meals consisted of hamburgers, hot dogs and potato chips or French fries. He drank coca cola instead of milk.

Debbie gave me the keys to her trailer and asked me to take Wim home, bathe him and put him to bed. When I walked into the disheveled trailer, I was shocked to find that the refrigerator contained a lonely half empty bottle of Jim Beam and no evidence of food products or milk for Wim and there was no food in any of the kitchen cabinets. I was sickened by WK's living conditions. I picked Wim up and drove to the local supermarket and bought food, milk, and other essential items. I stocked the refrigerator and waited for Debbie to come home from work.

When she arrived home from work, I questioned her about the negative environment she was exposing WK to. Our "discussion" was hostile to say the least and she kicked me out threatening to call the police if I did not leave.

I did not have the option to stay because of so many uncontrollable issues. WK did not need to witness this battle that I could not win and legally the police would support her demand for me to leave. And it would not benefit anyone for me to jeopardize my Air Force career a second time because of domestic disputes. All I could do was leave the scene of the crash. Empty, powerless, and helpless, I drove non-stop back to Edwards AFB. When I returned to my barracks room I was totally lost and the situation seemed hopeless.

Reluctantly and with a deep sense of dread I once more spoke with Colonel Prewitt and told him what happened. I was ashamed of myself and afraid that he would be disappointed in my inability to get a handle on my pitiful personal life and existence. With my heart deeply imbedded in my throat I asked him for advice on what I should do. He simply suggested that I might pray for guidance and invited me to go to church with his family. He prayed with me and I went to church to put my pain and suffering in God's hands. Prayers and church attendance became the norm for me and I found some peace. As the saying goes – "We fail to look up until we are flat on our back."

The Prewitt Family

Soon after returning to Edwards AFB and my trailer encounter with Debbie my phone rang at 2 AM on a Monday morning, jolting me awake. Debbie's familiar voice came through with a business-like precision. "Come and get your kid. I can't take care of him anymore." After a few seconds of clearing my head I realized what she was demanding. I was angry that she was using Wim like the pawn in a chess game but I was elated that I had some leverage now to put Wim under my protection and care. The ball finally seemed to be in my court.

"Sure, Debbie. If you give me complete, unconditional legal custody, I will board the next available plane to St. Louis Airport and you can hand him off to me. But you have to give me a Judge's order releasing Wim's custody to me."

"No problem, just let me know when and I'll get him there with the legal papers releasing parental custody to you."

I called Colonel Prewitt and awakened him from a dead sleep. The phone rang only a couple times when I heard his sleepy voice giving the standard military telephone response: "Colonel Prewitt Residence."

"Sir, this is TSgt Sergeant Wetzel. I am flying to St. Louis to pick up my son. I will explain when I return."

"Sergeant Wetzel, you do whatever is necessary to care for your son." He spoke.

"Thank you, sir. I'll see you and explain the situation first thing when I get back."

I drove to the LAX International Airport and caught the first available roundtrip flight to St. Louis and back. I had asked God for my son to be returned to me and He had answered and made provisions for me to get a direct flight within the hour to pick him up. I called Debbie with the flight information and she told me her mother would meet me at the airport with Wim.

I arrived at St. Louis and met my mother-in-law who handed me my son, the notarized legal documents, a childcare bag with the minimum essential diapers but no food of any kind. She turned around and walked away never uttering a single word to me.

My return flight was scheduled to leave later that day with a scheduled arrival at LAX at midnight. Upon arrival at the airport, I got into my car and drove us back to the base and slept next to Wim in my office. Where else could I go with an 18-month-old son who was not potty-trained?

God bless Colonel Prewitt and his entire family. Mrs. Jane Prewitt, Lisa, Lori, and Phillip all reached out to help me through this exceedingly difficult time. After explaining to him what had occurred Colonel Prewitt told me not to worry and that he and the Standardization Office team would help in every way possible. I reminded him that I lived in the barracks and had no other options.

He picked up the phone and called the Squadron Commander and asked for special permission for me to take Wim to the barracks until other accommodations could be arranged. The commander talked with the First Sergeant who agreed to let us stay in the barracks and better yet permitted me to take him to the dining hall for meals until we could arrange for another place to live. We moved into my barracks room and almost immediately the other guys in the dorm volunteered to help baby sit when needed. The other jilted single fathers or victims of Jodies, who also lost child custody were especially helpful.

Wim and I lived in the enlisted barracks and ate in the dining hall. The dining hall maintenance staff even set up a corner table with drop cloths under Wim's chair. We were blessed by the wealth of kindness shown towards us by everyone of the people on the base. But I knew that the situation would not continue to be acceptable and I had to find a more appropriate solution.

After three months of trying to find affordable housing for WK and me the First Sergeant could no longer ignore the younger Airmen who were complaining about living in a childcare center. He finally had no choice but to insist that I accelerate my move out of the barracks. Although I had no idea how I would do it and no clue how I would meet that commitment I thanked him for his patience and promised him I would move out quickly.

While visiting friends who lived in the base mobile home park, I noticed that their next-door neighbor had a For Sale sign in front of their home. I walked over to inquire about the price and asked to see the place. It was clean and well maintained. They were asking for $4000 and if I came up with $1200 as a down payment, they would carry the balance. Again, I did not have a clue how I would come up with the down payment but we shook hands on the deal on the spot pending the delivery of the down payment. God had just provided a home for us but He had not revealed any hint of where I would possibly find $1,200.

A fellow loadmaster, Al Capone and I had only recently become friends. He was single and was extremely helpful and sympathetic to my situation. He lived in the same barracks as Wim and me and knew why we were staying there. I do not think he fully understood that I literally did not have a pot to piss in or a window to throw it out of. Humiliated and embarrassed I explained my new dilemma. With compassion and understanding he asked, "How much is the down payment, Wim?'

I swallowed hard and plunged ahead. "Twelve hundred dollars." He stared at me in silence for a few minutes. Still silent, he stood up and walked behind me to his locker. I sat quietly with my head down still wondering how I was going to get that much money. I could hear him rifling through some papers then he came back to his chair and sat down facing me with a check book and pen in his hand and began to write. I assumed he was going to help me out with part of the down payment, maybe $50 or $100 but every little bit helped my cause and I was grateful for his willingness to help. While handing me the check he said. "Consider this as a gift. I do not want or need you to repay me; just take care of your son."

I could not believe what I saw. He had written a check for $1,200. "Al, this is a loan and I will pay you back with interest." He responded. "It is a gift and I don't want to discuss it any further. Take care of your son." God had provided for us once again.

I closed the sale and moved into our new home within the week. Neighbors helped to baby sit when needed. The Child Care Center manager made special provisions for his care if no one else was available. We were so blessed by the love and support of the Prewitt family. God was turning things around for us and our lives were starting to get better. Life was good again.

Colonel Prewitt told me that the Wing Commander was pleased with my job on the weekly standardization status report among other things that I had achieved. He suggested that Colonel Prewitt should nominate me for the Flight Test Center NCO of the Year. After successfully meeting two selection boards I was selected for the honor. To my surprise and with great gratitude, I was given the additional honor of being awarded the Antelope Valley Chamber of Commerce NCO of the year.

One day Colonel Prewitt asked to meet with me in private. I knew my job responsibilities were satisfactory and exceeded his expectations but he sounded somber. I reported to his office as requested. He looked up from his paperwork and greeted me in his friendly approachable manner and motioned for me to sit down.

"Have you ever considered going to college Wim?"

"Yes sir, of course, but in my present situation I have to put that on hold since I have to take care of Wim when I am not on duty."

I could not believe what he was offering me. "If you enroll in Cerro Coso Community College on base, you have my permission to take classes during your work hours and do your homework in the office. My only condition is that you will continue providing the weekly standardization status reports for the Wing Commander briefings."

The next day I enrolled in college classes and opened a whole new world with endless possibilities because of a kind, caring and loving friend and Air Force commander.

CHAPTER 35 – DOUBLE "E" TICKET RIDE

Dad had given me a priceless inheritance that followed me around like a persistent stalker. "If you want to be successful and earn respect; start by cleaning bathrooms and sweeping floors and do it with pride and dignity. And against everyone else's advice, volunteer for everything that no one else is willing to do."

I stood at attention while Colonel Prewitt presented me with the NCO of the year award and an unexpected second award for the AFFTC Suggestion Program of the year award. Thanks Dad, rest in peace.

Lt. Colonel George Prewitt

After receiving the award plaques, the Colonel told me that the NCO award meant that I could select to ride in any aircraft on the base. I was a civilian Commercial Pilot working on my FAA Flight and Instrument Instructor certifications and this was a once-in-a-lifetime opportunity beyond my wildest dreams.

It was quite a dilemma. Do I choose the Northrop T-38 Talon fighter jet, the world's first supersonic trainer and pride of the Thunderbirds? The one that is used to train Air Force pilots and astronauts, the same one used as a chase plane or…do I choose the McDonnell Douglas F-4 Phantom II, a combat supersonic jet interceptor and fighter-bomber with a top speed of over Mach 2.2?

Captain Lloyd Adams, our T-38 Test Pilot, was in the room. Colonel Prewitt was the F-4 Pilot. I hesitated but I knew what I wanted.

"Well Sergeant Wetzel, have you decided which aircraft you want to fly?" The Colonel asked.

"Honestly, Sir, why can't I fly in both?"

Colonel Prewitt shrugged and looked at Captain Adams to make sure he agreed to it. Captain Adams nodded his affirmation and I held my breath waiting for Colonel Prewitt's final word. "OK Wim, you got it."

"I'd like to pilot both of them, Sir."

The Colonel turned again to Captain Adams. Frowning with fake disapproval, the Captain said "Affirmative!"

To avoid the risk of being undignified I restrained myself from doing the happy dance.

Before I could become" King for a Day" I had to go through an orientation process that included ejection seat instructions and procedures, how to avoid blackouts during high G maneuvers and how to use the survival equipment if there was an accident. I was fitted with a special fighter pilot helmet and oxygen mask to cap off my "jet fighter pilot" persona.

After completing all the required training and class work, I was awarded the official "barf bag' that was not as elaborate as the garbage bag that I hung around my neck as a rookie Loadmaster, but now I was all grownup. I proudly assured the life support technician that it would not be needed. He told me to take it anyway because I would be required to clean up the mess.

With a "little" assistance from my heroes, they allowed me to taxi their aircraft to the runway and take command of the controls for takeoff into the wild blue yonder. Lloyd told me to look at the fuel gauges as he kicked the jet into afterburner. I watched in amazement as the fuel gauge dropped steadily and rapidly as we reached supersonic speed.

I was under close adult supervision and assistance but on both flights, they let me feel like it was just me and my plane.

Both pilots let me do acrobatic maneuvers and Colonel Prewitt let me conduct a couple of simulated bomb runs. The coup-de-gras was when I flew the F-4 the entire length of the emergency 30,000 plus foot long desert runway that was used by the Space Shuttle. With a bit more than a little help I landed the F-4 for the final landing.

The flight with Captain Adams was more challenging and surreal. He asked if I was interested in some aerobatics such as barrel rolls and other maneuvers and I said "absolutely!" He advised that the first barrel roll was to the left and without any further warning other than saying "Are you ready?" Captain Adams suddenly rolled the jet to the left for a couple of rolls and slamming my helmet against the overhead plexiglass window. He asked if I was OK and I responded with "Roger that Captain and are you ready to go to the right?" I knew it was now my turn to demonstrate what I could do and before he could instruct me on how to conduct the roll, I put the fighter into three rolls to the right slamming his helmet into the left side of the window. I got a big thumbs up.

We dove down to a long and winding river that ended at the base of 20,000 feet plus mountain. He weaved along the entire length at a couple of hundred feet off the river's surface and then he told me to hold on. Lloyd raised the nose and rocketed to the top of the mountain and sub-sonic speed. At the top he briefly leveled off before helping me fly the mini rocket down the other side. After taking over the aircraft we returned to Edwards where he allowed me to fly just above the entire length of the landing runway before helping me land on the final touchdown. For those of you that were born in the 50's and 60's you will know what I mean when I say they were "E" ticket rides. By the way, I returned the barf bag unused.

Colonel Prewitt Honor Flight Before and After

T-38 Honor Flight With Captain Adams

A few days later Colonel Prewitt offered to help me complete my training to obtain my flight instructor certifications through the Edwards AFB Aero Club. We flew several of the required long-distance "instrument only" flights with me under the hood. His expert instructions during those training flights, especially within the parameters of LAX, fully prepared me for the Instrument rating and ultimately the Instrument Instructor rating FAA examinations.

There is an old saying of debatable origins "Give a man a fish and he will eat for a day, teach him to fish and he will eat for a lifetime." There were never truer words spoken. I was truly blessed to have Colonel Prewitt and his caring family continuously there for me. I was willing to do the work to achieve my goals as well as raise my son to the best of my capability but the Prewitt family always had my back and were ready to clear any obstacles that would have otherwise blocked my way. They gave me the opportunity to eat for a lifetime and I grabbed on and ran with it like I was King bass. There was no way I was going to let this great man and war hero down. I wanted to make him proud.

Then one day at work he sprung the big question on me: "What are you going to do to give back to others as a way to say thank you for your opportunities?" I thought awhile about how to answer Colonel Prewitt's pointed question.

"Well, I was a Boy Scout and Explorer during my youth and always wanted to start a Scout unit."

***

There were no scouting organizations at Edwards AFB when I was stationed there but there were a lot of young families with teenagers. It was a perfect opportunity to offer those young people new and exciting adventures in life that they may not have otherwise had. The greatest honor I could give Col Prewitt and my own scout leader, Mr. Wildman was to give others what they had given me, life skills, self-confidence, and unlimited opportunities.

As a life-long Boy Scout and Explorer Scout I applied to the Boy Scouts of America (BSA) headquarters in Irving, TX for permission to create a co-ed Aviation Explorer Post 737. The fact that the Post was being created on the world's most prestigious Air Force Base and supported by numerous senior military commanders helped get the application approved quickly. Immediately after the application was approved with me as the designated Scoutmaster I had to get to work.

This was an Aviation Explorer Post on a base that trained the space shuttle astronauts and test pilots for every new innovative and powerful fighter and cargo aircraft. The local youth were hungry to have something of their own to allow them to be part of that environment. That made it easy to recruit members.

It helped that part of my job responsibility was to write, conduct and proctor the aircraft safety and emergency action written examinations for the pilots and test pilots at Edwards AFB. The job gave me direct access to the best pilots in the world to get the word out about the new scouting unit. As they say in today's world-the news went viral.

Setting up the logistics to get the Post off the ground took a lot of coordination and a lot of adult volunteers. We needed every possible resource available to get started and flying. The Flight Test Center provided us with space in the Test Pilot School for the meetings and several parents volunteered as my assistants. The BSA provided all the information necessary for us to meet their requirements and we had 35 extremely excited and highly motivated co-ed members who were extremely active in getting the post off the ground.

Colonel Prewitt was my assistant Scoutmaster and used his considerable influence and leverage to fast-track the approvals with the Base Commander and schedule the first Fly-In. It was an extraordinary example of the power of Dad's mantra: "Don't Ask – Don't Get."

Edwards AFB conducts an annual Open House to allow the public access to the many wonders and exciting events that the base is known for. We followed the same template used for the open house events. It was quickly approved and the Fly-In event was scheduled. Pilots from all over the area applied for approval to attend the event and land on the historic Edwards AFB runways. With the full support of all the members' parents and base personnel, the event became a rousing success.

***

At the request of the Edwards AFB hospital, I assisted them in applying for and establishing the Medical Explorer Post. I was already on overload but it was impossible to say no when I knew the rewards for the youth involved would outweigh my efforts.

It turned out to be a simple process of replicating my own request for an Aviation Explorer Post and the application was submitted at the same time. The approval came soon after my own application and the Medical Post was established. The unexpected rewards for my efforts paid off tenfold. In this case the reward for helping the hospital with their request came in a unique and most unexpected way.

The base Flight Surgeon owned a cabin at Mammoth Mountain Ski Resort and offered us the use of the place for a weekend. This was a great opportunity for the post members and I had never skied before and I was pumped and ready to go. The base motor pool gave me the keys to the 58 passenger Air Force bus. This time my bus privileges were used for more honorable purposes.

Twenty-two Explorer members and my best buddy WK participated in the skiing weekend. Once I initiated the trip, a well-oiled team of behind-the-scenes volunteers took off with the project. Parents contributed funds for the food purchases and the Air Force paid for the gasoline used for the bus.

My neighbor from the base mobile home park was one of the chaperones and she brought her two–eight and nine-year old sons. In return for her assistance, the cost for ski lift tickets and skiing for her sons were paid for by the Post.

Because of my karate training I understood the key to factors of shifting my weight for maximum stability and balance. I was overconfident because of that knowledge, but what I had not learned was the difference between a positive attitude and a cocky attitude. As the day proceeded my skills improved quickly and, in a few hours, I became a fairly competent skier.

After skiing together one last time as a group I decided to take one last ride on the highest slope. I told everyone my intentions and asked the chaperones to take the group back to the chalet where I would meet them for dinner. I got onto the ski-lift and returned to the top of the run. I did notice that I was the only skier on the lift as it reached the top. Smug, confident, and self-assured I exited the ski lift bench and immediately started down the run with abandonment and enjoying my own company.

As I started down the ski slope and looking ahead, something did not look quite right. *Whoa! It is really different looking down there from the higher elevation. I cannot even see the chalets or the people. Those trees are really big. I did not notice those trees before---wait a minute! There were not any trees on this slope before. Oh, shit, where am I? I am not on the slope. I am in the wilderness at a point of no return.*

Dodging trees and deep snowy rough terrain, I had no choice but to keep moving. My first priority was to get to the bottom in one piece before a tree jumped in front of me or I collapsed from exhaustion or froze to death. There seemed to be no end to the mountain slope as Mother Nature and I became intimately acquainted. I was on the wrong side of the mountain and it took so long that I was almost convinced that this side had no bottom.

When I reached the bottom of the non-existent darkened ski run, I stood there and wondered how I was going to survive. I panicked momentarily before gathering my thoughts about what to do next. I stood on the edge of a recently shoveled two-lane road so I counted my blessings and started walking. Walking in ski-boots and carrying my skis while wearing the minimum layer of clothing for sunny daytime skiing became problematic. The sun was long gone and temperatures plummeted and darkness took over. I walked for a long time and developed bad leg cramps and pain from walking in ski boots. I sat down on a big rock by the side of the road and prayed aloud for help. No sooner did I complete my prayer when headlights appeared.

I stood near the left center of the road waving my arms wildly. It worked and the driver pulled over and the passenger opened her window and said, "What the heck are you doing out here and where are you going?" I told them that I was lost after skiing down the back side of Mammoth on the last ride.

The four young skiers in the car were obviously amused and puzzled that anyone could make that mistake. I told them that I was staying at the Mammoth resort and asked for a ride. When the driver asked which cabin, I was staying in, my mind was as frozen as my body and I could not remember the address. At this point I am sure they were thinking--*That explains a lot.* When I mentioned that I was staying at a chalet owned by an Air Force Flight Surgeon, the driver knew immediately where to go. God had sent angels to save my hide one more time. On the long road trip back to the chalet I could not stop telling them how grateful I was for their kindness.

When we arrived back at Mammoth from my second "E" ticket ride it was 12:30 AM. The kind and generous driver dropped me off and refused my offer to pay for gas. Missing for eight hours and unprepared for what was waiting for me in the chalet, a representative from the mountain rescue team greeted me. "So, you are the missing Scout Master?"

I could not answer because all of the scouts surrounded and hugged me. Several had tears of joy after they had been imagining the worst. When everyone calmed down the rescue team leader made a radio call to the search team that the "Scoutmaster was home safe and sound!" His emphasis on the word scoutmaster was both embarrassing and comical.

I sat by the fireplace to warm up and share my comedy of errors with the scouts and the more responsible adult chaperones. It was a humbling and embarrassing experience but we were all grateful that they found me alive rather than frozen on the rock on the side of the road with a permanent dumb shit look on my face.

CHAPTER 36 - BLUE EYES

WK was the joy of my life. He was quite a character and I could not imagine my life without him. My social life hinged on him and for three precious years, when I was not working, we were joined at the hip and I even took him flying with me. He could not reach the pedals but he was a fearless flyer. He was the unofficial Aviation Explorer Post mascot and the members were all his big brothers and sisters and he followed them everywhere.

I received my promotion to Master Sergeant (MSgt) along with PCS orders to Altus AFB, OK. I know it was confusing for WK. He was too young to realize that he was being uprooted from his day care and Explorer friends and would not see them again. It was painful for me to leave my Edwards AFB family but orders are orders and we had to move.

I sold the mobile home for $5,200.00 and wrote a check to Al for $1,500.00. Al ripped up the check and repeated that it had been a gift. I thanked him profusely and told him that I would never forget him and his kind heart. Al continues to be one of my dearest friends today.

I contacted a real estate agent in the Altus area and she lined up prospective homes in my price range. I packed up our meager belongings and WK and I drove to Altus AFB in our surplus Air Force blue staff car. The trip took three days and we stayed in cheap motels, downed a lot of burgers, hot dogs, and greasy French fries. We stopped to visit the Grand Canyon and watched the mules carry inexperienced city slickers to the bottom of the canyon.

When we crossed the state line from Texas to Oklahoma late at night, we encountered several tornadoes lined up like rail cars. One of them found us and lifted the rear of our car off the ground and pummeled us with golf ball size hail stones. I tried to maintain my composure for WK's sake but he could sense that we were both very scared. Fortunately, the tornado went on its way to find someone or something else to terrorize.

***

After we arrived in Altus the first order of business was to meet with the real estate agent with whom I had been communicating. She had found a house in town on Mars Street and arranged for me to view the property. I was in a hurry to find housing to get us settled before I had to start my new job. I had no experience at buying real estate and she showed us a house that had all black interior walls and red ceilings with bamboo trim everywhere. She explained that the military owner's wife was Japanese. I considered what had to be done to make the hovel our home and made an offer below the asking price.

    The owner accepted the offer and I was able to get a good real estate loan with reasonable interest and low monthly payments. We purchased the minimum needed furniture from the base housing office and thrift shop, settled in, and started a new phase in our Air Force life together.

    Altus AFB was the location housing the primary school for all C-141A/B aircrew members including Pilots, Navigators, Flight Engineers and Loadmasters. The C-141 Loadmaster School trained new Loadmasters to become certified to serve on the Starlifter. My new boss was School Superintendent MSgt John Burkhardt which was a pleasant surprise because I had worked for him in aerial delivery earlier in my career. He had been a great mentor then and now I had another opportunity to glean from his knowledge and experience. My assignment was to teach at the school with the additional responsibility of Assistant Superintendent. As his assistant it was expected that I would be his replacement if and when he moved on to another position.

    I was either teaching classes or flying airdrop and air refueling missions every day or night. The Air Refueling (AR) missions were boring and tedious, especially the night missions. They lasted about four hours with repetitive connecting and disconnecting to the KC-135 refueling tanker aircraft or transferring fuel back to the tanker if there was an in-flight emergency requiring reducing fuel weight. But every crewmember looked forward to the overseas cargo and passenger flights in support of the Military Airlift Command's (MACs) worldwide mission.

    This repetitive process lasted about six months before John was re-assigned to another base and I became the School Superintendent. Thanks to John's mentoring I felt more than competent to handle the job. However, some things cannot be taught. The everyday challenges brought new leadership opportunities dealing with the students' antics as they were going through the program.

I was at Altus for four months when on June 1, 1980 I got a call from Debbie. She asked if Wim could come to Illinois and spend some time with her. She had remarried and sounded like she had finally pulled her life together. I still remembered how painful it was for me to be estranged from my mother during my teen years and I never wanted WK to experience that. My sixth sense warned me not to let him go but I chalked the feeling up to my selfishness. It was one of the most difficult decisions that I ever made but I put WK on a plane to fly to St. Louis.

***

Missing my best buddy and coming home to an empty house was not an appealing choice so I decided to get out of the house and go to the Altus AFB NCO club. June 5,1980 - I sat at the bar and ordered a beer and started a conversation with the bartender. A few minutes later I felt someone tapping on my shoulder. "Hi – I've not seen you here before. Are you a newcomer to the base?"

I turned in my bar stool to look into the most amazing blue eyes that I had ever seen. I could barely speak as I mumbled, "Yes, I reported to the base from Edwards AFB in March. I'm Wim Wetzel" I said, relieved that I could remember my name. I was shocked that such a beautiful woman would take the time to approach and talk to me.

"Welcome to Altus Wim, my name is Zee."

She continued to come over and make friendly conversation between serving drinks. She had the most beautiful eyes and I could not stop looking at her. She finally disappeared for about fifteen minutes so I decided it was time to go home. But before I left, I asked the bartender to tell Zee that I had to leave but I would see her again the following evening. I should have stayed longer because I really had no reason to go to my empty house and as a result could not sleep that night. All I could see with my eyes closed were her gorgeous blue eyes.

Zee

The next day I kept myself very busy. I probably accomplished more than I usually would in three days to keep myself from watching the clock. I do not think I hid my anticipation very well because my boss John sat amused watching me as I flitted about.

With a curious smirk and a twinkle of mischief in his eye he finally joked "You are in a good mood today. Slow down, you are making everyone look bad. What's going on Wim?"

"John, do you know anything about a girl named Zee that works at the NCO club?"

"Oh no, forget about her, Wim. She is a great gal and a straight arrow. She has held down two jobs as a single mom to three boys. They are probably all teenagers now and they are her whole life. I have never seen her date anyone and numerous Flight Engineers have tried to no avail. Trust me, she would not be interested in you." John's comments really piqued my interest and I resolved to prove him wrong.

That evening I returned to the NCO club and sat on the same barstool and waited for the opportunity to talk to her. It was out of character for me to strike up a conversation with a stranger. She spied me sitting at the bar and came over to talk. "Are you the person who told the bartender "Please tell Zee good night for me and that I will see her again?"

"Yes, I did."

"I teach at the Loadmaster School and am the Assistant Superintendent to MSgt John Burkhardt. I mentioned meeting you to John and he speaks very highly of you and he told me that you are raising three sons."

"I'm a single father raising a son and it piqued my interest. Knowing how hard it is to raise just one child, I can't imagine raising three sons by myself."

"They no longer live with me and are all on their own now. The two oldest are joining the Navy and my youngest is now living with his father in Georgia (GA). My younger sister has moved in with me for a while."

"Wim - How old is your son?"

"Four-going on twenty-four." We both laughed.

"Where is he now?" she asked.

"It's a long story but he is visiting his mother in Illinois for a few weeks. This is the first time that we have been apart since he was eighteen months old. And I am completely lost without him."

We talked about how I came to be legal guardian of WK. As a devoted mother she believed deep in her heart that no mother would ever abandon her child as I described. I could sense that Zee was never completely convinced about my story. It was difficult to graciously explain the circumstances without digging myself in deeper or sounding like I was vilifying my son's mother. Except for that one snag we were like-minded in every way.

Over time we became friends and shared son-raising stories.

***

I called WK often and during our telephone calls I told him about Zee, how much he would like her and how anxious she was to meet him. I allowed him to talk to her on the telephone and she had a calm and soothing voice that helped form a strong emotional connection before they even met. It was exactly the kind of motherly love Wim needed and missed for most of his life and she was exactly the stability I needed. I hoped she thought so too.

During the following weeks we spent every possible moment together and I learned that she too had suffered at the hands of two failed marriages. We really started to care for each other and the relationship was going well but we were both in an abyss of distrust and caution from our previous bad relationship experiences.

Zee introduced me to her sister who immediately referred to me as a dork and asked Zee where I learned to dress. I have never had a sense for fashion and was still wearing 60's era clothing when I met them.

Then one Saturday morning my doorbell rang at about 7 am. I answered it curious as to who might be coming to my house that early in the morning. Upon opening the door, I was pleasantly surprised to see Zee standing there with two palm plants under her arms.

She said, "Happy house-warming Wim."

Like a dork I just stood there with my mouth wide open unable to respond.

"Aren't you going to invite me in? These things are heavy."
Embarrassed standing in my bathrobe I stepped aside and let her in after grabbing one of the plants.

I asked her to sit down and I excused myself to get dressed and make myself look like less of a Dork. When I returned to the living room Zee was standing in the middle of the room, her head was slowly swiveling from side to side and those beautiful blue eyes were scanning the black walls and red ceiling. "Umm-who was your decorator Wim?"

"Nice, isn't it? Actually, it was the last owner and I haven't had the time or funds to change it yet."

"It looks like you could use some help here."

"Are you volunteering?"

"Maybe."

"Whose car is that parked out front?"

By her mocking tone I could tell that she was not impressed with my surplus hail-pitted Air Force staff car.

"Mine. It was in my price range."

She took a deep breath and blew it out to suppress a smile of amusement. "Oh, my. I see…" We both laughed.

I cooked breakfast for us and we spent the day together getting to know each other.

***

Zee invited me to spend the Fourth of July with her sister and their parents, Madge, and Ted Perryman, on the family farm. It seemed to be a great opportunity to get to know her family and enjoy a day on a working farm.

Madge was gracious and cordial but Ted was not an easy nut to crack. We all lingered at the kitchen table for more than an hour after the meal was over. I awkwardly tried to make conversation with Ted as he sat across from me with his arms folded, lips pursed and never making eye contact.

To my relief Madge finally suggested to Ted that he take me on a tour of the farm while he checked the livestock. I quickly responded. "Yes, if you do not mind. I would like to do that." That created an embarrassing long silence waiting for Ted's response and finally I think even Ted began to realize how ridiculous the scene was becoming and succumbed to the peer pressure. Without a word he got up from his chair, looked at me and nodded towards the door. I obediently followed his lead and we were on our way.

We walked in silence for at least fifteen minutes while I desperately reached into the farthest depths of my brain searching for something appropriate to say. Ted was not about to help me out with this struggle. I think on some level that he was enjoying my suffering. I began to ask him questions about farming, raising cattle and why he liked farming. He answered abruptly as if he were being interrogated and not wanting to reveal more information than his name, rank, and serial number. For me this was a huge breakthrough.

We strolled along the fringes of a newly plowed winter-wheat field taking in whiffs of the freshly turned rich moist soil. The sun warmed my face and the soft breeze gently swirled around us as we walked. Something seemed to catch his attention and he walked over to the fence rail, rested both arms on the rail fence and gazed out at the great expanse of farmland. I joined him and soaked in the beauty sprawled in front of us.

Neither of us took our eyes away from the beautiful scene in front of us and I finally broke the silence. "Ted, I think you need to know. I really am falling in love with Zee. I know that Zee had two very painful marriage experiences. I understand your concern and most of all I understand her pain because I too have come out of a very hurtful marriage. I do not take my relationship with Zee lightly. Please believe me when I say I understand why you would be worried but I am nothing like her ex-husbands and I know that I could never do anything to hurt her. I am in love with her." His demeanor softened and we began to talk more freely. He opened up about his relationship with his children and grandchildren.

By the time we returned to the house Ted and I were talking and smiling. The three women sat at the table dumbstruck by our now warm and cordial friendship.

***

So many things were falling into place. I had achieved my flight instructor rating but was still short 13 hours to meet the multi-engine instrument rating requirements. Under normal circumstances it was a goal that was just out of my financial reach. The 13 hours might as well have been 100 – I just could not afford it. My FAA flight examiner was a WWII bomber pilot and he was very generous with his compliments about my flight skills during the Commercial Pilot post check flight debriefing. He knew what was holding me back but he aggressively encouraged me to achieve this ultimate rating and we shook hands and parted ways. I never expected to hear from this WWII aviation hero again.

One day at about 4 pm I received a call at my base office from a civilian pilot based at Bluebird Airport in Dallas. I was referred to him by the WWII bomber pilot as someone who desperately needed some multi-engine instrument instructor flight time.

He asked how many hours I needed and I told him 12.5 hours-hood time. Hood time involves the use of a visor type devise referred to as a hood. It simulates poor visibility due to weather conditions.

"Well, if you accept my offer you will get more than that and you will be able to come to Bluebird to take the flight exam."

"I'm all ears, Sir!"

"Are you interested in flying my King Air to the John Wayne Airport in California – tonight. I will buy you a return airline ticket for helping me fly the aircraft at night. If so – we depart at midnight if you can make it to Bluebird."

"Yes. I will be there." He provided me with his location and the logistics of our rendezvous. I was so excited that I hung up without saying good-bye. I called my boss John Burkhardt to tell him about my opportunity and explain to him that I was going to be gone for two days. As I hung up from talking to John, I had a fleeting thought that I could not go. I had no one to care for WK. Then I remembered he was in Illinois visiting his mother.

I drove to Dallas, TX ignoring the speed limit signs and prayed that the entire highway patrol squad was on their coffee break or going through a shift change. The pilot found me waiting anxiously at our planned meeting place. We departed Bluebird on schedule and I made an instrument (hooded) takeoff for Albuquerque, New Mexico (NM) Airport (ABQ).

The entire flight and approach to ABQ was completed under the hood. Upon arrival at our destination the generous pilot signed my logbook with the total hours flown and a thorough description of the flight as required by the FAA. He handed me the airline ticket, shook my hand in congratulations in completing the FAA Certified Multi-Engine Instrument Flight Instructor Rating flight requirements. A week later I passed the FAA flight exam and became a single and multi-engine instrument rated flight instructor pilot.

The stars were in perfect alignment. I had all my pilot certifications and loved going to work every day, WK would be returning to me soon and I was quite sure I had met my dream soul mate.

CHAPTER 37 - WEDDING BELLS AND THE EX FROM HELL

I called Debbie to confirm Wim's return date and flight into Amarillo. I dreaded talking to her and as I expected, she did not want to return WK to me. She claimed that she had become a very good mother. I asked to speak with WK and he told me that he wanted to come home. She finally conceded. Although I had not threatened to do so, she understood that I was Wim's legal guardian and if she blocked his return it could result in serious legal consequences. Reluctantly, she put him on the plane as scheduled.

Zee and I had a long talk about me being a single father and how much I loved my son. She clearly stated that she already raised three sons and that she was not ready to raise another. I sensed that it was one of the factors that kept her from accepting my marriage proposals. She knew that I was a committed single father and that was the only thing I would never compromise on.

Zee and I drove the 100 miles to Amarillo to meet WK's arriving flight. My greatest fear was that Zee and WK would not like each other and that our deepening relationship may end before it had a chance to mature. I was tense and apprehensive but Zee sat waiting, relaxed, and calmly smoking her cigarettes. I did not smoke but my whole family did so I just accepted it as part of life.

We waited at the gate for the stewardess to deliver my son. The gateway door opened and I immediately saw WK. His eyes were darting back and forth searching for me. They finally locked on to me standing next to Zee. He bolted free from the stewardess and ran directly to Zee and hugged her. Zee was as shocked as I was at the abrupt welcome but she hugged him back. While hugging they turned and looked at me standing alone looking forlorn amidst all the offloading passengers.

Wim ran over to me, grabbed my hand, and dragged me to where Zee was standing. By this time, I was shedding happy tears and wondering what was going to happen next. I did not have to wait long. Wim looked at Zee adoringly and said, "I love you." Zee answered "I love you too WK." I knew her heart had softened and she turned to me with a relenting smile and a surrendering shrug. This moment was the deal breaker and things were going to be OK.

***

Before he went to visit his mother, Wim had been conditioned to having behavioral boundaries, rules, guidelines, and structure in his life. In the short time he was with Debbie he grew accustomed to Debbie's no rules, hands off parenting style and it was a challenge getting him to get back to following the rules in our home.

It was a major battle getting him to bathe or brush his teeth. He had become a connoisseur of junk foods and sugary drinks and had developed an aversion to the cooked meals that he had previously enjoyed. He became defiant when I denied him his fill of Coke, chips, and candy bars. Instead of the father and son relationship that I had cherished so much, it became a war of wills. It took some patience but the message did get from his ears to his hyperactive brain and things began to turn around.

Zee created a healthy environment for WK and me and WK responded to the structure, stability and nurturing she offered. I grew to love Zee more every day as she became a wonderful mother for WK and potential life partner for me.

***

We began to settle into the routine of a stable secure home life then Debbie began calling him at all hours of the night and day. Not wanting to come between him and his mother I was amiable at first. But she became more aggressive and started making him feel guilty for not being there for her. There was a role reversal as WK was becoming the parent and Debbie became the needy child.

He would be calm while they were conversing as Debbie cried and begged him to come back to her. After the phone calls we would have to console him and if she called at night he could not go back to sleep again. We thought Debbie's behavior would run its course but instead her obsessive behavior escalated as she constantly begged him to come back. Wim began to exhibit behavioral issues and I finally told her that she could not talk to him after 8 PM. Debbie used that to her advantage and told Wim that I would never allow her to call him again.

***

He began to act out in school and I was called into the principal's office to meet with his teachers. The school nurse wanted to have him prescribed for Ritalin to help control his Attention Deficit Hyperactivity Disorder (ADHD). I thanked her for her opinion and informed her that I would get a doctor's evaluation for my son's condition before throwing pills at him that he might not need.

I had Wim tested and as I suspected, the diagnosis was dyslexia. With treatment and special attention, the doctor believed that we could get some control of Wim's malady. He did recommend that Ritalin should be prescribed at the lowest possible dose to calm him down in the classroom. With the aid of a dyslexia therapist, he was able to learn some simple ways to improve his reading skills and over time we were able to wean him off the Ritalin.

For about four months we refused to let Debbie talk to WK by phone. We never told him that we were intercepting the calls and over time he started to calm down and forget about calling Debbie. His behavior and schoolwork improved and the stress in our home was significantly reduced.

Despite all of the interference and disruption Debbie caused in our lives, Zee was still convinced that I was grossly exaggerating Debbie's incompetent, non-nurturing, and neglectful parenting. It was the one ambiguity in our otherwise compatible relationship.

***

I wanted to marry Zee but after her two failed marriages she was very gun-shy at the prospect. Despite wanting to remain single she decided to move in with me in September. The arrangement was a good one but it was missing the stability that a marriage can bring to a long-term relationship.

One Saturday morning there was a loud banging at the front door. I answered the door to find her father, Ted, looking very agitated and angry.

"Hello, Ted."

"Is my daughter here?"

"Sure Ted, come in. I'll tell her you are here."

Ted folded his arms tightly across his chest and snorted "I'll wait for her out here!"

"All right, suit yourself Ted."

I went to the bedroom and told Zee that her father was outside and wanted to see her and that he seemed to be incredibly angry about something.

Zee came out of the bedroom and opened the front door. "Dad? Is everything all right?"

"No, I refuse to let my daughter live in sin with any man. Pack your bags and come home with me or I will disown you!"

"Well, you are sure going to miss me!" Zee shouted back and slammed the door in his face.

Ted stood outside for a few minutes as if he thought she would change her mind. Then he got into his old beat-up pickup-truck and peeled out of sight. As the truck tires squealed out of the driveway the phone rang and it was Madge warning Zee that her dad was on the way over to our house. Zee explained to her mother what had just occurred and Madge cried but then assured her that things would work out OK.

Just as Madge predicted on Thanksgiving Day, we got a call from Ted inviting us to Thanksgiving dinner. At the dinner he was much more reserved but friendly and voiced his concerns with our living arrangements. As a Deacon in his Southern Baptist Church, he talked to us about his conviction that we should be married.

I finally got an opportunity to speak with him privately as we took one of our, now traditional, walks around the farm. "Ted, I agree with you. Zee and I need to get married. I have proposed to her on more than one occasion. She is very gun shy and I cannot make the decision for her. Do you have some advice for me?"

"No, she's bullheaded just like me."

We both laughed and I continued. "Her reasoning is that she has been divorced twice and that she is concerned about our age difference. She keeps reminding me that she is six years older than me and she is worried that somewhere down the line it could be a problem."

Ted still was not happy about it but he understood.

***

A week before Christmas Zee was home with WK while I was at work and she called me. "Wim, you have to come home as soon as possible. WK has done something terrible."

"What happened Zee? Is he OK?" I asked.

"He is just fine but you need to come home right now."

Upon arriving at the house, I saw Wim sitting in the middle of the living room in front of the Christmas tree surrounded by torn and shredded wrapping paper. Every gift was unwrapped and laying haphazardly everywhere. He was startled to see me walk through the door and his face was a mixture of fear, apprehension, and guilt.

"Wim! What did you do? And why did you do that?"

He sat on the floor biting his lower lip, with a confused pitiful stare while fluttering his eyelids and mentally searching for a plausible explanation.

"I want you to re-wrap every one of those presents and put them back under the tree until Christmas morning.?

His chin began to quiver and his tears began to wet his eyelashes. "I don't know how."

I glanced over at Zee to catch her sporting a wistful grin and a loving but mischievous look in her eyes. I was baffled at how to realistically handle the situation but Zee sat down next to WK and wrapped him in her arms to calm him.

"We will help you re-wrap all of the presents if you promise to not touch them again until Christmas." He responded to her kindness by nodding tearfully sniffing and squeaking out a barely audible and humble "OK."

I gathered the presents in a big pile, recovered much of the minimally damaged wrapping paper and a lot of tape. The three of us re-wrapped all of the gifts and put them back under the tree. Without another word ever spoken again about his transgression, we hugged and I returned to work with one more reason to love Zee.

***

Not long after the holidays I realized she was softening on the subject of marriage when she asked jokingly "Would you still want to be with me when I am 70 and you are 64 and my boobs are hanging below my waist peeking out from under my blouse?" I knew she was feigning her lighthearted attitude and this was a real concern for her.

I answered seriously. "Yes - I would!"

Early in February of 1981 Zee brought up the subject of marriage without prompting. We talked about it at length and agreed that we could have a marriage that would last. I gave it one last shot and asked her once again to marry me and she accepted. Zee and I both believed in the sanctity of marriage and that no one should enter it only to walk away when things got tough. We both stood behind it and lived by that mantra.

We set the date for February 14, 1981, Valentine's Day at 10 AM. To be absolutely honest I selected Valentine's Day specifically because I could never forget the day and could kill two birds with one stone when it came to buying cards and anniversary gifts. Zee insisted she did not want any fanfare and did not want anyone to know about our wedding plans. Her philosophy was that an elaborate wedding does not guarantee a good marriage.

Early during the morning of our wedding Zee and I discussed whether her parents should attend and I encouraged her to call them. She agreed at the last minute and called her mother at 9 AM to tell her about the wedding in the Altus AFB chapel at 10 AM and asked her if she and Ted would honor us by being there. Madge did not hesitate to tell her "Yes!" and that they would be there on time. Zee never ceased to surprise me. Just before speaking our vows in front of the base Chaplain, Zee asked me once again if I were sure that I wanted to go through with our marriage and that she would understand if I said no.

Ready to start the ceremony, the chaplain jerked his head up from his notes in wide eyed surprise and then cocked his head in a scolding, questioning side glance. I responded to Zee in the affirmative and I assured him that we were ready. The ceremony was short and sweet and WK was the ring bearer. By this time WK and Zee had created an inseparable bond of love and trust.

Just as Zee wanted it, after the marriage ceremony we all drove to the NCO club for breakfast for the first time as Mr. and Mrs. Wim Wetzel.

Zee and Wim

CHAPTER 38 - NEWLY WEDS

After the wedding ceremony at the Altus AFB Chapel, we enjoyed a relaxing breakfast with family at the base NCO club and then returned home. At about noon I received a phone call from my Squadron Commander Lt. Colonel Milacek. His voice sounded urgent. "MSgt Wetzel, I need you to report to my office immediately."

"Sir! Zee and I were just married two hours ago and we have not had any time to celebrate. Is it possible for us to meet on Monday morning since I have extenuating circumstances that require me to remain at home?

"Congratulations Wim, but this is an urgent and mission-essential request and I need you to report to me right away!"

"Yes Sir! I understand and I'm on my way!"

I could not imagine what could be so urgent that it would require me to report on a Saturday afternoon on my wedding day, but orders are orders. When I reported to Colonel Milacek I found him shuffling through papers and making hurried notes. "Sorry to interrupt Colonel. What do you need from me?"

He finished his notes, put his pen down, looked up at me and said: "Congratulations Wim and I wish you and Zee a happy and productive life together. Unfortunately, I had to fire my First Sergeant earlier today. I decided that you are the most competent and efficient senior NCO under my command to replace him. Effective immediately you are now my new First Sergeant. Consider that you now have two wives to serve. I am absolutely confident that you will serve them well and with equally deep devotion. Enjoy your honeymoon First Sergeant." He grinned, handed me a beeper, and shook my hand. "You are now on 24-hour call as my new First Sergeant."

A few hours later my beeper went off. It was Colonel Milacek who advised me that one of our Master Sergeants was arrested for drunk driving and I had to go to town to get him out of jail.

The United States Air Force First Sergeant is not a rank, but a special duty held by a senior enlisted member of a military unit who reports directly to the Unit Commander often referred to as the "First Shirt"," Top' or "Shirt", he or she is responsible for maintaining and supporting the morale, welfare, and conduct of all the enlisted members in a military organization and is the advisor to the Commander concerning the unit's enlisted force.

***

Because the wedding date was planned so quickly, we had no immediate plans for a getaway honeymoon after our special day. But it would have been nice to spend some time with my new bride so instead I planned a special surprise for us to take a short honeymoon.

A week after our wedding I surprised Zee by stopping at the NCO club while she was working. With excitement and anticipation, I hugged her and announced "We are going to get away for a four-day break starting tomorrow morning. I have already arranged for Ted and Madge to have WK stay with them at the farm and we are going to drive to Las Vegas."

Zee smiled in appreciation. "That would be wonderful Wim, but there is no way I can just take off without a couple of weeks' advanced notice."

"Why? Just go to your boss and tell him that you are going to be away for four days. If he pushes back, tell him that you will be back. If you do not have a job when you return-it would be OK. Regardless, we are going."

Zee stared at me with those beautiful eyes contemplating the ultimatum and finally nodded her head in agreement. "OK, I'll try." She took a deep breath as if to inhale some courage and turned and walked into his office. I waited anxiously for what seemed like forever until she exited his office with a grin that covered her whole face. "He said have a good time, just do not get pregnant." We both laughed and she continued "He is going to pay me for the time off."

Zee was a loyal, hardworking employee and his best asset. The whole base would have been down on him if they found out that he had fired her for going on her honeymoon. She had no idea how special she was to those she touched every day. We were going to Vegas but I felt like I had already won the Grand Prize.

At daybreak we dropped WK off at the farm and drove Zee's car to Vegas where we spent two days and nights just chilling out. Zee played her favorite game – Bingo- when she was not sleeping and won a couple of grand. It was more than enough to pay for the impromptu trip. Before returning to our home, we stopped by the NCO club to find out if she still had her job. She did.

***

I gave Zee carte blanche to do whatever was necessary to fix up the house within my limited budget. The final result was spectacular.

Her sister had moved to Oklahoma City, OK to go to college and we rented out Zee's mobile home. We were approached by the mobile home park owner about leasing or purchasing the park and we immediately agreed. The park was designed to hold 50 trailers but only 15 families lived there, and the park was in disrepair and seriously needing care. Like everything else she did, Zee put every free minute into turning the park around while still working at the NCO club. Within six months we filled the park and the rental revenue significantly enhanced our bank accounts and we cleared all our debts.

In early May of 1982 WK was visiting his mother in Illinois and Zee and I had gone to visit my Mom in Florida. Returning from our long trip from Florida and exhausted from driving all day and we went to bed early. Our home was about 5 miles north of the base and out of range for hearing the tornado warnings. As soon as our heads hit the pillows, we were startled by a loud crashing sound and rumble similar to a train. A second loud crashing sound came from the roof and in a matter of seconds it was dead quiet.

I jumped out of bed and opened the back door and cautiously looked outside. The biggest pecan tree in our neighborhood resided in our back yard. The top of the tree was now lying a foot from our back door. The tree had been uprooted about 100 yards away and dropped at our doorstep only ten feet away from where we were about to drift off to dreamland. A second smaller pecan tree was imbedded in our roof directly above the guest bedroom.

We walked around the property to assess the damage and we could hear the faint sound of the tornado warnings coming from Altus AFB and the town of Altus. We went back inside and turned on the radio to hear the emergency action warnings. We learned that the tornado that visited our back yard was one of thirty the hit that night. It was my second tornado experience in two years. That was two too many.

After checking on our neighbors and ensuring that there was no additional damage to our home, we dropped into bed exhausted and fell asleep in spite of the new skylight in the guest room and a huge pecan tree transplanted on our back doorstep.

The next morning, Zee remained at home to arrange for removal of the trees and to attempt to find someone to repair the roof damage and I drove to the base to assess the damage. The base had suffered insurmountable damage. As far as I could see there was nothing but devastation. Aircraft had been severely damaged and some had been picked up and moved despite weighing hundreds of thousands of pounds. The direct hit caused billions of dollars in damage. There was a blessing in all the destruction since no one was killed or seriously injured and the majority of the buildings that were destroyed were the rat and termite infested wooden WWII era facilities. It was impossible not to cry thinking of all the history and all the memories gone in a blink of an eye.

Most of the WWII wooden structures were destroyed, but the brand-new concrete and brick constructed barracks and the Airmen living in them were spared. Thousands of Airmen and their dependents lost their homes on and off the base and places of work. There were no deaths or casualties on the base but a woman and her baby were killed just north of the base.

Expecting the worst, I went to my Loadmaster School building and to my relief found that it was undamaged.

When I returned home later that day, I discovered that our neighbors had come to our rescue and used chain saws to cut up and remove the large pecan tree. They removed the tree from our roof and temporarily sealed the large hole in it to prevent further damage from the rain.

Tornado Destruction At Altus AFB

Zee encouraged me to go back to school to complete my bachelor's degree and gave me her blessings to continue flying and to teach student pilots. With Zee's blessings we bought our own aircraft for personal and business use and purchased a two-seater Piper PA-28 Tomahawk aircraft. I used it for flight instruction and in a short period of time the revenue paid for the balance of the loan. In the first year we generated over 1,500 hours of flight training time and enough revenue to pay off the loan on the Piper. Together we were able to pay off the debt that Debbie had incurred by maxing out my credit cards and enhance our income.

My Baby - N23414 Piper PA 38 112

I had our plane locked in a hangar at the Altus municipal airport. One day I stopped by the NCO club to see Zee while she was working and one of the instructors who used my plane to train his students saw me and came to the bar to give me some bad news. One of his students broke the lock to the hangar, stole my aircraft keys and flew the airplane to a remote grassy landing strip.

He picked up two passengers in my two-seat aircraft and during the takeoff he ran through a barbed wire fence shredding the wings and fuel tanks and crashed. With the additional illegal passenger on board the airplane was too heavily loaded to be able to take off on a grass runway. No one was hurt during the crash and fortunately there was no fire because of the leaking fuel tanks.

A passing driver on a parallel road witnessed and reported the accident to the Mangum, OK police department. The two passengers were arrested for leaving the scene of an accident and the student pilot was arrested for stealing the plane and the FAA charged him for illegally flying an aircraft. The "pilot" called his wealthy father who bailed him out of jail and his rich Daddy paid cash for my totaled aircraft and the FAA grounded him. He got off without any repercussions but I decided the risk of owning an aircraft was too great. I put the money back into our bank account and regretfully never bought another aircraft.

I was serving my country as a full-time active crew member, conducting flight training, attending college two nights a week and on weekends as well as farming for my father-in-law. Zee worked at the NCO club at night and managed the growing mobile home park every day. We shared the responsibility of caring for WK.

Pursuing my goal to become a Senior Master Sergeant (SMSgt) I achieved three associate degrees in Airport Management, Traffic and Transportation Management, and Instructor in Technology and eventually earned a bachelor's degree graduating with a 3.8 grade point average (GPA) in Technical Occupational Education. Zee earned every credit hour along with me as she made it possible for me to achieve what would have been unachievable for me without her sacrifices.

***

We both loved and enjoyed the farm and considered farming as a great option for us after we retired from the Air Force. To determine whether this option was even reasonable or of true interest I completed a couple of college classes on agriculture and cattle ranching.

Ted's wheat crop yield had declined significantly when Zee's sons left home. Without their assistance he was averaging a disappointing 21 bushels per acre. But after the first year under

Ted's training and the completion of my college courses, together we were able to double the farm's wheat yield to 42 bushels per acre. Our share of the income from the wheat harvest and the sale of our share of the cattle sales gave us a financial boast.

Despite our love of farming Ted discouraged us from a farming career because with so many variables, not the least of them was the weather, the income was unreliable. After seriously considering his advice we decided that he was right and reset our future vision to stay in the Air Force.

Ted seemed to enjoy testing my moxie. One Saturday morning he called me to let me know he needed my help with "cutting" cows. To me that meant he had to separate the bulls from the rest of the herd and calves. I drove the 10 miles out to the ranch and was welcomed by Ted, his two brothers, a nephew, and a whole herd of young bulls. Madge was also waiting and gave me a brand-new pair of boots and coveralls. She said: "You are going to need these today and then she immediately left the scene." I began to grow suspicious as the guys avoided making eye contact with me but broke out in ornery sheepish looking grins. Ted asked if I had ever cut calves before and I responded with a shrugged shoulder and shook my head no. Ted responded with a big toothy grin. "Well Wim, you will today."

He proceeded to demonstrate how to "cut" a calf by having his older brother tackle and roll a small calf over onto his back. The other two guys grabbed one each of the calf's hind legs and spread them apart to display its small testicles. Ted brandished and unfolded an old and very dull pen knife and started "sawing" at the small calf's ball sack until he exposed the poor screaming calf's testicles. He grabbed them and pulled on them for what seemed forever while the calf screamed horribly. When he could not pull them out any further Ted cut the cord with the dull knife. He threw the testicles over his shoulder and said: "He will not need these anymore." He finished the job by throwing some anti septic powder on the open wound and the guys let the calf go.

Ted looked at me with a straight face and asked me if I thought I could do the next calf. I nodded my head in the affirmative but asked for a sharper knife. He handed me his knife and said that it was the only one they had. There is a farm cattle management gate system called a Squeeze Chute. It is designed to capture and hold a cow for various purposes such as milking, giving injections, doing pregnancy tests, and cutting calves – BIG calves. Ted signaled his brothers to bring up the next calf. It was a noticeably big one at least three times the size of the demonstration calf. It took two men and the nephew to drag this monster into the squeeze chute and to operate the squeeze holding function.

They did not tackle the calf to the ground. Instead, while it was standing, they activated the squeeze chute and holding the steer in place while each brother grabbed one of the rear legs to spread them apart. Ted led me to the back of the cow and told me I would need to get on my knees behind the cow while he held the tail up. He handed me the knife and directed me to start cutting – well sawing. I grabbed the large ball sack with my rather small hands and started cutting. It took forever, and the cow screamed at the top of its lungs as I imagined seeing his crossed eyes during the painful process. I finally got through the tough skin and spied the huge contents as they fell into my hands.

All the while I was working to "cut" the calf, he emptied his bowels over my head, face, and brand-new coveralls with the slimiest green material I had ever seen. Because of the slippery contents covering me from head to boots, it took some time to firmly grasp the testicles so that I could pull them out. I pulled and pulled and pulled for what seemed to be forever until I could pull no longer. I finally cut the cord, dropped the large contents on the ground while Ted handed me the antiseptic powder to apply it to the open wound. The nephew released the squeeze chute and the injured calf ran away with his hind legs barely touching the ground.

The calf had been grazing on green wheat which caused it to expel the horrible slimy green crap. The guys knew what they were doing when they set me up. Ted said: "Welcome to cattle ranching Son. Now let us finish the other 45 calves." It took over three hours to finish the task which was more than enough time for the slime to dry in my hair and on my face. My coverall bib kept falling causing me to stop numerous times to lift it up and interfering with the job. Enjoying my suffering, the entire group maintained a macabre satisfied grin during the entire calf cutting event.

When I arrived at our brand-new home, I opened the front door and walked in. Zee happened to be standing just inside the door and with panicked horror in her voice she yelled: "Don't move or take another step! Take your boots and coverall off right there and let me get you a towel." I complied and released the right-side clasp of the bib and then the left. As soon as the left clasp was released, the bib unfolded, and a huge green and wet cow patty fell out onto our new hallway carpet. I just stood and stared at it as Zee screamed. I removed my boots to find them filled with more caked crap and my white socks permanently stained green. That is how I learned to cut calves.

CHAPTER 39 - AIR FORCE OFFICER COMMISSIONING PROGRAM

After completing my bachelor's degree, I met all the requirements to attend the Officer Commissioning Program but officer candidates needed to be commissioned by the age of 35. I was 36 and needed a waiver to be accepted into the program.

The Chairman of the Senate Armed Forces Committee wrote a nomination letter of recommendation to attend the program and to waive the 35-year age limitation. I received written endorsements from the Governor of Oklahoma, the state's two Senators, my local Congressional Representative, four General officers and innumerable other senior Air Force officers. My application was impeccable. I had crossed every "T" and dotted every "I" and was loaded for bear. I left no room for rejection. Armed with a great deal of excitement I confidently submitted my officer commissioning application with its endorsements and waiver recommendations and a copy of my bachelor's degree diploma.

The last step of the process was to meet with the current Wing Commander for final approval. This was just a formality in order to meet the commissioning regulations and in my mind the final box to check off. I went into the meeting with full confidence that I would be accepted.

After reviewing my package, he looked at me and stated, "MSgt Wetzel I am disapproving your request." He checked off the disapproval box on the form and signed it.

I sat there staring at him stunned "Sir – what the Hell! Why are you disapproving the request with all the supporting gubernatorial, congressional and Air Force senior officer endorsements supporting my goal to become an officer?"

He leaned back in his chair and gave me a shrug and raise of his eyebrows as if he were about to scold my lack of respect. "To be candid, we have plenty of Second Lieutenants with no leadership and management experience. We do not have enough good senior NCOs with your experience. You will be a Chief sooner than later now that you have a promotion line number for Senior Master Sergeant. That is all Sergeant Wetzel and you are dismissed."

I left his office nauseous, disillusioned, and dejected. I knew any further attempt to bypass his disapproval would be futile. Out of character for me, I gave up any further attempts to pursue an Air Force officer commission but I have never gotten over it.

***

Zee brought me down to earth by reminding me that we had a plan B. Undaunted by the disappointment, we went full speed ahead for the remaining three years of my tour at Altus AFB. We were happy, content and satisfied with our busy lifestyle. But I was worn out and had no desire to continue going to college. But Zee was not ready for me to quit going to school and urged me to pursue my master's degree.

I resisted out of pure exhaustion but I knew that Zee was just as tired. She was driven to support my career and she was willing to carry the heavy load of our day-to-day life so that I could pursue a master's degree. She reasoned that it would be helpful in accelerating my advancement to CMSgt.

I enrolled for the two-year weekend program and challenged all the credit hours humanly possible. Both of us maintained the same hectic schedule for two more years.

I completed the Webster University on-base campus program for my master's degree in Human Resources Development and graduated with collegiate Honors. During that period of time, I was promoted to SMSgt.

Zee had the vision to see in me the person who I could become – not who I was at any point in time. I doubt that I would have ever been as successful without Zee's support and constant encouragement. She was confident that I would achieve our goal to be promoted to Chief Master Sgt.

There is not one specific thing that can make a marriage work but I can attest to the fact that working hard toward the same goals can play a big part in maintaining a good relationship.

CHAPTER 40 - TIME TO MOVE ON

I received a call from the Air Force Personnel Office about a possible higher headquarters assignment at Scott AFB, IL. The CMSgt position had been vacant for a long time and every Chief who was offered the role turned it down. Several SMSgt's had also turned the offer down.

After I accepted the unexpected offer the Personnel Officer asked me, "Would you be interested with a 30-day report date?"

"Yes, I will. What date do you want me to report – Sir?"

This was the first time in our marriage when I made a decision without discussing it with Zee first. So, when I got home, I had a double bouquet of flowers and a thank you card in hand. Puzzled, she opened the card and immediately started to cry and hug me with joy.

"When do we leave for Scott?"

"In thirty days."

"I need more time than that to pack, sell the house and move. Can you report early because I can do all that myself."

"Yes."

***

Just prior to leaving Altus we sold my beloved Air Force staff car and we purchased Zee her dream car, a new Buick LeSabre. I bought a Volkswagen Rabbit for me. As we planned, Zee stayed in Altus to take care of the loose ends. I arrived at Scott in the middle of the night and out of curiosity as to where I would be working, I drove to the Headquarters (HQ) Military Airlift Command (HQ MAC) building and stopped in front of the massive building at the same moment a tornado warning had been sounded. I immediately stopped the Rabbit and waited for it to pass. The edge of the tornado briefly lifted the car's rear bumper off the ground and giving me a full front windshield view of the road below me before releasing the car and slamming it to the pavement. The good thing was that I was not driving Zee's new pride and joy. She was so proud of her new Buick.

***

Thanks to Zee's renovating and decorating skills we made a handsome profit when we sold our house. Her mobile home was in pristine condition so we decided to ship it to Scott rather than sell it. Zee arrived before the mobile home was delivered so we stayed in guest housing for a week.

We had not heard about the status of the delivery so I contacted the shipper to determine when we could expect its arrival at the base mobile home park. The shipper advised me that the driver towing the mobile home had decided to park it and abandon it at a roadside rest near Oklahoma City. The shipper was frantically searching for another tow vehicle and driver.

Three days later we received the good news that the new driver would deliver our mobile home sometime the next day. Looking on the positive side, we knew that at least when it did arrive that set up would be a turn-key operation. We were so excited to finally sleep in our own place. We prepared the parking spot for arrival the next morning and we waited and waited and waited. It did not arrive that day.

The shipper called to tell me that there was a slight delay. Two of the tires had blown during the last leg of the journey and the driver had to find new tires and someone to replace them. The new Estimated Time to Arrive (ETA) was the next day by noon at the latest.

The next morning Zee parked her treasured new car near our driveway while we waited for the arrival of our home. I laughed at her as she spied a small smudge on the hood and used her wetted finger to wipe it clean. The base was in the process of installing a STOP sign near our driveway close to where Zee had parked. In the process of lowering the sign into its permanent home the forklift driver lost control of the forks and dropped the sign onto Zee's smudge free new Buick. The trunk hatch caved in, the rear window was smashed and the soft-top was torn.

We both stood there speechless as the forklift driver drove away without saying a word. Thirty minutes later his supervisor showed up, apologized, and handed us some accident claims paperwork to complete for Air Force reimbursement for the damage repairs.

***

As the supervisor was driving away, we saw a wide load escort vehicle for a mobile home come into sight. Following it was a mobile home that appeared to have been damaged by a tornado. It had several of the exterior panels missing and other panels flopped haphazardly along both sides. Zee and I commented to each other about how sad it was that some poor family had just lost their home to a tornado and now they must be removing it from the park.

The driver slowed in front of our spot and started to back in as we watched in horror as two more panels fell off. The driver stepped out of his vehicle and apologized, explaining that he found the home in its current condition at the roadside rest and gave us Polaroid pictures of the evidence for home insurance purposes.

He got back into the cab of the truck to finish backing the mobile home into its permanent location: a cement foundation that is imbedded with several steel hooks to allow the mobile home to be tied down securely with heavy cables.

This maneuver was done with the guiding assistance of the wide load escort vehicle driver that probably would not have need of a razor for a few more years. Before I could stop him, the kid pointed his arm in the wrong direction guiding the tow truck driver to back into the parking space and directly over the steel hooks located on the left side of the parking space destroying both tires.

The tow vehicle was unable to move any further since one of the tie-down hooks had imbedded itself in the cheap tire rim. The tow vehicle was now blocking half of the busy road causing a traffic back-up. Base Security Police (SP) stopped by and kindly directed the tow driver to disconnect his vehicle from the mobile home to clear the roadblock. The SPs contacted the motor pool and asked for a heavy-duty forklift to lift the mobile home up and off the damaged rim.

The spectacle attracted a large number of appreciative base mobile home park residents and other curiosity seekers at the gate to watch the mobile home caper that was unfolding before them. We finally finished parking the previously beautiful home in its resting place. The positive side was that gracious neighbors stopped by with welcome gifts of food and assistance in getting us settled in for the night and allowing us to finally get to sleep in our own place.

***

My last requirement before qualifying for promotion to Chief Master Sergeant was completion of the in-residence Senior NCO Academy. I was waiting for an opportunity to attend the resident Air Force Senior NCO Academy and was informed that I could volunteer to attend a sister service Senior NCO Academy. Always interested in new challenges, I applied for the 13-week Navy Senior Enlisted Academy class located in Newport, Rhode Island. I was approved for the class starting in October of 1987.

The men in my class were the best that the Navy had to offer. I was accepted as their peer and treated as a brother and equal. During the second week of training, I had the honor of being asked by the most senior Navy Chief of our flight to go through the Navy's Senior and Master Chief orientation program. The Air Force did not have a similar program so it was an honorary role but none the less I felt very privileged to be asked.

It turned out to be a brutal eight-week program. But as most of my teammates, I am not ashamed to say that during the pinning ceremony as an Honorary Navy Senior Chief I shed tears of pride along with several others who completed the program. On graduation day I was presented with honors for Leadership.

Navy Senior NCO Academy, Newport Rhode Island

I returned to Scott AFB and resumed my position. Zee's parents were still living in Oklahoma and her mother Madge was in the rapidly declining advanced stages of Alzheimer's. Her dad, Ted, was completely overwhelmed and incapable of the caregiving involved with the horrendous disease. After more than 50 years of marriage Ted was lost without Madge to help him make simple day to day decisions.

Her three siblings lived close by their parents and Zee reached out to them for help hoping that they could all work together and distribute the burden of their ever-increasing caregiving needs. Her pleas for help fell on deaf ears and Zee became the soul caregiver, driving ten hours one-way to Oklahoma on a regular basis, leaving WK and me to care for each other for weeks at a time.

Zee carried her burden of guilt as she felt pressured to balance our family life and caring for her parents. Even when she was home, she was on the phone for hours at a time, managing their care long distance and watching painfully as her mother rapidly slipped away into mental and emotional oblivion.

Debbie was like carrying a python in my pocket. She would lie quietly waiting until I let my guard down and then sneak up unnoticed to squeeze the life out of me. Her constant harassing telephone calls to WK never let up causing his emotional and mental health to continue to decline.

The inherent stress of caregiving is hard is on any marriage but the deterioration of our marital relationship began as a direct result of the interference by my ex-wife. She again started to call at all hours of the day and night to talk with WK. There was a role reversal between Debbie and WK. Debbie convinced him that it was his responsibility to take care of her and he should be with her. This never-ending flood of disruptive calls wore WK down and he again became extremely agitated and upset during and after the calls.

Zee and I would spend hours after each phone call calming him down and letting him know that we loved him. Each telephone call became more intrusive, heart rending and painful for all of us as we watched WK agonize over needing to take care of his mother when he should have been being a carefree kid. This began to have a negative influence on our otherwise happy marriage and we decided to get professional counseling before it damaged our relationship any further. We valued what we had together and wanted to learn how to cope with the increasingly difficult situation WK's mother was creating in our relationship.

Unfortunately, the counselor made a volatile deteriorating situation worse. I was intensely distraught over WK's emotional turmoil and the counselor asked me, "If you had to choose between your wife and your son, who would you choose?"

I hesitated for several minutes contemplating my answer. It was a no-win situation because I was anticipating that if I chose Zee the counselor would recommend that I give up my son to live with his unfit mother. I did not want to hurt Zee by choosing WK but in the end I could not take a chance of losing WK again. So, I answered. "I would have to choose my son."

It was that single phrase that started the erosion of our marriage. Devastated, hurt and angry Zee stood up and left the office. My answer would haunt our marriage for many years as Zee's warmth toward me became lukewarm and distrustful from that point on. Her skepticism grew concerning my claim that Debbie was an uncaring, unfit mother and an incompetent guardian to WK. She began to believe that I was keeping WK to somehow spite Debbie.

Seeking help from a professional counselor caused Zee to suffer a great deal of emotional pain and disappointment in me. The ongoing unending turmoil created by Debbie and the love and devotion I had for my son caused a rift between us that would never fully heal.

As always, we worked hard together but things had changed. There was now a chasm between us and we just never moved beyond that day in the counselor's office and it raised its ugly head on numerous occasions. We were committed to our marriage vows but the dark cloud remained hanging over heads for the remainder of our 32-year marriage. We still loved each other but with the help of a professional family counselor our marriage suffered a major blow that neither of us fully recovered from.

CHAPTER 41 – THE ROCKY ROAD TO CHIEF MASTER SERGEANT

The process for achieving the rank of Chief Master Sergeant is a grueling system of exams, reviews, and promotion recommendations. In spite of all the personal and family upheaval Zee always stood by me. With the MAC Commander's strong recommendation of "Promote to Chief Now", I was promoted to Chief Master Sergeant at minimum time in grade.

Promotion Ceremony at Scott AFB, IL

About a month after receiving my promotion "line number" the Squadron Commander at Scott AFB called and gave me a direct order to report to her immediately. She made no attempt to hide her fury and refused to tell me what I had done to cause it. Searching in the depths of my mind I could not think of anything I could have done to provoke her anger.

Upon reporting to her she read a letter that Debbie sent to the HQ. The letter stated that I had never paid her child support and alimony payments. Debbie told the Commander during a follow-up telephone call that I owed several thousand dollars in back child support and alimony. I stood speechless, shocked by the false accusation. She glared at me defiantly with pursed lips and squinted eyes as if she had caught me stealing from her piggy bank.

"Ma'am, I'm sorry but you are mistaken. I have always paid monthly child support payments through the Air Force Finance Office allotment program and I have records to prove it." I continued. "I have always honored my commitment to my son. The divorce decree clearly stated that there were no requirements for child support or alimony payments but I paid monthly child support payments since our divorce even though I was not legally bound to do so."

"Sergeant Wetzel, your ex-wife has no reason to lie to me. You leave me no choice but to redline your promotion orders to Chief and have you processed for discharge from the Air Force for failure to meet your family financial obligations. You are dismissed!"

I responded with frustration and anger. "Ma'am, I will return with proof of my child-care payments and a copy of the divorce decree."

Before returning to her office with my documents I saw my boss, a full Colonel. I explained the situation and gave him all my documents. He was stunned at the unprofessional and unwarranted disrespect that the Squadron Commander unleased on me.

"Calm down Wim. Go home and I will take care of this."

"Thank you, Sir." Still seething, I turned towards the door to leave and he called out to me. "Sergeant Wetzel."

I turned to face him again. "Yes Sir."

His expression had softened. "You will be promoted on schedule."

"Thank you, Sir."

A few days after the incident we had a new Squadron Commander.

The Colonel was true to his word. My promotion date came on schedule, and my boss awarded me the Chief stripes in a Command ceremony and Zee proudly sewed them onto my uniform. She had earned them.

***

Our marriage was in crises and we were discussing a trial separation. As Zee selflessly traveled back and forth to Oklahoma, she never pressured me to retire from the Air Force or to find a way to get back to Altus. But our marital survival needed my attention if it was going to remain intact. It was a time of transition for both of us. I had over 20 years on active duty and enough years in grade as a CMSgt to retire with a Chief's pension but I did not have it in my heart to walk away from the career I loved. But I knew the ball was in my court if I wanted to keep our marriage on course.

I desperately wanted to find a solution to this dilemma short of retiring. I had one last card to play. I made the decision to talk with my Commander about my options. He gave me confirmation that I was absolutely correct on my path to care for my family above all other options.

"Family comes first Chief. Because of the significant improvements you made in your current position at MAC we will have no problem finding a replacement for you. Have you considered applying for a humanitarian reassignment to Altus?"

"No Sir I had not because I have a loyalty to the Air Force and you, I felt that my professional responsibility is to stay here to do my job. Until now I always held the position that my job was more important than my personal life."

"Chief. I do not want to lose you but I suggest that you go to the Consolidated Base Personnel Office (CBPO) and have this discussion with the assignments section. My best wishes in whatever decision you make."

I was disheartened at the thought of giving up my cherished HQ MAC position but the commander made a profound statement, bringing me back down to earth. As much as I valued my marriage, I had always put the Air Force first. My priorities for living my life had always been led by "Service to Country." Apparently, I had been wrong and was advised that the proper sequence of priorities for living life are: GOD - FAMILY - COUNTRY.

For the first time in my adult life, I made the difficult decision to set aside my career goals and applied for a humanitarian reassignment back to Altus AFB to be near Zee's parents. The request was accepted and Altus AFB once again became our home.

CHAPTER 42 - OUT OF MY COMFORT ZONE

I checked into the Altus AFB personnel office and was advised that the Base Commander wanted to see me at the first opportunity. I was mentally prepared for a challenging and rewarding position as the 443rd Military Airlift Wing (MAWs) Chief Loadmaster and looked forward to being briefed on my new assignment.

I was able to arrange a meeting with the Commander's Executive Officer as soon as I arrived at Altus and my instinctive response was to stand at attention and salute. "At ease Wim and please dispense with the reporting formalities." He offered a friendly handshake and invited me into his office. "Welcome back to Altus, Wim. Please sit down."

"Thank you, Sir. It is good to be back."

"I am not sure how to approach this but we've known each other for many years and flown innumerable missions together so I think I can be candid. Personally, I am glad to see you again, but there is a problem."

"Sir?"

"Altus is a small base with one primary MAC mission to train C-141B aircrews. We currently have no positions for another CMSgt Loadmaster. Since all the Chief positions are filled what am I going to do with you Chief Wetzel?"

Completely out of character for me, I was at a loss for words. Remaining awkwardly silent and dumbstruck, he broke the impasse "You bring a wealth of executive management experience to Altus after your tour at HQ MAC HQ and I want to take advantage of that experience so, what would you like to do here Wim? Are you interested in any other jobs other than aircrew management?"

"Sir. Since I was unaware of the situation, I had not considered any other option. What positions and responsibilities are available for me to consider?"

"Here is a list of six organizations on the base that need a Chief's immediate attention. I have to warn you that they are the worst units at Altus including a couple that have a critical mission of supporting flight operations. We cannot have a CMSgt at Altus just sitting in an office without a job. I regret to advise you that your decision will need to be made by choosing one of the options from the list."

I was so steeped in my career in aircrew management that doing something else never crossed my mind. "I would certainly consider it, Sir." I spoke. "Since it is Friday, may I have the weekend to go over the list, do some investigation and come back Monday with my decision."

He watched me as I sat there scanning the list as if it were a menu from a bad restaurant. "Of course, Wim, have a good weekend and good luck with your investigation. We will talk Monday."

On the way back home, my mind was spinning and I had a long pity party with myself. *I was going to be relegated to one of the worst jobs on base. A job I would most likely hate and I had to choose which poison pill I want to take. I am going to retire.*

I stomped through the front door, slammed it behind me, headed for the kitchen, opened the refrigerator, grabbed a beer, plopped down in my favorite chair, popped the beer can open and took several gulps.

"What's wrong Wim?"

"I quit! We are retiring and leaving the Air Force for civilian life."

"Oh no we are not! What's the matter?"

I threw the list on the table next to her. "These are the jobs available to me. The Commander told me they were the worst run organizations on the base. And none of them require my Loadmaster skills and I am not about to start a new career this late in life. Especially not one that I will hate, even if they were the best run organizations on the base."

"Pick the worst job on the list and get back to work. We are not retiring from the Air Force!" Zee always knew what to say, no matter how much I did not want to hear it and she was right. I still had a choice. I could accept the challenge or leave the Air Force.

Over the weekend, I called everyone I knew on the base to investigate why the six units were on this list. Every unit on the list had one thing in common: poor leadership or poor management.

After much investigation I concluded that the worst unit on the base was the Aircrew Life Support and Survival Training Branch. I had a shocking revelation. The life of every crew member on this base hung in the balance based on the efficiency or lack of it in this unit.

I constructed a business plan consisting of a list of requirements that the Base Commander would need to approve. No NCO had ever filled the position of Life Support Officer (LSO) and I did not want to be a straw boss so, I drafted a contingency letter of resignation from the Air Force in the event that the commander rejected my conditions.

Early Monday morning I reported to the commander. "Good morning Sir."

"Good morning Wim. Have a seat. I trust you have made a decision?"

"I will take the Life Support and Survival Training branch."

"OK…?"

"I have some conditions." I stated firmly.

The Commander leaned back in his chair appearing skeptical but curious.

"Go on, Chief!"

I gave him a copy of my business plan and I laid out my action plan.

"If you approve of this proposal, I will take on your challenge". I took a deep breath and continued "I request full control of the organization without interference in my decision and personnel assignment decisions as the Wing Life Support and Survival Training Officer (LSO). Since the LSO position has always been assigned to an officer it will be necessary for you to advise your Unit Commanders that a Chief is now running the unit."

"To re-establish a sense of pride and military discipline this unit will fall back on daily physical training exercises and weekly uniform inspections. In line with that program, I will schedule monthly personnel full dress open-rank inspections. With your direct support those monthly inspections will be conducted by a different full Colonel assigned to the base. To kick this off I would like you to be the first Colonel to conduct the inspection one week after I assume the position as LSO. After your inspection I respectfully request that you assign a different Colonel from the base to conduct the inspection each month until further notice. I want the ability to communicate with you directly about any issue, including budgeting, without having to go through another subordinate Commander."

The Wing Commander sat quietly assessing me as if waiting for more and I could sense he was suppressing a grin. He finally spoke. "Why the monthly inspections by my Commanders and me? What is that going to do for you and your unit?"

"Sir, during my research I contacted several of the Chiefs of each unit affected by Life Support and asked them what their most pressing concerns were about life support. Every one of them advised me that they were concerned that the lack of discipline and attention to detail in their jobs was going to cause serious injuries or even the death of our crewmembers. In their estimation it was not "if" but WHEN!"

"Sir, the Life Support branch had failed every local, numbered command and HQ inspection for over two years. Officers assigned to life support stayed long enough to check off their promotion records eligibility squares. Few if any took the time or interest to become involved with the enlisted personnel in the organization. Until that process changes there is no hope for the unit and valuable Air Force men and women will sustain serious injuries, become permanently disabled or die."

"Chief, to be honest, I was aware of the failures of inspections and the records of disciplinary action within the unit, but this new information shocks the conscience."

"I can't stress the seriousness enough. To make matters worse I discovered that the Life Support facility is rife with vermin such as rats and mice. It is out of control. Rat and termite feces have been discovered in oxygen masks and survival gear. Rats have damaged survival rafts and the termites are destroying the facility infrastructure. Oxygen equipment is routinely returned to the inspection unit due to failures because of damage caused by the vermin. In my professional opinion you do not have any other option but to take drastic action to resolve the crises. I commit to fixing the problem within three months and if I fail to meet that commitment, I will resign from the Air Force."

"Thank you, Chief. This has been very enlightening. You are officially designated as the LSO effective today. You have the authority and my personal support to turn this disaster around in any way you deem necessary. Keep me fully briefed on your progress and advise me of any issues that keep you from being successful. I will see you next Monday morning for my Open Ranks inspection."

CHAPTER 43 - WHAT THE HELL DID I GET MYSELF INTO?

Reporting to my new unit on the first day I realized that every bad thing I had heard about this unit was a lie. It was worse: so much worse.

What the Hell had I gotten myself into. There is no way this single shop of 39 enlisted personnel was responsible for supporting aircraft and survival training equipment for three different Air Force major commands – Military Airlift Command (MAC), Strategic Air Command (SAC) and Air Training Command (ATC). But they were and they were doing so with no evidence of any realistic adult supervision.

The LSO position was a prized role for young, commissioned officers. It was popular with most young officers in order to record the position in their career-development records. They were just passing through on the way up the ladder and wanted the title of LSO to fill a square in their promotion folders. Because they knew it was a short-term position for them, they had little concern for the overall operations of the organization or the personal welfare of the people they were allegedly leading.

***

It was readily apparent that the condition of the shop directly contributed to major personnel problems. The morale was as bad and sometimes worse than any I had seen in my combat days and a general apathy permeated every part of the unit.

Several of the airmen and women had filed for bankruptcy. Twenty seven of the 39 members had disciplinary actions pending and/or records on file. One of the airmen was in the stockade and had been there for 30-days of a 60-day sentence. I was surprised there was only one in the stockade.

I was appalled to think these were the people who were responsible for maintaining, servicing, and installing aircrew survival equipment such as oxygen masks, parachutes, aircrew helmets, life preservers, life rafts and other critical survival supplies. To make matters even worse the unit failed every major command inspection during the past several years.

Thankfully, there was one gold nugget shining through the rubble, the NCOIC, TSgt Michael Black. His credentials included having been named the Air Force Recruiter of the Year. He was the cream of the crop and a man of substance who knew there was great potential in the organization, but he never had an LSO to back him up.

No one had ever unleashed Mike's skills, talent and leadership capability or the authority and resources that he needed to effect any changes. He was fighting hard to survive and keep the unit from collapsing under its own weight.

Mike's responsibility was to oversee the well-being of the NCOs and Airmen by motivating, teaching, and guiding them to achieve and maintain an attitude of excellence at work and in their personal life. Without the back- up of an engaged LSO Mike's effort were futile and the unit was limping along.

I met with Mike and introduced myself. He was respectful but a strong personality and had been through a lot of LSOs He was rightfully wary of another one coming through the revolving door. Mike was especially concerned about a new LSO NCO who had ZERO experience in the Life Support field. He already investigated my personal and professional history by contacting other Chiefs who worked with me during my career.

"No insult intended but what makes you think you are qualified to run this unit Chief Wetzel?"

"I know how to lead and train people to be the best they can be Mike. It does not matter to me what technical skills they possess because it basically comes down to professionalism and pride in their work. Either they have it, do not have it, and can be trained and motivated to have it, or they do not care to ever have it. You and I are going to get rid of the latter and you know better than I who they are. We are getting rid of the "I do not give a shit!" people, starting right now."

Mike was a trustworthy man of integrity and I affirmed what my fellow Chiefs had told him about me. With my back-up support he was ready to turn his shop around. We had an unspoken agreement; the organization would always be Mike's and I was just the figure head.

"INVEST IN THE HUMAN SOUL. WHO KNOWS, IT MGHT BE A DIAMOND IN THE ROUGH." — Mary McLeod Bethune

"Have every person assigned to us report at 0700 tomorrow morning in full dress blues and bring along their work clothes, and tennis shoes to work out in."

In my new office I found a desk drawer filled with personnel files. I read each disciplinary file and discovered numerous warning letters and other documentation confirming the history of this rag tag bunch. I asked Mike to provide me with each airman's personal history including information about who was single, who was married, their spouse's full names and birth dates, children's names and birth dates, anniversaries, hobbies, and school activities such as college or trade schools.

Before I met with the team, I had Mike bring an empty garbage can and some lighter fluid. On a table, next to me I stacked all their office personnel and disciplinary folders and one blank sheet of paper.

At 0655 hours Mike and I were standing at attention in our dress blues and spit shined shoes waiting in the open bay work area. The slovenly dressed crew wandered in aimlessly. Mike ordered them to fall in and come to attention. They appeared confused and dumb founded, but Mike reminded them of their basic training and helped them to fall in properly. It was difficult to keep a straight face watching this version of the Keystone Cops as they struggled to comply.

I then introduced myself. "I am Chief Master Sergeant Wim Wetzel and I am the bastard in charge of this bastard organization!" It got their attention and the air was thick with silent simultaneous - "Oh, Shits!"

"Collectively this unit has a reputation for being the worst unit on the base. That is going to change NOW!"

"Mike, please pick up the files."

"These are all of your disciplinary files."

"Mike, please drop all of the folders in the trash can, pour the lighter fluid over them, and burn the files."

The team stood at attention, wide-eye and confused as Mike lit the flame and we all watched them burn.

I picked up a blank sheet of paper and said: "This represents a clean disciplinary record for every one of you present."

"Now that you all have a clean slate; I want to see clean urine samples as well. For your convenience we have medics from the hospital standing by to conduct urinalysis tests near the men's and ladies' bathrooms. You will all line up near the appropriate restroom and stand at attention until your turn comes up for the test. Mike and I will go first since there are no exceptions. I will review the test results and meet with anyone who fails it".

"If you fail the test, you will be given ten days to get clean and rid of the drugs from your life. In eleven days, we will all, including me, be given another drug test and if you fail, you will be processed for discharge from the Air Force. The Base Security Police will come to your on-base home or barracks room with the drug detection dogs tomorrow morning to search for illegal drugs. They will take the appropriate actions if drugs are found because it will be out of my control."

"Starting tomorrow morning, and until further notice, you will report to work an hour early every day for calisthenics. Unless you can provide a doctor's excuse, we will all participate. Bring workout clothes with you each morning."

"Next Monday morning you will all participate in a full-dress open rank's inspection being conducted by the Wing Commander. Mike will retrain you on that process during the rest of this week to avoid embarrassing yourselves and us. On the first Monday of every month until further notice you will participate in open ranks inspections conducted by a randomly selected or volunteer full Colonel assigned from a different unit on the base. After this morning's drug test, you will fall into formation again for your first refresher lesson on how to conduct an open ranks inspection taught by TSgt Black. Fall Out and get in line for your urinalysis."

Test results proved two participants had drugs in their systems. No one tested positive after the follow-up tests. No drugs were found in the on-base homes or in the barracks. Giving them a day to clean up any illicit drugs may have helped in getting these residents clean. There was little pushback by anyone in the organization. In fact, I sensed an air of relief that someone actually cared about them and their shop.

Mike scheduled personal meetings with me for every one of the team members. I used the information Mike provided on the fact sheets to meet and interview each one of the LS members. I shared my military experience and personal life with them as well.

Mike and I discussed the issues each member of the team had at work and at home. When I asked him about an Airman in the base stockade, his answer astounded and sickened me. The Airman had been incarcerated for 30 of the 60 days of his confinement. During that time, his wife had a baby boy and she had not been allowed to see her incarcerated husband nor let him see his new son.

I visited the confined Airman and asked him if anyone had been to the stockade to visit. "Only Sergeant Black visited me regularly Chief." I asked if the First Sergeant, the commander, Chaplain or LSO had visited. The answer was "No."

I met with the stockade NCOIC and discussed my concerns about the failure of anyone to come by to visit the prisoner. Incensed by his haughty indifference I said, "Prepare to release the prisoner into my custody before the end of the day and I will have his release papers when I return."

He flashed me an arrogant grin, sniffed mockingly and dismissed my instructions. Ignoring his insubordination, I left the facility to begin the process of getting the release papers.

I called the Wing Commander and asked for an emergency meeting and we met for lunch. I explained the Airman's incarceration and being denied visitation from his wife or the new son he had not yet met. I also expressed my dissatisfaction with the dereliction of duty of the First Sergeant who neglected to visit the Airman. Distressed with my report, the Wing Commander leaned back in his chair contemplating the situation.

"What is it that you want me to do Chief?"

"I have already told the NCOIC of the stockade to release the Airman to me today. You can order his release into my custody by setting aside the remainder of his sentence by written order approved by the Judge Advocate General (JAG). The justification is basically due to his chain of command's (the First Sergeant) failure to conduct due diligence in his responsibilities to care for his subordinates and their families. This Airman and his family have suffered enough. He paid his dues and served his penalty with good behavior."

"I'll have the order typed up for you to deliver this afternoon."

"Not necessary Sir. The JAG gave me the letter for you to sign. He agreed that a release is appropriate."

I handed the Commander the letter, he signed it and said: "You are a piece of work Chief!"

I thanked him and let him pay for my lunch and left.

Assuming that I would not be back with a release order when I returned, the stockade NCOIC was totally unprepared to release the Airman. He did not hide his hubris as he alluded to the release order as being phony. I reached in my pocket, pulled out a slip of paper and slid it across the desk.

"Here is the Wing Commander's direct telephone number and if you don't understand the written order to release my Airman - CALL HIM." He will be glad to explain his written order verbally." The NCOIC opened his mouth to protest but nothing squeaked out.

The airman was released into my custody and I drove him home to meet his new son. Six months later we nominated him for the Air Force Leadership School where he graduated with the highest honor; the John Levitow Award. John Levitow was a Loadmaster Medal of Honor recipient in Vietnam for saving his entire C-47 flight crew's lives.

Zee and I often discussed the family situations of the unit, their dire financial situations and how it was destroying their self-worth and family cohesion. She was busy with her parent's caretaking situation but she never failed to surprise me when she went above and beyond to reach out, teach and encourage others. She went to work tirelessly to help the wives. She asked Mike's wife to gather the spouses for a meeting and the wives complied.

She began teaching and mentoring the young women in financial management and budget planning. I had heard this story before in the form of a bad joke but pathetically Zee experienced it first-hand.

One of the wives actually stated "Mrs. Wetzel I don't understand what the problem is. I had all these checks in my check book and they are all being rejected." Zee asked how much money she and her husband had in the bank." Frustrated and confused the young wife retorted "As long as I have checks in my checkbook then we have money in the bank."

Zee's success in reaching out to the families' by helping them confront and improve their financial life was a huge help in changing the course of the troubled unit.

***

As I suspected, the majority of our Life Support people were unpolished diamonds waiting to be ground down and polished. Nothing brings out the brilliance of a diamond like gold. And under the gold standard leadership of SSgt Michael Black, they began to shine.

The facility and working conditions were still an embarrassment to the USAF and Altus AFB. After a great deal of research Mike and I found an exceptionally large, but little used facility on the base that needed a lot of elbow grease, tender Loving Care (TLC) and required funding that could rival the national debt. But the building was still a great improvement over the rat and termite infested environment that we were plagued with.

We had some major competition for getting the building and I pled my case to the Wing Commander, the entire command staff, and their Chiefs. I won approval hands down but the approval came with conditions. We had to supply all the elbow grease and TLC. The project funding, in a word, was nonexistent.

***

Mike and I were not deterred. With my blessing Mike set out with his crew on a world-class scavenger hunt. He and the entire Life Support team connected with their fellow NCOs in all the sister organizations on the base and collected all the supplies they needed to refurbish Building 444. Mike was like the Pied Piper, as every crew member followed Mike's lead and eagerly participated in the refurbishing of the hangar in record time and in glorious fashion. I just sat back and watched the "Mike Black Show" with pride. The residual results included the crew's morale hitting an all-time high exhibiting a sense of accomplishment, teamwork, and a sense of pride.

The end result was more than I could have hoped for as the functions of Life Support were now under the same roof as the Aircrew Chemical Defense and Survival Training sections.

***

The Fabrication Branch is responsible for major repairs to the life support equipment such as the parachutes, life rafts and life preservers. It was located an unacceptable distance from our new location but soon moved into the remaining third of our new facility.

For the remainder of my tour at Altus the Life Support shop passed every Operational Readiness Inspection (ORI) and Operational Readiness Evaluation (ORE) with Outstanding or Excellent ratings.

Mike was promoted to Master Sergeant and selected as Aircrew Life Support NCO of the Year as I sat back and continued to watch the Mike Black show.

I love it when a plan comes together.

CHAPTER 44 – TIDES OF CHANGE

Thanks to Mike Black's leadership skills and the hard work of the entire crew the Life Support unit was standing on solid ground and becoming less of a challenge. However, there were increasing political power struggles rising between senior NCOs and commanding officers, making the job less rewarding. At the same time, because of external distractions that seemed beyond our control, Zee and I were slowly drifting apart.

WK had been gone for three years. Birthday cards, Christmas cards and gifts were sent but I never received a response. Phone calls were futile since Debbie would intercept the calls, dominate the visit, and make WK's life miserable with guilt after talking to me. I was not about to make WK a human ping pong ball.

Zee tried to reassure me that it was always better for a child to be with his mother. I know she was sincere and I believe that she had WK's best interest at heart but I also knew that Zee was very wrong, WK was where he wanted to be and not where he needed to be.

The Wing Commander had kept his word. I had full responsibility for the unit and the Wing Commander never interfered in my decisions about staff disciplinary actions or the day-to-day operations. Everything ran as smoothly as possible even with so many competing logistics in play. My personal life, however, was suffering.

***

I had been able to keep my thoughts of WK from flooding in by drowning myself in my job but then the dam broke. I was at work one day when I received a phone call. "Are you the father of a nine-year-old boy named Wim Wetzel."

"Yes Sir. What is wrong? Is he all right?"

"Yes, he is all right, but there is a problem. I am Detective Roush from the Santa Maria, CA police department and we have just arrested your son's mother. She is a fugitive from Illinois for check kiting and we understand that you have legal custody. What do you want me to do with your son?"

I was not sure that I was hearing correctly. "Excuse me but I do not understand."

"His mother is in jail sir. Do you want to come and get him, or do you want me to put him on a plane to Oklahoma?"

"Of course, I'll arrange for his airline ticket and you can put him on the next plane. May I have your direct contact phone number so I can call you back with the flight details."

I quickly wrote it down. Numbed by the shock; I hung up without saying goodbye.

After confirming the flight and working out the logistics Zee and I drove to the airport and waited anxiously at the Oklahoma City airport for WK's arrival. We watched as the flight attendant escorted WK from the plane. He was much taller and was maturing into his tween stage of life. I had overwhelming waves of guilt and my heart was in my throat when I saw his red tear- filled eyes, full of fear, torment, and confusion. Zee and I rushed toward him relieved and heartbroken at the same time. *Why the hell had I let him go to her?*

The flight attendant handed him over to us. "I'm sorry Sir, but Wim has been crying nonstop from California to Oklahoma and nothing anyone tried to do could calm him down."

We thanked her and she left us to our family reunion. Zee hugged him and told him how much we loved him. His quivering lips, jerking shoulders and erratic convulsed breathing began to subside as he relaxed in Zee's arms.

Zee still could not wrap her head around the magnitude of Debbie's disregard for our son's welfare. It was impossible to convince her that Debbie would never be nominated Mother of the Year. Zee just wanted to take WK home and make him feel loved and wanted. She wanted that for everyone.

The car ride home was quiet. Zee held WK, occasionally reassuring him while I drove in silence with the weight of guilt pressing in on me. Why the Hell did I let him go?

The days ahead were awkward as we tried to make WK welcome and comfortable but things were different. There was always the elephant in the room: What had happened to him over the last three years? We were careful not to press him for information and hoped when he was ready to share it his story would trickle out one drip at a time. Eventually the ugly truth unraveled without much coaxing from us.

WK started to gradually unfold the events of the last three years and even I was stunned by the life of crime that my son had been forced to lead. The layers peeled back slowly and he began to share stories that were hard to believe but were easy to verify.

***

Debbie had a job at the local Sears store and before she left work for home each day, she unlocked a window in the ladies' bathroom so she could come back after closing and pilfer the store undetected. Since the window was too small for an adult to fit through, WK became her accomplice in her breaking and entering scheme.

After a scheduled store inventory, it became obvious that there was a huge disparity between the low inventory and the sales for that time period. That prompted management to study the security cameras. The images solved the mystery. Debbie and WK were arrested but because she was a single mother, she was given a light sentence followed by a short probation and they were barred from ever entering the store again. I had no idea she was capable of sinking this low. But she did and continued her downward spiral taking my son with her.

***

Debbie had an impressive list of clients in her new enterprise of drug sales and distribution. She rolled the drugs into a paper napkin and gave WK specific instructions on where and to whom to deliver the products. He was expected to deliver these products Cash on Delivery (COD) and return to her with the money. She was exploiting an already broken eight-year-old child and risking his life as a drug mule.

Now we had the monumental task of attempting to reverse my damaged son. The next few years were trying as WK exhibited behavior that reflected Debbie's negative parenting. But he was responding to his structured life and our intervention. We were convinced that he turned the corner for a stable life and loving environment. But soon after celebrating his fourteenth birthday, with no prior warning to prepare WK or us, Debbie was released from jail.

The phone calls at all hours of the day and night started all over again. I did not want WK to experience the guilt of having to choose between parents, so being naïve about what was happening I did not intervene. But Debbie knew WK's vulnerabilities and knew what to say to convince him that he needed to be "home" taking care of his mother. Gradually he began to digress by having serious behavioral issues at home and school, including drug issues, scrapes with the law and making dangerous life decisions.

I received a phone call at work from a friend who owns a small gas station in Blair, Oklahoma. "Hi Wim, it's Sam at the gas station in Blair. How are you?"

"Hello Sam! I am good, thanks. What can I do for you?"

"Ah, sorry to bother you at work but I just wanted to verify that you wrote a check for $15 cash. The signature is your name but it looks forged to me. Can you come by and check it out and confirm the handwriting?"

"Sure Sam, I'll be right there." I knew exactly what had happened.

I drove straight to the gas station and picked up the check, reimbursed him the $15, apologized, and thanked him for his call.

I do not remember driving home, because I was mentally debating with myself how to approach the crime. I could not help but asked myself if Debbie, through her annoying phone calls, had set up the check-kiting with WK to give me a reason to want to get rid of my son. I put the thought out of my head. There is no way that even Debbie would do such a terrible thing.

When I walked in the front door WK was sitting in the living room doing what boys his age do: watch TV and eat.

"I think we need to talk Son."

"What about Dad?" he answered innocently.

What a good liar he was! I was so angry it was hard to look at him.

I had already called Zee from work and told her what happened so she had been waiting for me to come home. She walked in from the next room ready to confront WK with me. I held up the check. "Whatever possessed you to steal this from us? Why did you try to cash a stolen check?"

"I don't know what you are talking about."

I handed him the check. "This is what I am talking about Wim."

He examined the check as if he had never laid eyes on it before. "I never saw this before.'

"That is interesting because you signed it."

He became defiant and belligerent. "I did not steal this check. That is not my handwriting. Why are you blaming it on me? I did not do anything. Why do I get blamed for everything?"

This was the last straw in a long chain of negative events and Zee had an aha moment with the realization that everything I had shared about Debbie was true.

This was beyond our abilities to handle effectively and we had to take him to a child psychologist. After a lengthy and painful session his recommendation was that we put WK in a home for troubled youth located in San Marcos, Texas. Devastated, we knew we did not have a choice. WK needed serious intervention.

The heart-rending realization came when we were told that WK would be there for a minimum of six months and we should not expect to see him on a regular basis. WK did not take the news well. Zee had always been his confidant and defender but this time was different. He begged Zee not put him in this home and Zee told him that we did not have a choice and he would have to go there to get help.

He went into an uncontrollable rage. His white knuckled fists, red face, insane screaming, and ranting was all directed at me. WK's anger towards me was almost more than I could bear. I was experiencing Debbie's violent and explosive rants all over again.

We were told when we delivered him to the home that we could not call him or see him for at least six weeks and he was not permitted to call or see us during that time. I was shattered. The emotional turmoil was insufferable.

Six Hellish weeks went by before we received permission to visit WK and take him out for a probationary visit day. Surprisingly when we met him for our visit WK was in a good and positive mood. As always Zee got the first loving hug and I received the cursory kiss on my cheek. We took him to the local Canyon lake campground, went swimming and picnicked. It took him a while to loosen up and talk about his experience and when he did – he was remorseful and apologetic about the check-kiting incident that got him there. He had me believing that I should sign him out of the facility and take him home.

When we did take him back to the center, we met with the counselor and discussed our concern for having WK stay for the full six months because he appeared to be "Healed." The counselor told us that it was not unusual for parents to come back hopeful from these visits with their wayward children. We were being conned. The teens get together and discuss their visits and how to manipulate their parents in the exact same manner. I had seen WK's manipulation skills before and I had to face the reality that WK had graduated with honors from his mother's "University of Deceit and Parental Manipulation." The counselor made it clear that we should leave without saying good-by. I expressed my appreciation for the honest feedback and left the facility. I do not know how I would have managed to get through it without Zee's love. She hugged me and assured me that I was doing the right thing.

***

While WK was under the care of professionals, things at work were becoming more complicated and contentious. While formal events dictate a public display of military decorum and some pomp and circumstance, it is just not practical nor efficient for any Chief to stand at attention, salute and wait for the command to be at ease before approaching their Commanders for every-day business issues. A CMSgt is rarely expected or required to "officially report" to his or her Wing Commander, Colonel or even a General using formal military decorum on a day-to-day basis.

I knew my place in the pecking order but my regular Wing Commander and I enjoyed an informal working relationship as do most Chiefs and commanding officers. The only exception to this relaxed protocol in the ranks is if the commanding officer happens to have an ego bigger than the national debt.

The Wing Commander was attending a 22nd Air Force meeting at Travis AFB, California and the Vice Wing Commander was in temporary command of the base. Unfortunately for everyone at Altus, this Colonel could have produced the training video on how to destroy morale and lead subordinates into a spiral of failure.

He despised enlisted personnel and treated them with derision and disrespect that earned him the nickname, "H. Hitler." His reputation followed him from base to base as being arrogant, power hungry and self-serving. He had his lights punched out more than once by NCOs who thought the satisfaction of doing so outweighed the consequences. I was about to understand why.

One unfortunate day when my office was in its usual organized chaotic state, I was interrupted by the phone ringing. I answered, "Chief Wetzel here, can I help you?"

It was the Vice Wing Commander and he seemed more than slightly perturbed.

"Chief Wetzel – Report to me immediately!"
"Yes, sir. I'll be right there."

When I arrived at the Wing Headquarters his secretary told me to go right in because the Colonel was expecting me. I knocked on the door and he directed me to come in. As I had done numerous times before I walked in and said: 'Good Morning, Sir what can I do for you?"

He glared up at me and without missing a beat he retorted sternly "Have you forgotten military decorum Chief? Leave my office and report properly."

I was caught completely off-guard by his direct order and responded formally "Yes Sir!" I then stood at attention, did an about face and left the office. I waited a moment and knocked again. Hitler stated, "Report Chief!"

I marched in, stood at attention, saluted, and reported "Chief Wetzel reporting as ordered Sir!"

"At ease Chief!" he ordered.

"I prefer to remain at attention Sir."

Colonel Hitler was a short man and had a platform built behind his desk to elevate his chair to a level equal to or higher than anyone visiting him. With a look of obvious distain, he looked down at me from his self-appointed throne.

"Have it your way Chief." he said in a condescending tone. "I see Airman John Doe received a second Driving While Intoxicated (DWI) and you recommended an Article 15 (non-judicial punishment). I want him to receive a court martial since he did not learn from his first DWI."

"Sir I have already discussed this matter with the Wing Commander who already supported my recommendation for the Article 15 since there appears to be extenuating circumstances related to the charge."

"The Wing Commander is at Travis AFB and I am in charge here." He replied through clenched teeth. "You will support my recommendation for a Court Martial. You are dismissed!"

"With due respect Colonel this offense does not justify a court martial and I cannot in good conscience or by my professional judgment comply with your request. Can this decision be deferred until the Wing Commander returns? He and I have already discussed this matter and I believe it is inappropriate for anyone to reverse his previous decision during his absence."

"No! It will not be deferred, and I affirm my order for judicial punishment."

"In that case Sir, you will have my retirement request papers on your desk by noon tomorrow." I saluted, did an about face, and marched out of the office.

He screamed "Chief – get your ass back in here. You are not dismissed!". I ignored his order and continued to leave. I knew that I was done and my career had come to an unfortunate and premature end.

As I walked out of his office the Executive Officer (XO), a captain, and the two secretaries stood up and gave me a silent standing ovation. The captain shook my hand and I left.

My direct supervisor, the Wing Director of Operations (DO) had his office on the second floor of the HQ building immediately above the Wing Commander's executive office. I climbed the stairway, knocked on his door and entered.

At the exact same time the infuriated red-faced Vice Commander entered the DO's office through the private entrance from the executive suite stairway.

"What's up Chief?" the DO asked me just as Hitler was also entering from the private entrance.

"Ask the Colonel Sir – he can probably answer your question better than me."

Colonel "Hitler" was puffed up with anger. I could see his clenching jaws moving and his breathing was getting faster as his hostility built up steam. "I want to press charges against the Chief for insubordination." he demanded, spitting as he spoke.

The DO told him to calm down and tell him what happened. The Vice Commander gave his slanted rendition of the incident making it appear that I instigated the encounter.

The DO then nodded in my direction and calmly asked "Chief, is what the Colonel says true?"

"No Sir, but it does not matter at this point. When a senior noncommissioned officer can no longer take care of his troops it is time for him to depart the "fix." I am submitting my retirement papers and will be delivering them to your office on Monday for approval."

"Don't be hasty, Chief," the DO advised, "and please reconsider. I am sure we can resolve this issue to everyone's satisfaction. Go home and think about it and see me on Monday."

I promised to think about my decision over the weekend but I knew, in my heart, that my career was over. If I stayed, I instinctively knew that Colonel Hitler would make my life a living Hell from this day forth. "I will give you my final decision on Monday Sir." I stood at attention, respectfully saluted him, and did an about face and left his office.

***

Zee and I talked about my decision all weekend and she begged me to stay in the Air Force. I had 24 years behind me and had already been approved for a special enlistment extension from the standard 30 years to 33. There were other considerations. I had to find a job with good health insurance for all of us but especially right now while WK was still going through treatment. It would be way above my means to pay for his mental health treatment out of pocket.

Zee was devastated. With our combined time as Air Force spouses and her time with her first husband, Zee had served our nation for over 30 years. She loved the Air Force; possibly more than I did. Her dedication to our country as an Air Force spouse was unchallenged by her peers. But I had always promised myself that once it was no longer fun or enjoyable to be in any job, civilian or military, that I would quit and move on to better things. I needed to be true to myself and this was not fun anymore. Each day had become a chore and I needed a change in my life and this incident was simply the last nail in the coffin.

Monday morning, I handed my retirement request over to my boss. He advised me that Colonel Hitler had withdrawn his suggestion to have me charged with insubordination to a superior officer. But it was too late. My decision to retire at 42 years of age at the 24-year point of a successful career that I loved was final. As a last demonstration of the DO's respect for my service he handed me a personal letter addressed to Mr. Ross Perot. It was a job recommendation.

CHAPTER 45 - THE JOB INTERVIEW

During my tour of duty at Altus I worked under Major Skip Orwell and he offered to give me a job reference when I retired. He now worked for Hughes Training Inc in Arlington TX so I called to ask him for a job reference. He arranged for and asked me to come in for an interview. I put on my crisp white shirt, tie, sports jacket, dress pants and spit shined shoes and wasted no time getting to Hughes Training, Inc.

Hughes was on the cutting edge of technology, offering Computer Based Training (CBT) for employees of businesses worldwide. Hughes had recently nailed down a $650 million Air Force contract for aircrew on-line courseware development. My loadmaster expertise enhanced by my bachelor's degree in Technical/Occupational Education, and master's degree in Human Resources Management were the credentials that they were looking for.

The interviewer for my position was a retired Air Force Lieutenant Colonel F-4 fighter pilot. I walked in the human resource office dressed for success, a bit nervous but confident. A friendly secretary greeted me. "Good Morning. You must be Mr. Wetzel. Come with me." She led me down a long hallway and I looked around amused at the color scheme that was obviously not chosen by any military person.

I was jolted back from my musing as the secretary tapped on an office door and opened it. She smiled at the man sitting behind the desk "Excuse me Jack, Mr. Wetzel is here for his interview."

He was a rotund man and not at all what I would have expected from a former F-4 fighter pilot. He stood up and walked from behind his desk and motioned for me to come in. He was well-groomed but his relaxed casual clothing was in sharp contrast to my board room executive look. I felt like a Dork. *It must be casual Friday.*

I instinctively had the urge to present myself in formal military fashion but I caught myself, apparently not soon enough. Recognizing my attempt to shake off my instinctive military decorum, the retired officer laughed and offered a hospitable handshake. "At ease Chief. You are a civilian now. It is nice to meet you. I am the head recruiter for courseware design and development. How does it feel to be a civilian?"

"Honestly, sir? I do not know yet. It has been less than 48 hours since I started my terminal leave from the Air Force. For the next 90 days I will still be on active duty."

"You'll get used to it." He smiled knowingly as I stood there fighting to appear relaxed. "Skip has filled me in on all I need to know about your credentials, character and extensive experience in teaching and management. This interview is simply a formality and all that is left to do is to negotiate a starting salary that is satisfactory to both of us."

A paycheck was important but my most pressing concern was to provide medical insurance for my son. He confirmed that my employee medical insurance covered pre-conditions including WK's treatment and I was happy with the salary we agreed on.

"How computer literate are you Wim?"

"I have a Commodore 64 at home."

"Well then you are computer-keyboard literate. You are assigned to the Hughes prototype courseware development team and will be reporting to Mr. Tom Mahoney. He is expecting you and welcome to Hughes."

I was shocked at the speed with which I was hired. However, I had a bad feeling that I was in way over my head after the question about computer literacy. I had no clue about computers and I barely knew how to use the Commodore 64 gaming computer. A little voice in my brain told me to run like Hell.

***

I introduced myself to Tom and he introduced me to his team. As he walked me to my new computer workstation, he proudly explained that Hughes had just purchased two 40 MB hard drive computers with a price tag of $250,000 each for the prototype team. I was now the "lucky" owner of one of the two leading-edge training and development computer-based-training (CBT) units at Hughes. I stood stupefied gawking at the machine but finally took a deep breath and forced myself to sit down and face my nemesis. Tom was talking to me but I was in a trance-like state gaping at the amazing contraption, tuning him out and having my own personal mental conversation that Tom was not privy to.

Hmm. So-this is what a real computer looks like. What the Hell are all these buttons for? The keyboard looks familiar. Houston, we have a problem. I do not have a clue what to do with this thing.

Tom's voice brought me back to Earth. Gesturing towards my personal quarter million-dollar monster he asked; "How much computer experience do you have Wim?"

We were both staring at the high-tech electronic beast and I gave him my stock answer. "I have a Commodore 64."

"You *are* kidding, right Wim?"

"Nope."

There was an audible gasp followed by an exhale of exasperation.

OK, I just got fired from my first civilian job before I even started.

"All right let us do this. Sit down, turn it on and become familiar with it. He turned to walk away then glanced back. "By the way, nix the coat and tie. We work in a casual environment here Wim." With that he walked away and left me to my misery.

Thirty minutes passed, and it was time for lunch. Tom returned to find me sitting at the computer literally twiddling my thumbs. "What are you doing? Why is the computer not turned on yet?"

"I do not know where the power switch is Mr. Mahoney."

Tom drew in a big breath and blew it out and inhaled another exasperated breath. He paused briefly and I wondered if he was counting to ten to gain his composure before either showing me the exit door or the location of the power button. He reached down hit the power button and proceeded to show me how to log in with my new password before telling me to "Play with it and get familiar with the disk operating system (DOS) programming language using these manuals." I asked the obvious question "How do you spell DOS and what does it mean?" Tom shook his head in disbelief but took the time to walk me through the login process, introduced me to DOS and showed me where to find the information I needed in the brand-new plastic sealed manuals.

"There is nothing you can do to hurt the computer or damage our network systems because of all the safeguards that are programmed into it. I will be back at noon to take you to lunch and introduce you to the entire CBT prototype team." With that he left me to find my way through the wondrous world of DOS.

What the Hell is a network system? I started experimenting by pressing keys to see what they would do. I began to notice messages on the monitor that seemed to be warning indicators. Then all of the sudden everything disappeared from the computer screen and it turned green. Everyone around me started freaking out and Tom rushed back to my station and asked me what I had done. "Tom, I don't have a clue."

"Oh Shit, Wim! You just brought down the entire Hughes network system. Whatever you did I will fix it. Can you come back tomorrow morning and Sunday to learn how to use these systems? I will teach you what you need to know. You do realize the success of all of Hughes' $650 million Air Force contract for aircrew on-line courseware development will be based on our prototype team's efforts?"

"Yes."

Tom told me to take the rest of the day off and that he would see me on Saturday morning at 8 AM. I complied and left discouraged and disheartened. Walking through the parking lot I seriously pondered, *I wonder if the Air Force would allow me to cancel my retirement request.*

Zee and I were temporarily living in our 28-foot motor home at the Grand Prairie, TX Flea Market while searching for a home to buy. I walked into the motor home and grabbed a beer from the refrigerator and plopped down on the couch silently staring into space for several minutes. Zee was waiting to hear how it went and if I was hired. She took a long drag on her cigarette. Exhaling the smoke and swatting it away with her other hand she asked "Well, how did it go today Wim? Did you get the job? How much is our salary and do we have medical benefits?"

I chugged another swig of beer swallowed hard and began my confession. "Zee this job is way over my head. I am nowhere near competent to work at Hughes. I will be embarrassed to go back there let alone collect a paycheck. That is, even if they decide to keep me. I crashed the whole computer system Zee. Everyone was freaking out."

Zee was undaunted by my tale of calamity and calmly puffed away letting me explain the whole disastrous scenario. In her usual tough love way, she finally responded. "Go back to the office in the morning as you committed to do and learn how to use these new-fangled computers. Give it a week to learn what you can and if it does not work for you, then we can discuss any other options. You still have the recommending letter to Ross Perot to fall back on."

That night I did not get much sleep dreading having to face Tom again. I got up at 0500 hours and put on my crisp shirt, coat and tie and drove to the office. You can take the man out of the Air Force, but you cannot take the Air Force out of the man.

"Good morning Tom." Tom turned around from working on his computer and looked at my attire as if I were wearing a clown costume. He rolled his eyes and smiled. "Are you kidding me Wim? Don't let me see you wearing that monkey suit again as long as you work with me."

***

Over the first weekend and every night after work for over three weeks Tom taught me everything I needed to know about the new computers, DOS, and the software development programs. In spite of myself, when he was done teaching me, I was competent enough to use all the courseware development systems and became very proficient under Tom's tutelage.

Soon I was able to teach the other new team members how to use the complicated network systems. Our Loadmaster CBT prototype team set the standard and created the screen templates for all of the C-141B courses.

CBT development became a new passion for me and teaching others to create them opened up greater opportunities for employment if my Hughes job did not work out. My computer skills grew exponentially and I went to work every day excited to be there.

***

Pleased with my performance, Senior Management assigned me to Doctor Sue Arnold's advanced courseware and development team where I met and became friends with Doctor Kenneth Roadman. Ken and Sue became wonderful mentors and friends and through them, I was assigned to an advanced software development team at the headquarters in Sacramento, California. To my amazement and Zee's delight I was promoted twice and my salary grew exponentially with the promotions.

***

At the end of WK's six month stay at the facility he was released and we picked him up to take him home. He seemed to be recovered from his traumatic experience and things were improving on the surface. There was an underlying discontent and disconnect from us that was hard to read. I could only pray that he would finally come around to see that what had happened was in his best interest. Just before WK's fifteenth birthday the phone calls from Debbie started all over again.

Debbie was remarried and told us that she wanted to have WK visit her in Illinois for a couple of weeks during the school Spring break. Initially we told her "NO." After many harassing phone calls from her to WK, I realized that although legally I could stop him, nothing short of locking him in his room indefinitely was going to change his mind about going. We both finally realized that WK was physically in our home but emotionally with his mother. I knew how painful it was to be estranged from a parent at his age and emotionally I could not stop him from seeing his mother.

We both struggled with how to convince WK that he was making the wrong decision but it was only making him angrier and more rebellious. His mother's skills at lying and manipulation became more prevalent with every phone call. He hated the boundaries, structure and discipline in his life and hated us for keeping him away from his mother. We knew he had passed the point of no return. He was convinced that he needed to take care of his mother and we had lost him. Debbie had won many battles over the years and now I was just too emotionally and physically exhausted to fight one more battle. She had finally won the war.

At fifteen years old I knew the war was over, I had done all I could. I bought him a one-way ticket to Hell. Under the mis-guided philosophy of "Tough Love" during those days I resolved to let him go.

***

Four months later the phone rang.

"Dad."

"WK? How are you son?"

"Dad, I want to come home."

"What's the matter WK?"

"Mom is too strict She will not allow me to do anything."

Either Debbie had made a 180 degree turn in her parenting pattern or WK was conning me again. Debbie had trained him well in the fine art of being a consummate liar.

"I miss you and Zee so much. I want to be with you - not Mom."

Zee was listening on the other line as I gave WK the conditions for returning. "We would love to see you come back son but there are some conditions you will be expected to meet."

"What do you mean, Dad?"

"You must stop lying and stealing from us. You will do your best at school to get better grades and D's are not acceptable. It does not matter to us whether you always get A's and B's. It does matter that you give it your best effort. Also, you are expected to contribute to this household by doing chores and helping Zee and me."

"Can you follow these three basic rules of behavior?"

Zee listened on the extension line as a long silence screamed back at us. I had called his bluff and prayed for an affirmative positive response.

WK confirmed my suspicion. "No Dad, I don't think I can follow those rules."

I had to give him credit for that. At least for once in his tragic life he did not lie.

I choked back tears. I knew if I gave in to him again, WK would go back to his mother like dog to its own vomit. Zee was exhausted and had already sacrificed a huge portion of her life for him without his appreciation. I swallowed hard and answered. "Then, son, you are no longer welcome in my house." I hung up the phone, collapsed on the couch a completely broken man crying uncontrollably. Zee sat beside me hugging me close and telling me how she loved me and that I did the right thing. Logically, I knew she was right but my heart was filled with overwhelming guilt that just maybe I had not done enough to save my son.

CHAPTER 46 - ROY'S FINAL YEAR

We moved into our dream home on a double lot that was an oasis of nature's beauty. It had a back yard that was cascaded with huge trees and led to a private dock on the river that meandered into Lake Granbury in Granbury, TX.

Zee was overwhelmed and exhausted with caring for her parents who had finally come to live with us. I helped her as much as I could. Zee and her sister were now living in close proximity to each other and they became remarkably close but her sister made little effort to help care for their parents.

Zee's relationship with her sister should have been a positive part of all our lives but she was selfish, spoiled, manipulative, and self-serving in contrast to Zee's selfless, giving, and self-sacrificing nature. It became a cause for my concern that Zee was becoming easy prey to her sister's schemes.

The wounds left from WK's departure began to heal but never completely scarred over. My challenging and satisfying career at Hughes/Raytheon helped to ward off the sadness but Zee was on overload taking care of our household, her parents but not taking care of herself.

Eventually, taking care of her mom became overwhelming and we were faced with the difficult decision to move her back into a care facility. Madge died soon after moving back to Oklahoma and was buried on the family plot near the farm. Ted married an old family friend a few weeks after the funeral and lived a quiet life for several years until he passed away and was buried next to Madge.

Early in July of 1994 we invited Roy to come to Texas to enjoy some down time and get away from the hectic schedule of running the schools, planning Karate tournaments and teaching. The only thing Roy was more passionate about than fishing was teaching so it was an invitation he could not resist.

Being the family alpha male, other than his war injuries, he was always the poster boy of perfect health. I was electrified with excitement when he accepted the invitation. I was already anticipating his competitive spirit kicking in and I was prepared for him to challenge me to a two-man private fishing tournament and nothing could please me more.

The day finally arrived to pick Roy up at the Dallas Fort Worth Airport. When he walked toward me it was hard to disguise my shock. He had not mentioned any new health issues when we talked on the phone, but I would not expect him to. That just was not Roy's style. He had always been trim and well-muscled but he now appeared sickly, pale, and drawn. His usual perfect posture and assured confident stride had morphed into a slumped slow guarded shuffle. I was aware that he had been having additional heart issues from his exposure to Agent Orange but this was much worse than he had ever let on.

We greeted each other with hugs, handshakes, and tears of joy. I said, "I love you Roy!" Roy issued his stock answer; "I love you more!" He attempted in vain to hide his weakened condition with his infectious easy laugh and a few brotherly verbal jabs accusing me of getting soft in my cushy executive position. But it was evident that this might be our last fishing trip and deep in my gut I felt that this might be the last time I would see him alive.

On the ride home Roy was quiet and anxiously stared out the window, his eyes were darting back and forth as if he were searching for something. Finally, he blurted out. "Hey, where are all the cowboys and Indians? I was expecting to see cowboys and Indians all over the place in Texas." At first, I thought that he was joking but then realized he was really expecting Texas to have cowboys and Indians around every corner like a wild west scene on television.

To curtail his disappointment, we took him to Fort Worth's stockyards to Billy Bob's Bar and Restaurant and toured the yards. We managed a photo-op of Roy sitting astride a Long Horn Bull. He had the biggest smile I have ever seen on his pale face.

Our week together was spent engaging in antics and laughter as we spent every waking moment fishing and boating all over Lake Granbury. We shared stories, enjoyed our passion for fishing and recounted memories of our youth together on the Ohio River in Beaver and the many Pennsylvania lakes we frequented. We reminisced about raising worms to fish on the canal banks in Holland and feeding the leftover worms to Jane to keep her healthy. When it was over, the seven-day visit felt like seven minutes.

When it was time for Roy to leave there was an unspoken melancholy as we both knew it was unlikely that we would ever see each other again. It was difficult for both of us to stop hugging and kissing each other before he boarded the plane to Pittsburgh. He finally said; "I love you!" and I responded immediately with tears streaming down my face; "I love you more!"

The days after his departure I returned to my routine with a heavy heart and a pocket full of memories that no one could ever steal from me.

Roy returned home and continued teaching and taking care of the business affairs of the Karate school. His cardiologist, Doctor Joe Nawrocki, was one of Roy's students and a family friend. Joe was continuously monitoring the progression of Roy's condition and a week after returning home Roy met with him for an evaluation. While in his office Roy's bulging aortic aneurism finally won the battle. Roy collapsed in the cardiologist's office. To everyone's amazement he survived the trip to Allegheny General Hospital in Pittsburgh and the extensive surgery to repair the aneurism and replace a damaged heart valve with a mechanical valve.

Roy called me from the Intensive Care Unit and proudly held the phone up to his chest for me to hear his new life-giving mechanical valve. I can still hear the rhythmic clicking. Proof that Roy had once again defied the odds in his human game of Russian roulette. He was still alive.

The doctor released him from the hospital with strict post-operative orders to refrain from any strenuous activity and begin closely supervised physical therapy until his doctor gave him permission to resume normal activities.

To everyone's horror, one week after his release from the hospital Roy did some crunch-it-ups causing the surgical staples to tear loose and protrude through his abdomen. Zee and I visited him that Christmas and he proudly displayed the outline of his still clearly visible staples. Undaunted by his experience Roy was enjoying his journey towards a successful recovery.

Roy started dating again and began to enjoy his life. I finally breathed a sigh of relief, anticipating that I would indeed have many opportunities to challenge Roy's fishing expertise against my own.

***

During the summer of 1995 Roy was scheduled to host a highly anticipated Karate tournament but failed to show up for its opening ceremony. Dr. Joe was participating in the event. Worried about his friend and patient's uncharacteristic absence, Joe drove to Roy's home to check on him. He found Roy lying on the floor, dressed in his Gi, conscious but too weak to stand. Joe carried him to his car and drove Roy to the Allegheny General Hospital in Pittsburgh where he had his emergency open-heart surgery the previous summer.

Joe knew the dire nature of the situation and as they approached the hospital, he said to Roy: "I have to be honest with you Roy, have you been baptized?"

"Yes! - Dutch Reformed." Roy managed to whisper weakly between gasps for air.

Joe had called ahead to the Emergency Room (ER) and let them know he was on his way with a critical patient. When they arrived, a medical team was waiting with a stretcher. Joe filled them in on Roy's medical history and what had just occurred as the medical team helped Roy onto the gurney and swooped him off for tests and treatment. It was the last time Joe saw Roy alive.

My stepsister Janice called me in Texas and told me that Roy was dying and had asked for me. Twenty-five hours after a non-stop drive from Plano, TX I entered his isolation room at the Allegheny General hospital in Pittsburgh. I saw "fear" in Roy's eyes for the first time in our lives. He could not speak but was able to squeeze my hand. His exposed skin was covered with chicken skin-like bumps that I was told later was a reaction to his body fighting the infection. As I held his hand I said, "I'm here Roy and will stay here as long as you need me."

He was laboring for breath and I sensed that he was wrestling with death and losing the war. "It's OK Roy! Let it go! I will make sure that the kids will be taken care of. I love you!" The fear left his eyes and his body relaxed and Roy fell asleep. He passed from this life soon after I left his side. As I write this my tears well up and fall down my cheeks uncontrollably. My best friend and brother, gone too soon at forty-seven years of age.

Heart issues like Roy's require caution when having a simple dental exam. Not only had Roy not taken prophylactic antibiotic before his dental appointments but after the fact he ignored the warning signs that may have saved his life.

The autopsy revealed that the cause of death was due to a major staph infection growing behind the mechanical heart valve. It could not be seen through X-rays and it ultimately grew large enough to separate the valve from Roy's heart causing his death. Taking the prescribed antibiotics before his routine dental care would have prevented the staph infection and Roy's death.

Dad may have set up the first Karate school but Roy is the one who made the Oriental Arts of Self-Defense part of the American fabric. He will always be remembered by anyone who ever met him or was touched by his teaching. Even today when I allow myself to dwell on Roy and his short life, I feel a terrible emptiness in my heart and soul and often repeat our shared phrase of love, "I love you more."

1968 NIAGARA, PA REGIONAL GRAND CHAMPION

Roy Wetzel in Hall of Fame

V.T. 6-10-95

Roy E. Wetzel, 46, of New Brighton was inducted into The World Martial Arts Hall of Fame May 6 at the Hilton Hotel in Akron, Ohio.

Wetzel is active in community affairs including the area crime watch organization and lectures and gives demonstrations for schools, organizations and civic groups. He provides self defense training to various law enforcement officials such as local, state and county police, the FBI and undercover agents.

He also heads a program known as Kung Fu and Karate for Kids, a private foundation that allows underprivileged children to learn and participate in the martial arts at no cost. Candidates are identified through various organizations in the community.

Wetzel was born Aug. 9, 1948, in Jok, Jakarta, Indonesia, the birthplace of Pentjak Silat for which he began training from the time he could walk. He continues to teach and train at his martial arts school, Self Defense Systems, Inc., 128 Brighton Ave., Rochester.

ROY WETZEL INDUCTED TO THE WORLD MARTIAL ARTS HALL OF FAME – 1995

ROY E WETZEL
LCPL US MARINE CORPS
VIETNAM
AUG 9 1948   MAY 22 1996
PURPLE HEART
SEMPER FIDELIS

CHAPTER 47 – "CALL 911 – I'M HAVING A HEART ATTACK"

It was our eighteenth wedding anniversary. Zee's youngest son Jeff and his wife Mina were preparing to move in with us. He had just left the Army and they were still transitioning to the civilian world. It was my day off and Jeff and I were working fast and furious to finish painting their bedroom when we both heard Zee's voice in the next room.

"Wim! Wim! I am having a heart attack. Wim, I need to go to the ER."

Jeff and I looked at each other questioning the validity of her complaint and stupidly went back to painting furiously. Again, we heard her voice. "Wim, I am serious I need to go to the ER." Still not taking the situation seriously I said casually "We are almost done painting the bedroom, can it wait for a few minutes?"

"No! We need to go now, and it is too late to call 911."

It finally got through to Jeff and me that she was not joking. We both dropped our rollers and brushes splattering paint everywhere and took off towards her panicked voice.

We loaded Zee into the car and called 911 on the way to the Arlington, Texas hospital. Immediately upon arrival they put her on a stretcher and rushed her into an operating room. Someone was taking her blood pressure, while she was being hooked up to monitors and IV fluids. The cardiologist was in the room barking orders to the medical staff.

Jeff and I stood back helplessly gawking as the heart monitor went silent and the cardiologist tore open her blouse, lifted her bra and pounded on her chest twice before inserting a long needle directly into her heart. He waited a couple of minutes and gave her another injection. Jeff and I stood there paralyzed at the surreal scene. Zee took a deep breath and came back to life.

After a few minutes she became responsive and alert. Her eyes scanned the room with curiosity and spied the doctor staring back at her. He tapped her on the forehead and said, "Lady you have smoked your last cigarette." She flashed him a cynical smile and announced, "No I haven't!"

After recovering from the heart attack, we brought her home. Her compromised heart turned out to be one of many health issues including Chronic Obstructive Pulmonary Disease (COPD), asthma, and degenerative arthritis. I spent the next thirteen years watching her as she slowly deteriorated before my eyes.

***

I was attending an executive meeting with numerous PhDs present, Ken asked me why I was not pursuing my doctorate. I was the only non-PhD in the meeting and being my normal smart-ass self, I expressed my position on the matter. "I was going to pursue my doctorate until I was told that in exchange for that diploma, I would be required to give up my common sense." As I looked around the room at several pairs of PhD eyes glaring back at me, I determined that the loss of one's sense of humor was also a prerequisite. But common sense told me to keep that observation to myself. Ken was the only member present who laughed.

My job at Hughes did not require me to have a Doctorate but I was surrounded by colleagues with PhD titles after their name. Zee was concerned that not having my Doctorate might mean being passed up for future promotions even if I was more qualified for the job than my colleagues. Zee insisted that I earn my Doctorate and I reluctantly trekked back into academia.

***

As she developed increasing signs of dementia or Alzheimer's, Zee began to gradually drift away from me. While she was unaware of what was happening to her, we both knew that her health was as good as it would ever be. She became an unwilling repeat hospital emergency care customer as her body gradually began to succumb to her arterial disease. We spent so much time in the ER that the medical staff and I were on a first name basis. They all loved Zee because she had such a good attitude and encouraged others while playing down her own adversities.

She was still able to take care of herself but I was watching her grow weaker every day and gradually fade away from me into her own world of dementia and confusion. My best friend and life partner was quickly slipping away into mental oblivion.

***

My career gave me some solace. Dr. Sue Arnold, my immediate boss had a laissez-faire leadership style that gave me an opportunity to use my skills, creativity, and imagination without interference. Sue supported all my decisions and gave me the freedom to do my job without restrictions.

Sue accepted an offer for a better position at Citizens Communications in Stamford, Connecticut (CT) to take over the company's organizational development (E&OD) and employee training programs. Leaving us was a devastating blow for the entire Raytheon team and a personal loss of a great friend and mentor.

About two weeks after Sue left the company, she called me at my home. "Wim, I need you and Ken to come work for me again. My company is moving into Plano, Texas and I have the charge to set up and run the E&OD and employee training programs. I want to hire you as Citizens Communications' Manager of Training. Would you like to work for me again?"

I was hesitant in accepting the offer because the drive from Arlington to Plano was long and tortuous through the heart of Dallas on nightmarish congested freeways. Sue sensed my hesitation and said: "I will double your current salary and start you off with 30 days of annual vacation and a very good annual bonus."

"Let me give my two-week notice and I will report to you then."

"Thank you Wim and I look forward to working with you and Ken again."

***

With the management position at Citizens Communications came a lot more responsibility, opportunity, and a long leash. I was trusted with a huge budget to design and develop an employee and organizational development program under Dr. Arnold. Sue made sure that I received every opportunity to have a say at the executive decision table.

I was given full reign to recruit new employees from across the country to support the rapidly expanding telecommunications company. Having already developed a great working and personal relationship with Dr. Ken, we traveled to New Mexico, Arizona, Utah, and Nevada American Indian reservations to interview and hire native Americans to service the telecommunications infrastructure.

We traveled to a severely economically depressed central Pennsylvania town with high expectations of finding quality young people that would be ready to sign up for the opportunity to leave behind a life of joblessness and an uncertain financial future. We interviewed forty young high school graduates for telephone linemen, service, and maintenance positions. The various jobs started at an annual salary of over $30,000 (equivalent to $46,216 as of 2018) with great benefits.

After Ken and I finished conducting the interviews we left mentally scratching our heads. The most startling question the recruits wanted answered was: "Do I have to leave home to work for your company?" When I answered "Yes." Not a single candidate accepted the job offer. The apron strings were just too tight. No one wanted to leave Pennsylvania and their friends and family. I could not help thinking about my last year living in Pennsylvania before serving in the Air Force. *If I had not made the painful choice to leave Beaver Valley where would I be today?*

At risk of using a cliché - I will anyway. *"All good things must come to an end."* Because of Dr. Sue's leadership and our quality team E&OD became extraordinarily successful and significantly increased the company's bottom line. Internal political rivalry and power struggles began to cause a rift to rise up causing Dr. Sue to accept a position with a competing company. Her replacement was a demon sent from Hell and if anyone at Citizens liked her, they certainly were not talking about it. The Human Resources department was told to use a "hands off" approach with her. For reasons no one understood she was Citizen's darling and appeared to have full control of her superiors.

She often bragged about being a preacher's wife but then on two separate occasions she slapped female employees who displeased her and received no consequences for her unacceptable behavior. Everyone I knew at Citizens who was under her thumb was looking for a way out. The destruction left in her wake seemed as if she were intentionally out to destroy what our team had accomplished.

I could not wait to leave the company as the only accommodating thing she ever did for me was to get me fired. When I got the word of my dismissal, the Human Resources Director told me that the company will give me another 30 extra days of employment if I would train my replacement about everything I knew about training and development.

"Sure!" (*Sure. I can teach my replacement all my accumulated 30 years' experience in just 30 days - no problem*).

Unfortunately for the company and my youthful high school diploma replacement, I stayed too busy and did not have time to train him on all that I knew about training and organizational development.

Only a few days into my thirty days things quickly went from bad to disaster. My new supervisor slapped one of my employees, fired her on the spot, called security and had her removed from the building. It took every bit of moral strength and courage to prevent me from striking the "Boss" in response. After I watched my employee walk out to her car in tears I went straight to Human Resources and demanded that they allow me to leave the company immediately and without prejudice. I explained why I needed to leave and was given approval to do so by the end of the week.

I went back to my office and boxed up my personal library of valuable life experience material and training and development work. A collection that I had started as far back as my Air Force days and accumulated up this point at Hughes/Raytheon. It was a significant collection and a lifetime of work. I decided to wait until the next morning to pick up my boxes and load them in my truck.

When I came to work the next morning, I discovered that everything that I had boxed for departure had been removed from my office. I called security to help me find my things but they just factually told me that my "boss" had directed them to remove my boxes and take them to her office. Telling them that everything in the boxes was company property and that security was directed to escort me to HR and then out the front door.

It was the only time in my life that I really, REALLY wanted to hurt someone without a shred of remorse, but by the grace of God, I was not given that opportunity as two company security men, one on each side of me, escorted me to my car.

***

For the first time in my adult life on May 1, 2000 I was unemployed and collected my first unemployment check two weeks later. I was mortified and felt ashamed cashing it. I received the second check and never cashed it. I still have it in my safe as a stark reminder of how blessed I am to not to have needed it.

I found a job advertisement in the Dallas Morning News Sunday edition: $600 per month- Will Train-No Experience Required. It was a job and I did not have one.

I drove to the Crest Isuzu dealership in Plano with my resume in hand and spoke with the sales manager. After reviewing the resume, he hired me on the spot pending completion of training that started the following Monday. The automobile sales associate training class lasted five days and I graduated at 4 PM on Friday. I sold my first used car at 5 PM the same day for $1,000 more than the used car cost new a year earlier.

It was hard and hot work six days a week and often 16 hours a day. I had to leave Zee alone which gave her sister plenty of time to exploit Zee's declining mental state and her ability to reason.

The summer months in Texas often exceed 110 degrees and the black asphalt sales lot increased the temperature by 20 or more degrees. The day started at 8 AM but I always showed up at 6:30 or 7:00, made coffee and walked around the yard to learn all I could about the inventory.

During my rookie month and despite all the negative factors related to selling cars, I sold 11.5 cars. The .5 car was the second new car that I sold and it meant that I needed help to close the sale and had to share ½ the commission. The sale closed at 2:30 AM since the dealership's policy was to stay open until any active sale was closed.

My worst commission was $25.00 after working with the customer for three days. The customer for this sale was a leader of the Holy Land Foundation (terrorist finance organization) in Dallas. He and his cronies were later arrested and convicted for collecting donations for terror organizations. My commission was actually

$50.00 but the service department billed me $25 for my failure to get the second set of keys for the terrorist's trade-in vehicle.

One day I was eating lunch at my desk while the other Associates had gone out for their lunch. I noticed a skimpily clad young woman wandering around the parking lot. Of course, out of "professional" courtesy, I postponed finishing the last half of my sandwich. As I approached her, I realized she was a server at "Hooters" restaurant across the street. In case you were wondering how I knew she worked at Hooters, well, she had big-umm… letters on her chest that spelled out HOOTERS that adequately described where she worked.

"Hello and welcome to Crest Isuzu. I'm Wim Wetzel, can I help you with anything?"

"Yes, you can." She pointed to the Isuzu VehiCROSS. "How much is this pretty yellow car?"

"You have good taste. That one is pretty pricey." I answered not wanting the sticker price to discourage a possible sales opportunity.

"Well, how much is it?"

"The base price is $52,000. But maybe I can interest you in something more affordable."

"No, I want this one and I will get my friend at work to come over today to pay cash for it. Do you have a business card? I'll make sure that he asks for you." I handed her my card and she honored me with a peck on the cheek and turned to leave. She stopped and turned around as if she had forgotten something. "Thank you for helping me." I stood there slack jawed and stunned as she casually walked back across the street as if she just purchased a pack of gum. The whole experience lasted less than 10 minutes.

Within the hour her "friend" met with the dealership finance officer, paid cash for the hybrid off-the-road vehicle in her name and drove off the lot. I later found out that her "friend" was married to someone else but promised her she could pick out any car on the lot across the street and he would buy it for her. It was the largest sales commission I received during my short tenure at the dealership. Selling cars was not the best paying job in the world but it was entertaining at times.

I have a lot of respect for car salespeople. It is a job that I am glad to have experienced but was even more delighted when that short career ended. I knew this was temporary but over my lifetime I never mentally discounted even the most menial jobs. Each one became a part of my survival arsenal and this job was no exception. It pushed me out of my introverted shell and I became friendlier and more transparent with strangers.

While still working at Crest Isuzu I put my resume out everywhere I could think of that would be a good fit. I threw mud at every wall, hoping something would stick. Three months after starting my sales job I received "The" call.

"Wim Wetzel?"

"Yes sir? How may I help you?"

"This is Vic Lauerman- a recruiter at NEC. What are you doing for work?"

"For right now I am a car Sales Associate at the Crest Isuzu dealership in Plano, Texas."

"You are kidding of course?"

"No sir, I am not."

"Why, are you wasting your skills and talent selling cars?"

"I needed a job and they gave me one, Sir."

"Well, your resume has come across my desk and you appear to meet every qualification we are looking for. Can you come in for an interview and meet the NEC Human Resources (HR) Vice President (VP)?"

CHAPTER 48 - THIRD JOB'S A CHARM

I had my first interview with Vic who then set up a second interview with the HR VP. A third interview was set up with the company president.

By the fifth interview I had already exhaustively answered every question more than once. I even referred him to the internet and the myriad of well-known publications that interviewed me over the years, including The Wall Street Journal, Dallas Morning News, Beaver County Times, and several trade magazines. By the time I was called back for my sixth interview I was at the end of my patience but with Vic's coaxing I reluctantly returned.

After the sixth interview I was confident the next call would be a job offer and salary proposal but I was wrong. Vic called me to come in for a seventh interview because the HR VP wanted a seventh interview.

"I am sorry Vic but I am no longer interested." Undeterred, Vic persuaded me to return.

Exasperated, I said to the HR VP: "If you hire me today and provide me with the adequate resources to set up the employee development office, my department will pay for itself, my salary and my assistant's salary in six months. If I am unable to meet this commitment in that time frame, I will personally hand you my resignation."

He accepted my proposal and hired me as the NEC Manager of Employee Development.

On 9/11/2000 at 8AM I reported to NEC's human resources (HR) department for in-processing. As I waited in the lobby several senior Japanese executives entered the building. The reality struck me. I might be working for living survivors and offspring of the Japanese empire of World War II. Mom and Dad will be rolling over in their graves.

Having exceeded all my commitments in less than six months I presented him with the status reports and he highly commended me for my performance. I thanked him and added.

"Based on my reports and success, I am asking for a promotion to Director Employee and Organizational Development and a pay raise to match the position."

"Wim, I can't do that. That kind of promotion typically takes several years - not six months."

"I understand but, in that case, I will be happy to train someone else for the position before I leave the company."

The matter was settled and I was immediately promoted to the position of Director Employee and Organizational Development in Human Resources.

Customer service was a critical weakness in the company and it became my biggest initial challenge. The term "service" was far from the correct word to describe the department's performance. Customers were constantly complaining about the terrible service and how blatantly discourteous the staff was to them.

I set up customer advocacy and support training for every employee in the company regardless of whether they even remotely dealt with customers. The NEC product service practices continued to be a problem and I knew my limitations with my small staff of trainers. However, I was still holding on to one last ace and it was time to call in the A-team of Doctor Sherry Buffington of Quantum Leap Systems.

Sherry had successfully completed an employee analysis and development program for me at Citizens Communications and she with her daughter, Gina Morgan, turned the severely problematic department into a highly professional and successful customer service machine.

As I moved up the senior management chain, I developed personal and professional relationships with the Japanese employees at every level. My NEC HQ counterpart Director of Training and Employee Development and I worked closely together. During the course of our developing relationship, we talked about WWII and I told him about Dad's experiences as a POW in Tokyo and throughout southeast Asia. He, in turn, told me that his grandfather was killed at Iwo Jima.

Not long after that discussion the divisional Vice President asked me to meet with him in his office. To my surprise he asked me about Dad and my family's history in Indonesia. After listening intently, he asked. "Wim, why would you accept a position working for any Japanese company considering what happened to the Wetzel's during the war?"

I was uncomfortable with the question but as calm and professional as I could be, I answered.

"Sir, any hate for the Japanese my parents had was buried with Dad's ashes and Mom's casket. We live in a new world where we learned from the past and resolved never to make those terrible mistakes again." The answer seemed to satisfy him as the discussion continued about my department's goals for the corporation.

***

Zee's health was rapidly declining but she was still able to travel. I had been at NEC for three years and Mom was remarried and moved to Okeechobee, Florida. Everything was running smoothly at NEC and the timing was right to take a break from work so we decided to take a trip to Florida. I was glad to see Mom, and she was overwhelmed with excitement to see her wayward son.

The visit started out wonderfully but was interrupted when I received an emergency phone call from Decatur, Illinois. It had been ten years since my "tough love" conversation with my son. WK had been taken to the hospital by ambulance from his construction job and at 27 years old he was brain dead. During the process of re-roofing a customer's house he was raising an aluminum ladder through some tree branches. The ladder struck a 7500-volt power line electrocuting him, blowing a shoe off his foot as he collapsed to the ground holding onto the ladder. On life support, with no brain activity he would not survive much longer. I knew the decision I had to make, but I wanted to see him one more time before I let him go forever.

His mother, Debbie, had died from a brain tumor a few years earlier and he had two beautiful children – Tyler and Kali. He was engaged to a wonderful woman - Amber who was seven months pregnant with Carlie. Since Wim and Amber were not yet married, I was the next-of-kin and needed to decide whether or not to take him off life support.

We left immediately and drove almost non-stop to Decatur and went straight to the hospital. We met with the doctors and Wim's fiancée. The medical team advised me that there was no chance for Wim's recovery. Zee and I sat with my beloved precious son for a long time. After an agonizing and painful time holding Wim's hand, I asked the doctors to disconnect him from life support. On August 29, 2003 WK left us for the last time and his painful life struggles ended while my grief and heartful pain grew exponentially. This time I knew that he left us for a better place in peace.

My grief was unbearable. I had always harbored a burden of guilt and regret about my "tough love decision" to shut him out of my life. Now I swore that the rest of my life would be dedicated to ensuring that his children would be financially set for facing adulthood.

We decided to donate his remains to the hospital to use any part for the benefit of others. We learned that his eyes and his skin had made a difference in several people's lives. That knowledge gave me some peace but I doubt that I will ever be able to make peace with myself that maybe things could have been different- *if only*.

The accident was caused by improperly installed powerlines. I found a lawyer to sue the power company and the state of Illinois for his wrongful death. We won the lawsuit and Wim's three children were awarded a significant sum of money and with the assistance of the court we set up savings accounts for each grandchild to be accessed by each upon reaching the age of 21. A separate account was established by Amber to access for any expenses necessary to raise the children.

God graced us all by bringing Amber into WK's life as she was a wonderful, dedicated, and loving mother who raised Carlie and Tyler in the most spectacular way. My WK would be extremely proud of his family and his first wife, Kali's mother, raised Kali.

Tyler, Kali and WK

Carlie, Opa and Amber – 2019

CHAPTER 49 – CELEBRATING AND HONORING A LIFE WELL-LIVED

One day after completing my Doctorate I was making the rounds at NEC and networking with the General Managers. The Engineering Manager, Steve Fisher, stopped to congratulate me and asked if he could read my dissertation on building a corporate university. After reading it he asked me for permission to use parts of it for an executive presentation. He wanted to recommend the establishment of a corporate university at NEC.

The Japanese executive staff accepted his proposal to include offering me the position pending my salary requirements. Initially I told Steve – "Thanks but no thanks. I am not interested and besides, you cannot afford what I want for my salary and other requirements." He asked me what I wanted.

"I need $130,000 worth of audio-visual and on-line infrastructure improvements and a complete autonomy and no interference in running the organization. The project would need a staff of up to 10 employees to develop and convert all classroom courses to computer and distance delivery training and a 40% salary increase."

"Wim how can you justify the cost for the infrastructure in the audio/video delivery center as well as the cost of your salary which would be more than mine."

"I'm sorry Steve but those are my requests. I need the infrastructure investment to convert the more than 100 instructor-led customer courses to computer-based and distance learning training. The company will receive its return on that investment within six months after it is implemented."

"OK Wim, I'll approach the corporate executives. But do not expect a positive response on this. I'll let you know."

I knew Steve was excited about the project and about the prospect of us working on it together. We were both skeptical because my conditions may have been more than the executives were willing to shell out.

Two days later Steve called me for another meeting. I was sure it was going to be a counteroffer and I was prepared to decline. I sat down and observed his demeanor across the desk while trying to guess what he had to offer.

He sat leaning forward, his hands folded on the desk and shaking his head in amazement. His lips curled up slightly then broke out in a full-blown grin. "Congratulations, they accepted your offer, Wim - the whole package."

With Steve's friendship and support my department surpassed those expectations and the National Training Center was launched successfully. We converted 106 instructor-led classroom NEC product courses to on-line training within the first year. The cost for training every vendor employee dropped from an average of $3,500 to $1,000 not including the cost of travel, lodging, and meals for a two-week course. My department enjoyed an annual income of over $6 million in training revenue until the time of my retirement.

My career was better than I could have ever planned for. I loved the job and the people I worked with but the love of my life was suffering terribly.

***

Zee had three cardiac incidents and all of them caused her to flat line but she always bounced back. It was an emotional rollercoaster. We knew that the worst was inevitable and we drew up wills and made each other the executor. It would give us both peace of mind knowing that our entire estate would belong to the surviving spouse. We decided together that the wills would go in our home safe and only the two of us would have the combination.

Twenty-two years after our marriage Zee's overall health declined precipitously. Her chain smoking left her with COPD and vascular disease that caused her unbearable leg pains when she tried to walk. Her advanced osteoporosis caused multiple painful bone fractures and she developed colitis and an intestinal blockage and had to have most of her colon removed. One of her hospital stays lasted forty-five days as her weakened immune system gave in to Methicillin-resistant Staphylococcus aureus (MRSA).

I was commuting 45 minutes one way for work every day. My exhaustion from the round-trip commutes to work and caring for Zee had finally broken my spirit but I could not let Zee go to a care facility. I had no choice and had to talk to my boss and good friend Steve about my dilemma.

I walked into his office feeling defeated and ashamed that I had let him down. "Hi Steve. Do you have a minute?'

"Of course, Come in and sit down. What's up?"

I held back tears until I thought my face would burst. "Steve, I can't do this anymore. I have to quit. Zee is getting worse and requires more time than I can give her and still come here every day. I am sorry, Steve. I am really worried about how I can pay the medical bills if I quit but I know I have to."

"Wim, you do not have to quit. The office is running smoothly and you have trained your employees well and they are more than capable of continuing without your daily presence. You can do just about everything from home and just come in for mandatory executive meetings."

I broke into uncontrollable tears of relief. "Thank you, Steve." I choked out the words. I knew Steve had a heart as big as the state of Texas and he had been a good friend and confidant for several years but now we had a bond that was closer than brothers and I honestly believe to this day that I would die for him.

Zee's primary care doctor advised me to have Zee admitted to a full-time care facility. Against the doctor's recommendation I insisted on caring for her at home. He explained in detail what that would mean for me. But I was unrelenting. He finally agreed to let me try if I was willing to go through some extensive training.

Our living room had to be converted into a hospital room. He ordered a hospital bed, bedside potty, oxygen equipment and a bedside stand for medicine and drip delivery.

A professional nurse and home health care assistant were scheduled to briefly visit us several times a week to assess her condition.

I learned to drain the tube inserted through her back and inject saline into the tube to flush it out several times a day. She never complained as I injected the saline but her contorted face told the story. I administered her injections, changed her drainage tubing, bathed her, and attended to her bathroom needs for over two years while working from home.

Her full-time oxygen lifeline followed her everywhere but she continued her life-long two to three pack smoking habit and I often caught her smoking while she was breathing oxygen.

She knew her time was coming soon but she never stopped her crusade to encourage and uplift others and she stayed engaged in every life she touched. But in 2008 the woman that had always given her all for everyone else had no more strength left to give. We chose to fight together until her last breath. She hated that she was becoming so dependent on me and she suggested that I take her to a nursing home, drop her off and to forget about her. That was not an option that I could live with. Not yet and hopefully not ever.

***

After only a few days of performing this procedure my wrists began to hurt badly and the fingers of my right hand alternately went numb or had sharp pain. The diagnosis was carpal tunnel syndrome (CTS) in both wrists caused by my 24-year career as a Loadmaster handling heavy chains and tiedown devices.

A hand specialist recommended that both wrists be repaired, one at a time over a couple of months. That was not an option I could live with. So, since CTS surgery heals quickly, I elected to have both wrists repaired on a Friday and our friend and housekeeper, Chris, helped me care for Zee over that recovery weekend. The surgery results were positive and no time was lost in my caregiver responsibilities.

One day while lifting Zee from the wheelchair to her bed I felt a pop and sharp pain in my left groin. I was in agony but I knew I had to gently finish transferring her to the bed. The pain subsided but I had a bulge in my lower abdomen. I called Chris to come and stay with Zee while I went to the ER. The diagnosis was a hernia and surgical repair was required quickly. I planned with Chris to be with Zee and the next week I had the surgical repair.

My Prostate-specific Antigen (PSA) was rising rapidly with every doctor visit and my physical "finger-wave" prostate exam result was very suspicious for cancer. Contrary to my doctor's advice I opted out of more extensive testing. I felt that I had no choice as

Zee's only caretaker and did not feel that I had the luxury of time to do anything about it.

Out of her three sons only Zee's youngest son, Jeff, made any attempt to help take care of her. Throughout her life she was always the first one they turned to in their times of need and she was always there for them. I could not believe that her two oldest sons had become invisible and unavailable now that she was no longer useful to them.

In the midst of this chaos, I was diagnosed with life threatening heart problems. The doctor wanted to schedule me for surgery to repair or replace three leaking heart valves as soon as possible. It was nearly impossible for me to even find time for a doctor's appointment let alone find time for immediate major open-heart surgery. When I explained my dilemma with being Zee's sole caregiver, he reluctantly offered me the only other option. Treat it with medication until I was able to have the surgery.

I knew too well that I was playing Russian Roulette with my heart issues but I had no choice, Zee was completely dependent on me and this was where the rubber met the road. Until death do us part. For the next 13-months my breathing became more compromised due to the heart issues.

Zee was admitted to rehabilitation facilities three times during that year. It was like jumping from the frying pan into the fire and exactly why I had resisted the recommendation. Zee needed constant undivided attention that was not an option in the rehab setting.

The last straw was when she was admitted to a recovery facility and Zee fell out of bed and broke her arm, suffered a concussion, and tore various intravenous needles from her arms. I could no longer live knowing she was getting substandard care and I demanded her to be released to me and took her home for the last time and contacted the local hospice organization.

A stream of hospice team doctors, nurses and medics visited us and assessed her condition. They explained to me that her life expectancy was about two weeks but they would make her comfortable and promised to keep her pain free as medically possible. Feeling defeated and exhausted I conceded to the hospice care if they indeed promised me that they would keep her pain free. With the senior doctor's assurance, I agreed and I gave them approval to start immediately. It was a Tuesday afternoon and after two years of caring for Zee on my own, the first nurse reported and immediately relieved me of my 24-hour, 7 day a week nursing duty. I pulled my recliner next to the hospital bed and made it my home.

Our pastor, Alice Coder, routinely came to the hospital to visit and pray with us. Zee told Pastor Alice that she would not be with us much longer and asked Alice to preside over the funeral. When Pastor Alice asked Zee which bible verses, she wanted her to share with her friends and family at the memorial service, Zee simply said, "You have known me long enough to determine that." Even in her state of dementia she did not want anyone to be sad but to celebrate where she had been in her temporal life and where she was going from here. "Just pick positive passages that most clearly define who I am."

For someone who has never stood by and watched a loved one suffer like this it would be hard to understand but Zee was past living without extreme pain and watching her suffer was killing me. I was begging God to take her and I was angry that He was allowing her to linger.

The first night under Hospice care Zee screamed in pain as she rolled over in bed and broke two ribs. The Hospice nurse gave her pain medications and injected additional medications into her drip. Early that next morning Zee broke her foot trying to roll over as her ankle was tangled in the bed sheet. I panicked and lost my cool.

I called the Hospice care doctor and reminded her of her promise to keep Zee pain free and that the nurse had failed to do so. I insisted that she needed to intercede immediately and she came to the house with several other medical personnel to assess Zee's condition.

"Mr. Wetzel, the only way Zee will remain pain free is if we put her into an induced coma. You must understand that decision has irreversible consequences and there will be no turning back. Be sure that you understand that she will never wake up again." I watched Zee lie there writhing in pain and accepted the fact that this was an irreversible situation no matter what I decided and said, "OK – do it now!"

For the next two days Zee did not move and on Thursday morning I saw more blood in her urine bag. The medical staff re-evaluated her condition and told me that Zee's kidneys were failing and that she had less than five days left.

Amazingly, in true Zee style at 7 PM on Friday night she suddenly came out of her coma and started talking to me in the clearest voice. She looked at me with those beautiful eyes and said, "I love you."

The Hospice nurse stood up and watched dumbstruck. She had never seen a patient come out of an induced coma and I never expected to hear her voice again.

She began to reminisce about our life together as if she were not even ill and clearly said; "I saw my mom, dad and WK and everything is going to be all right. Mom is sitting next to you right now and smiling. I love you so much."

"I love you too Zee.". Those were the last words we shared as she slipped back into her coma as quickly as she had come out of it.

***

Zee's life-clock was counting down and Saturday morning the Hospice staff re-evaluated her condition. The Hospice doctor told me that she had 24 to 48 hours left but to expect less than 24 hours. Now I was even more angry at God and asked Him "Why are you making her suffer so much? Zee deserves so much better for the wonderful and Godly life she lived."

I was counseled that it was time to call any family members or friends that may want to see her. I called each of her family members and told them this would be their last chance to say their goodbyes and that they needed to come to the house now.

Some responded in disbelief and advised me that I had cried "wolf" about her health condition before. Losing my patience, I tried to calmly explain what the senior hospice doctor had told me but my pleas fell on deaf ears. I finally gave up and put the hospice nurse on the phone to confirm what I was saying. She finally convinced them I was not overreacting.

Zee stood by her sister through good and bad times over the years and had been her encourager and mentor throughout their lives. Her sister had always exhibited self-centered traits but now it was important to put that aside. I felt that of all the people that needed to say good-bye to Zee that her sister was the most important. But now my sister-in-law showed her true colors.

She told me that she and her husband were on their way to a gambling casino in Choctaw, Oklahoma and were not coming back until Sunday. She assured me that they would swing by to see Zee the next day on their way home. I reiterated the urgency for them to see Zee now explaining once more that the doctors did not expect Zee to make it through the night and that tomorrow would be too late. Cold-heartedly she told me that she was not willing to forfeit her vacation opportunity and hung up the phone. I was numbed by her heartless response. It appeared that since Zee did not serve a useful purpose for her any longer and she had no time for her.

Zee's sons, grandson, nephew, and brothers did come and stayed until late that Saturday night. I knew that Zee could still hear us and that she was enjoying all the laughter, the many heartwarming funny moments, and happy memories we were sharing about our life with her. She positively impacted so many people. It was a time for celebrating what she meant to all of us and there would be plenty of time for grieving later.

After everyone left, I fell back into a restless sleep in my recliner while holding Zee's hand. Our Schnauzer "Lindsey" was lying next to Zee with her head resting across her right arm occasionally whimpering softly and licking Zee's hand. Lindsey had not eaten in three days and rarely left Zee's side. She instinctively knew that something was very wrong. The night nurse awakened me at 2 AM to tell me that Zee's breathing had become erratic and very shallow and that she would soon be gone.

She suggested that I get up on the edge of the bed, hold her hand and talk to her until her last breath. I did so and in the most loving way that I could I shared how much she meant to me, how much I loved her over all our years together and that it was OK to let go. Her breathing became more and more erratic and her eyes stared into mine. It is a moment I will take to my grave. I repeated several times until her last breath "Honey I love you so much. It's time to let go."

Even though I had been warned about what was about to happen when her breathing stopped - it startled me. I looked over to the nurse. And asked: "Is she gone?"

"No, I don't think so. As hard as she has fought, I believe she will try to breathe again."

Right after she uttered those words Zee took three deep breaths, stared deep into my eyes, and stopped breathing for the last time. I collapsed over her body crying and sobbing uncontrollably for several minutes. In a moment that I will never forget, I gained my composure, reached up and closed her eyes for the last time.

The nurse calmly reached down and turned off the oxygen machine putting an end to the familiar continuous rhythmic pulsing, blanketing the room with an eerie stillness that seemed to announce to the world the end of a human life. That simple act of silencing the never-ending sound of pumping oxygen was another one of the hardest things I ever experienced. Dutifully, but respectfully, the nurse quietly picked up the chart and entered the last entry in Zee's chart - Time of death; 2:20 AM February 27, 2011.

At 2:40 I began making phone calls to relay the news that Zee was gone. Her sister was nowhere to be found. Baffled by her only sister's lack of sensitivity, I finished making the calls to the rest of the family and stood zombie-like watching the recovery team prepare Zee's body for transport.

Before Zee's last breath and while I was asleep in the chair next to her, the nurse had discretely summoned the ambulance in anticipation of the inevitable and it was already waiting in our driveway. The mortuary team quickly entered our home; prepared Zee's remains for her final earthly trip and took her out of the house.

I watched stupefied as the hospice team collected and destroyed all her medications by mixing them with coffee grounds and putting them in a container. Then they hugged me sympathetically and left me standing with only my grief as a companion. The medical supplies, oxygen and hospital bed disappeared almost magically and the temporary hospital setting quickly went from the dying room to the living room once more. There was nothing more to say and nothing more to do. "Death leaves a heartache no one can heal; love leaves a memory no one can steal." It is not an original quote but whoever first said it; thank you! It is a fitting statement.

CHAPTER 50 – BETRAYED

The memorial service was held at our church in Plano. Family, friends, and colleagues from my company attended. Zee's brother Bill gave a beautiful eulogy which celebrated Zee's life and how she impacted people's lives so positively. I had a hard time holding myself together and sobbed uncontrollably for a moment. For thirty-three years Zee had always been the wind in my sails and the feeder bands from that wind positively touched every life around her.

I was relieved and comforted by the fact that years before Zee became unable to make rational decisions, we had decided that we needed to get our affairs in order ensuring that everything that we had worked so hard for together would go to the surviving spouse. This made it so much easier to know that everything was already prearranged. Exhaustion and grieving were enough to deal with. The one consolation in this painful time of grieving was that once the initial proprieties were over, I knew the wills that we had drawn up were in our safe at home and it would be easy to settle the estate.

My three stepsons, Zee's sister, and I met in my home after the funeral for what I thought was a time to grieve and console each other after our loss. While we were reminiscing, I shared my thoughts openly "I do not know what I will do next with my life, but as much as I dread it, I do have to go through the papers that we have in our safe and find Zee's will. I am so grateful Zee and I had preplanned for this. As executor it should not be a complicated process."

"Wim, you are not the executor." My sister-in-law said coldly.

The statement snapped me out of my vegetative stupor. I was stunned and sure that she was confused. "Of course, I am. Zee and I took care of all of that a few years back before her mental state diminished. The will is in our safe."

"The will is not in the safe anymore Wim. Zee changed her will. I have the latest will and I am the executor."

I sat staring across the room watching her lips dribble out the words like honey while her forked tongue spewed out deceit and hate that flowed like a river. I realized then that her past devious behavior was a practice run for this, the grand finale, the sting.

Indeed, the will had been removed from our combination safe that only Zee and I had the combination to. I can only speculate on how that played out but I did find out that her sister convinced Zee to change her will on the pretense that I would not treat Zee's grown sons, from her previous marriage, fairly. As the pieces of the puzzle began to unfold, I realized what had been happening while I was at work and too busy caring for Zee and too exhausted to watch my own back. Zee's dysfunctional greedy family had cashed in on our years of hard work, blood, sweat and tears. Even the executor would get her fair share.

I met with the executrix's attorney to read the new will and ask some questions. After reading the new will I noticed that the two witnesses who signed it were Spanish speaking workers from the nursing home where Zee was a patient at the time. The date the will was signed was during a time when Zee's dementia was far advanced and she was heavily sedated to make her more comfortable. I knew exactly when this was signed. I handed the will back to him and suppressing my rage I asked. "I was Zee's sole caretaker and I know that Zee was not coherent and able to make rational decisions when this was drawn up and signed. How did you determine whether Zee was of sound mind? Can you explain that to me?"

He sat back in his chair with an exaggerated condescending arrogance and shrugged his shoulders. "She answered the two questions correctly – What is your name? And what is your date of birth? That by Texas law, is all that is required." It took all my will power to not reach across the desk and wipe the smug self-satisfied grin off his face.

I sat there processing the fact that everything I had worked for all my life was now controlled by my ungrateful greedy sister-in-law. My entire financial future was at the mercy of my grown stepsons and Zee's sister. My total lifelong investments, retirement funds, savings and even my real estate were at stake and I had no recourse. I would get what was left over after my three stepsons and Zee's sister took what they wanted. I would get what was left over when the court saw fit to give it to me. That was Texas law.

The phone rang one day and her sweet syrupy voice came through the receiver. "Wim, how are you?"

"Fine What do you want?"

"I thought you might like to know that I will be meeting with the probate judge soon."

"I need to attend the probate hearing because I intend to challenge the Will."

"Fine, you will be told when the hearing is scheduled. Goodbye Wim."

Numbed, I hung up feeling betrayed and beaten down by Zee and her entire family. I still could not wrap my head around the vicious deception. All I could do was wait.

After a few weeks of anxiously waiting, I called her. "Do you have any idea when the hearing will be?"

"Yes." She said flatly and gave me the date and told me it was scheduled for 8 AM at the Collin County Courthouse.

"Thank you for letting me know." I hung up the phone frustrated and angry that she had not called me as soon as she knew.

On the date of the scheduled hearing, I went to the courthouse at 7:45 AM prepared to challenge the legality of the will. I spotted a Bailiff and asked where the hearing was going to be held. "I'm sorry sir. The hearing is over." He showed me where to go to inquire about it. As I entered the hearing room, I saw the probate judge meeting with her. I introduced myself and mentioned that the executrix advised me that the hearing was scheduled for 8 AM and that I had arrived early.

He peered above his glasses as if scolding a school child. "Mr. Wetzel you are late and I have already ruled in favor of the Executor named in the document."

"She has a conflict of interest in the estate and should and could not be the Executor. Furthermore, that Will was written when Zee was under heavy mind-altering medication and, therefore, unfit to write a rational will.

"I have ruled in the case and if you want to challenge the ruling, feel free to do so. Get a good lawyer and be prepared to spend a lot of money. Dismissed!"

With the exception of Zee's youngest son Jeff and his wife, when Zee needed them the most her family had disappeared into obscurity, leaving Zee and me to fend for ourselves during the peak of her illness until the sweet smell of money lured them from under their rocks. Zee's two adult sons and sister did next to nothing for Zee or me while she was living. As Navy retirees they both enjoyed a financially comfortable life and now they were pursuing as much as possible from my estate. In God's own time I would find out how much of my accumulated estate would be forfeited to satisfy a family's greed.

CHAPTER 51 – "DOCTOR - HOW DO YOU FIX A BROKEN HEART?"

Living in a house of fractured memories and broken dreams, Zee, WK and Roy were following me from room to room as every tangible and intangible part of the life that Zee and I had built together was about to fade into a cloud of calculated greed and legal dust. It was not so much that Zee made the decision or agreed to change her will; but the betrayal of trust that had totally broken my spirit. *How does one deal emotionally with losing your soul mate and trusted best friend and simultaneously bear the pain of unfathomable deception that you never saw coming?*

***

The doctors were monitoring my leaking heart valve and my untreated military back injuries. My broken back was now pushing my maximum pain threshold and the pain in my back and legs had become intolerable. The MRI scans indicated that my L-5/S-1 vertebral body was broken in two places causing significant pressure on the spinal cord. My personal life and medical problems were rapidly declining into a crisis with no sign of a positive outcome. I repeatedly asked God, "Why?"

Before moving ahead with the radical-360-degree back surgery, I had to get clearance from my cardiologist. The pre-operation sonogram revealed a 5.6 CM aortic aneurysm, but I was still cleared for the back surgery. After I was rolled into the surgery suite the five-doctor team reviewed my chart one last time while the medical staff was prepping me for the operation.

***

Anesthesiologists have one job, keeping the patient asleep and alive during a surgical procedure. The anesthesiologist assigned to me studied my chart and medical history, weighed the odds of me not waking up and reconsidered the possibility that putting me to sleep that day may have been a bad day for all of us due to my aortic aneurism. Just as a pilot has the last word on whether or not to fly an airplane- the anesthesiologist has the last word in the decisions made in the operating room. His final assessment was that the aneurism made the back surgery too risky. I had to get the aortic aneurism repaired before an anesthesiologist would consent to such a lengthy and complicated procedure. Surgeons are at the mercy of the "gas passer" so I was back to square one.

***

Because I was considered a statistically high-risk patient, my thoracic surgeon had decided to give me a mechanical valve and scheduled me for emergency surgery. I was offered the option of a mechanical, pig or bovine valve. The fact that Roy had died from complications caused by a mechanical valve and the fact that I would be required to take Warfarin to thin my blood and that required a regimen of frequent blood testing, the mechanical valve did not seem like an option. The limitations of Warfarin certainly did not coincide with my active lifestyle of being an avid hunter, fisherman and outdoorsman.

I agreed to the surgery but asked for a few days to research the valve options. I met with Dr. Wallace about my decision to have a bovine valve replacement. The day before the surgery he advised me that he was going to repair my valve instead of replacing it. His success rate with this cutting-edge procedure was exemplary. His patients recovered faster than when their valves were replaced, it required no blood thinners and had a higher rate if life expectancy. After a detailed explanation of the procedure, I told him to "git-r-done!"

***

October 27, 2012 and on the eighth month anniversary of Zee's passing I was lying on my back feeling very vulnerable as I looked up at the surgical team that, in a few minutes, would literally hold my heart in their hands. Before passing out from the medication Dr. Wallace told me that I was in good hands and asked if I had any questions.

I answered: "No Doc. See you on the other side!"

He laughed and repeated the sentiment.

As was the case during my entire life, the surgery did not go smoothly. During surgery I lost 1300 CCs of blood (about 1 1/2 quarts) and the team had to work frantically to stop the hemorrhaging. Eight hours later I was transported to the recovery room with a repaired aorta and heart valve.

I spent seven days in the hospital recovering and going through cardiac rehabilitation. I was sent home and was scheduled for rehabilitation for the next twelve weeks.

My best friend, neighbor and golfing buddy in Plano was Jim Thompson, also known as JT. He and his wife, Nancy, had committed to care for me and to help me through my recovery. JT moved in with me, treated my wounds, and fed me every day for a couple of weeks.

He escorted me for my first walk outside the second day. My legs and feet were swollen so badly that it appeared I had elephantiasis. After walking about 200 feet I started to pass out from the pain in my legs and JT helped me back to my bed. We decided that a return to the ER was prudent.

X-rays revealed that a significant amount of fluid had built up around my lungs which triggered another procedure called a thoracentesis. The doctor drained 1000 CCs of fluid from my chest cavity giving me immediate relief. I was sent home to continue my recovery.

I improved so rapidly that I did not finish all the rehab sessions but still proudly received my heart surgery rehabilitation graduation T-shirt in the mail.

JT's wife, Nancy, continued to cook me amazing, tasty meals and JT never left my side until I was able to care for myself. There is no way to express gratitude to someone for such compassion and unconditional love and kindness.

CHAPTER 52 - CHRISTMAS AT FIVE GUYS

Having time to process what had happened after Zee's death I had an "Aha!" moment. Zee's sister had not been focused on hurting Zee at all, she had been targeting me and getting her revenge for me coming between them. Her subterfuge and influence over Zee in recent years was the primary cause for Zee drifting away from me long before she took her last breath.

I missed Zee terribly but I was still thankful that we had both been spared another Christmas consumed by her desperate struggle for every breath and constant writhing in pain. I pray that God forgives me for actually praying that he would take her home. The past few years had taken an emotional and physical toll on both of us and even though I had not been alone the past few holiday seasons, I had been very lonely.

***

I had no interest or thought of dating again. I did not believe it was possible that anyone would be interested in an old man, especially when they discovered all about my medical issues and surgeries.

It is said that after the death of a spouse each "first" is a painful hurdle to be conquered. The first birthday, first holiday or first trip without your life partner all have an impact on the grieving process. My first holiday season was approaching quickly and December was a mix of emotions for me.

Chris Koleber, our housekeeper, stood by Zee and me for so many years. Chris became our guardian angel and would stay with Zee to give me a mental health break from taking care of her. After Zee's death Chris stayed on to take care of the domestic duties and had become a trusted caring friend.

Chris and her husband Dennis invited me to dinner for my first solo Christmas day. I did not want to go and actually had decided to call Chris at the last minute to cancel. I even got lost looking for their house and knocking on the door of the wrong address caused me to be uncharacteristically late. When I finally found the correct address, Chris answered the door and warmly welcomed me into their home and quickly introduced me to another dinner guest. Her name was Vikie Jordon, an attractive and charming lady with a warm inviting smile.

I had the feeling that Vikie was thinking the same thing that I was. This is a set up. But I also got the feeling neither of us minded. Her warm and friendly demeanor piqued my interest and I wished to know her better. We were both amazed that we had so many shared interests. At the time I thought that if nothing else came out of it, it had turned out to be a delightful "first" Christmas day.

Vikie

The day after Christmas I called Chris and asked her to contact Vikie to request whether I could have her email and phone number. After calling Vikie, Chris called me back and gave me Vikie's contact information and I called her later that day to ask her out for dinner. I intended to take her to a nice restaurant but had not made dinner reservations. Being married for 32 years left me inexperienced at dating. I had not considered that it was the Christmas holiday and every restaurant would be booked full.

We drove around the Plano area for quite a while which gave us an opportunity to talk and get to know each other better until finally discovering the only place not booked full was the 5 Guys Hamburger restaurant. We shared a double order of fries in a brown paper bag and a couple of great burgers for our first date. I doubted that Vikie was impressed but it did not keep us from dating again.

***

Our courtship was delayed as I went back to the hospital for the 360-degree radical back surgery. My research indicated that this is an extremely dangerous surgery. Regardless and after years of unbearable pain, the risk was worth the reward and I was ready. On February 28, 2012, one year and one day after Zee's death, the anesthesiologist and five surgeons that previously opted out of the risky surgery were now on board with my plan to "git-r-done!" I was a much lower risk now that my aortic aneurism and heart valve were repaired and it was now time for lift off.

The surgery lasted two hours longer than planned and the recovery was lengthy. My doctor told me to expect a least an 18-month recovery and rehab. After the surgery I did follow the weightlifting restrictions to the letter but every other restriction such as walking and going up stairs were pushed to the limit. Partially due to my post heart surgery rehab and extended walking on the treadmill my back muscles were strong and that ultimately shortened my recovery time. Once again, my dear friends JT and Nancy stepped up to the plate and were by my side throughout the first two weeks after surgery. They provided physical and moral support during my critical recovery time. Nancy's cooking was so good that the thought crossed my mind to milk my recovery for a little while longer.

I did not realize at the time that Vikie and Chris had set up a prayer chain for me to petition God to put his healing hands on me and for a successful surgery and a full recovery.

***

In April I was still on a medical leave of absence (MLA) when I received a call from my boss and dear friend Steve Fisher advising me that I had to lay off three employees because NEC was going through a downsizing process. The department was already functioning with a minimum workforce and it would be unrealistic to expect it to maintain its previous standard of excellence while being understaffed. Secondly, I could not bear the thought of how devastating it would be for my young employees and their growing families. One of my employees was dealing with going blind and another was battling several critical medical issues. The thoughts of putting them on the street without medical benefits haunted me and I could not lay them off. I had an epiphany that might save their jobs.

I discussed the situation with Steve and asked him to make Human Resources a counteroffer. If NEC would keep the employees on the payroll in exchange for my job and immediate retirement - then I would retire.

Later that day Steve called and told me that HR had fully accepted the offer and we set a retirement date of June 1, 2012.

On the heels of NEC accepting my offer, Steve made his own generous offer to retire in exchange for not laying off eight employees. Human Resources accepted his offer as well and Steve spoke with two other senior executives about our initiatives to save jobs and they both did the same thing. Ultimately 15 or more employees' jobs were saved at the worthwhile expense of several good leaders and none of us ever regretted our decision.

In my personal life, Vikie's love and support got me through a very painful period as I healed from the emotional and physical trauma of the past year. She is a strong, independent, intelligent Christian woman with a heart of gold. She loves the outdoors, travel, and thrives on new challenges and adventures. I knew I had met a gem and I did not want her to slip away. We were married on June 20, 2012 by Dennis who is a lay preacher with only our closest friends present. My best friends Blain and Linda Sheppard attended through Skype.

CHAPTER 53 – MY POST-TRAUMATIC-STRESS-DISORDER (PTSD) TRIGGER

While we were still in limbo waiting for the outcome of the estate probate, we were beginning our new married life together with a fresh outlook to the future for both of us. Before our wedding plans had been arranged Vikie had planned a trip to see her daughter and two nephews in Coeur D Alene, Idaho (ID) and I had arranged to spend a week with Steve at his lake cabin in Deer Lake, Washington (WA). We decided that even though the plans took us in different directions we would stay on that course. We flew to Spokane, WA together and upon our arrival at Spokane International Airport we were met by my friend Steve and Vikie's daughter. We went our separate ways with the understanding that I would catch up with Vikie at her daughter's home in a week.

I was swept away by the beauty of the state of Washington. It seemed like every new area I ventured into was more beautiful than the last. I called Vikie a day later and told her; "I'm ready to move to Washington." Vikie was happy to hear that because it was closer to her daughter and she loved the Washington state wilderness as much as I did.

As planned, I stayed with Steve to go rainbow trout fishing and to just relax on the boat or the dock at Deer Lake. Steve had other plans for me. From the first day to the last he had me walking on the mountain side trails and roads to build up my strength from the recent surgeries. It was a tough slog walking up on the trails. I do not recall any trails that went downhill and found myself frequently stopping to catch my breath. But slowly and surely with Steve's constant encouragement the walks started to get easier and have a positive effect. I started to enjoy them.

Vikie arrived on the evening of the last day at Deer Lake driving a Dodge RAM pickup truck that she had rented to take me back to her daughter Leslie's home in Coeur d' Alene, ID. I was happy to see Vikie was as enthralled as I was by the beauty of the Deer Lake mountains and the clear water lake. My only regret was that we only spent one day with Steve.

While we were visiting Vikie's daughter we started house hunting and found a piece of paradise near a lake in Idaho but the timing was not right. The unknowns revolving around the estate settlement made it impossible to purchase any property.

***

We still lived in our Texas home and Vikie was longing for a recreational vehicle (RV) trip to Alaska. To me, it seemed daunting. I was not fully recovered from all my surgery and the probate procedures were still pending. But with my neurosurgeon's assurance that I would not negate his handy work while fishing for salmon and one-hundred-pound halibut, I felt more confident about making the trip.

En route to Alaska we took a side trip to explore Washington and to look again for our new home. Our joint goal was to find a cedar-built or log home over 2,000 square feet on timbered acreage.

We finally settled on property that more than met our requirements. It was a 2800 square foot cedar-built home situated on the side of a mountain on 40 acres of heavy pine timber overlooking the valley surrounding Springdale, WA. The beauty of the property took our breath away and the home was exactly what we both dreamed of. It was owned by a realtor named Kathy and the bonus was that Kathy also owned 80 acres of virgin pine timberland adjacent to the 40 acres and she offered to hold a seller-carried loan on the 80 acres. I was already picking out a place for my tree stands and imagining many beautiful days of hunting elk, deer, bear, and moose on my own property.

We made an offer and it was accepted on contingency based on selling our Plano home and arranged to purchase the additional 80 acres on a personal loan. Before leaving for Alaska, we called a realtor in Plano, TX and put our home on the market before continuing our Alaskan RV trip.

***

Three months later we returned to Plano to discover that the house had not been shown. I had documented the real estate value in the property listing for Zee's Probate but the executrix, Zee's sister, insisted that I had greatly underestimated the real estate value. She presented me with a court order from the Probate Court ordering me to obtain a new appraisal to be done by an appraiser of her choice at my expense. I reluctantly paid for another appraisal and the appraiser supported my initial appraisal price.

Every financial and material asset that was held jointly prior to Zee's passing was frozen until the probate process was concluded. The executrix reminded me often that she intended to stretch the probate process out for the full three years allowed by Texas law to maximize the value of my home and gain the greatest possible price at closing. When I tried to challenge that decision, she made it clear to me that whatever anxiety or inconvenience that the three years may cause me was none of her concern.

I had a personal life insurance policy for $75,000 that was in effect before Zee and I married and I had made Zee the beneficiary. Since there was no need to continue it and my assets were tied up in probate, I cashed it out for $7,500 and used it to pay for funeral expenses.

The Executrix told me that I had no authority to use estate money to pay for the funeral without her approval and she directed her lawyer to have the Probate Court order me to repay the money to the estate. He in turn told her that she was going too far with that request and refused to comply.

She attempted to pillage my 401Ks but the retirement funds were spared because of IRS rules and regulations. Then under the guise of a court order she came into my home and appropriated treasured gifts that I had given Zee over the years including jewelry and many of Zee's other personal effects. Her claim on the final probate property listing was that the booty she retrieved was worth about 10% of its actual value.

Everything I owned was fair game including a small annuity from my two-year stint at Citizens Communications, 50% of my home value and household goods, a 60-acre farm that Zee and I had purchased, half of all our checking and savings accounts and half of the previous year's federal tax refund that I received shortly after Zee's passing.

Besides forfeiting half of everything that Zee and I had built together for 31 years, my personal legal fees as the surviving spouse exceeded $40,000 and I had to sell several personal items to settle the estate. My savings account was wiped out with one settlement check.

Jeff, Zee's youngest son, offered to sign his inheritance check back over to me. It was a wonderful and generous offer but I asked him to apply it to his son's college education fund.

After the probate was settled, the executrix sent me a birthday card telling me how much she loved me.

***

A few months after the estate was settled, we successfully sold the house for our asking price and Vikie and I sold almost everything we owned through an estate sale for about ten cents on the dollar.

As painful as that small check was - I was done! We left Texas and never looked back.

***

After settling into our new mountain home my PSA levels reached a point where I could not ignore the reality that cancer had raised its ugly head and I had prostatectomy surgery. I have now reached the five-year cancer free mark.

***

To Vikie's dismay and concern after we had settled into our new calmer lifestyle, without warning I began to explode into unexplainable anger, grief, fear, depression, and feelings of deep loss that had no connection to our life together. I will never really know what triggered these deep emotions but I was wracked by vivid visions of the repressed horrors of war. Nightmares, and flashbacks of combat events began to take control of my life. My mind had hit a brick wall and I had nowhere to turn.

Through the VA I was tested for PTSD related to my military service and I entered the VA 12-week PTSD management program. Since completing the intense program, I can now recognize the triggers that cause the flashbacks and nightmares. (There is more information about PTSD and how to get help in a supplemental chapter at the end of this book.)

CHAPTER 54 – DOES THIS MEAN THAT I CAN GET A NEW CAR?

October 1, 2013, we moved into our mountain house and spent our first fall and winter making the house our home. Living on top of a mountain afforded us the most magnificent view imaginable but it also had its challenges. Our one-mile road leading to our mountainside home required plowing whenever we had more than two inches of snow so we decided to trade Vikie's car in for a four-wheel drive vehicle.

When the calendar page flipped to March. we decided to venture out on a quest to search for a Jeep to replace Vikie's 2013 GMC Terrain. The nearest car dealership was in Spokane about an hour drive from our mountain paradise. We made plans to head out at zero dark thirty AM one Wednesday morning to take full advantage of spending as much time in town as possible. To get to the main road we needed to drive down our very steep one-mile-long serpentine road.

Warmer weather had melted the ice and snow and turned the road to slush a few days before our planned excursion. The GMC Terrain was garaged and protected from the elements so when we headed out for the day, we were unaware that a freezing rain had solidified the previously melted snow on our road.

Since it was Vikie's car she volunteered to drive. Unmindful of the freezing rain that had frozen our driveway the night before, we approached the first and steepest downhill slope. That downhill section is always in the shadow of massive pine trees, leaving that 25% of the road a sheet of ice suitable for an Olympic bobsled run and now it was camouflaged with a deceivingly thin layer slush.

As we started down the hill it became immediately apparent that we were in trouble and I advised Vikie not to hit the brakes to prevent the car from skidding on the ice. Not using the brakes caused us to pick up speed as we coasted down the steep ice-covered hillside. Despite Vikie's excellent driving skills our speed continued to accelerate and the situation became unmanageable.

The right front tire hit a snowbank and the right rear tire left the road causing the car to skid into an uncontrollable roll. After the second roll I started counting as I listened to the sound of twisting metal, cracking tree branches, and the loud thumping that occurred with every roll sending us down the embankment like a slinky toy going down a set of stairs. We tumbled into the unknown and I kept reassuring Vikie that it was going to be OK. Suddenly the car landed upside down and slammed against three huge pine trees causing twelve of the thirteen airbags to deploy simultaneously while windshield and three of the side door window glass panes exploded. That was followed by an eerie stillness and soft hum of the running car engine.

I felt some pain in my shoulder but I did not seem to have any other injuries. Sometime during the crash and subsequent rolls Vikie lost consciousness for a few minutes. I had a sense of foreboding as I hung helplessly upside down from my seatbelt and watched Vikie dangling upside down beside me as lifeless as an abandoned rag doll. When she finally regained consciousness, she gingerly smacked her bloody swelling lips and rubbed her tongue over her gums where her front teeth had been just moments before. "Hmm…I guess this means that I will get a new car, huh?" she said with a toothless lisp. I breathed a sigh of relief. She was OK. Simultaneously we both thanked God out loud for saving us.

We hung upside down in the dark for a few minutes while processing what had just happened and wondering what to do next. Vikie's panicked voice broke the silence, "I smell smoke!" She somehow managed to reach the ignition key and cut the engine. The humming stopped, creating a foreboding quiet.

We hung upside down trapped in our seats waiting for the fire but it never came. I finally managed to reach my seatbelt release and dropped to the ceiling with a painful thud and then searched for an escape route. All the windows and doors were pinned either against the ground or against the three trees where the car was imbedded.

I found one intact window next to the back-seat passenger side and crawled across the ceiling, which was now the floor. I tried in vain to break the glass with a large hunting knife and several kicks. Frustrated with my failure and acutely aware that Vikie was still tethered upside-down to her seatbelt in pain.

I crawled back to the front seat and studied her situation trying to figure out how to free her from her seatbelt without causing her more injuries. Her thighs were supported by the bottom of the steering wheel and blood was pouring from her head onto the car's ceiling. I started to panic as I imagined the worst for her condition.

I crawled under her body and raised her as high as possible before releasing her seat belt. She fell relatively gently into my arms and we just hugged and cried while thanking the Lord. The reality remained that we were stilled trapped and I began verbally beating myself up over not being able to rescue Vikie from the dangerous situation. Vikie's calm demeanor put everything in perspective. She was sure God would provide a way for us to get out of the car safely and that was enough for me to get my act together again.

Because of the heavy underbrush we knew that there was no way anyone would see where we had exited the road and our car was too far down the embankment to be noticed by someone passing. It was Wednesday morning and no one that we knew would expect to hear from us until Saturday. The thought that we could freeze to death occurred to both of us and I said, "I guess that this may be the end for us." With that thought we crawled onto the back-seat passenger ceiling and together we made several attempts to free ourselves from the car. We finally gave up exhausted and sat holding each other's hands, feeling defeated and helpless to save ourselves.

As we sat there comforting each other I could sense that Vikie was praying. Suddenly, without human intervention, the rear hatch door opened and the sunlight shone into the car. It was as if a direct message from God said, "Come this way! It is not time for either of you to leave this physical world."

As we exited the car and looked past the trees that were holding the car in place, we saw nothing else beyond them that could have stopped us from plunging to our death. God and the well-built GM car that He had provided us had protected us from being crushed. Neither of us doubted the presence of God during the entire event.

The impact of the exploding steering wheel airbag had hurt Vikie badly. Her nose was broken, her right eye was bleeding and damaged, three of her top front teeth were missing, her right leg was hurting, and blood was dripping from her scalp soaking her hair with blood. A tree branch had penetrated the windshield and struck her on the right side of her hairline and broke off causing her to bleed profusely. I must have had a premonition because I still had half my wits about me to quickly photograph Vikie's injuries, the crash scene and the damaged vehicle for insurance and historical documentation.

I knew that no one would believe what happened without proof. Why would they? Heck, I still did not believe it myself.

GMC Terrain Could Not Be Seen From the Road Above

We had to climb several hundred feet back up the hill to the road and Vikie was my inspiration as she fought her way up the hill in two-foot-deep snow and climbed through heavy brush while in severe pain. There was no way she was going to allow me to go to the house to get help or call an ambulance without her.

Then we walked and crawled another quarter of a mile on the icy slushy road to the house. After slipping and sliding all the way back to the house we took an inventory of our injuries. I escaped almost unscathed, but Vikie was severely injured.

We knew that any help or ambulance could not come up the steep icy road, so we decided to go to the house and get the truck with the mounted snowplow to go to the hospital. Vikie was reticent. She did not want to get into another vehicle and drive down that icy road again. She insisted on walking down and having me meet her at the bottom of the hill. She hesitantly changed her mind after I promised her that I would put chains on the tires and drop the snowplow onto the road and drive as slowly as possible. The plow would prevent the truck from sliding or increasing speed during the descent.

We traversed the icy slushy obstacle course safely and headed directly to the Spokane hospital an hour away. I intended to drop her off at the ER and then park the truck, but Vikie would have none of that. She insisted on going with me to park the truck and then walk into the Providence Holy Family Hospital ER together.

I parked the truck and accompanied her on a very painful walk to the ER. The waiting room was standing room only. All the chatter stopped when we limped through the door with Vikie covered in blood-soaked clothing, blood matted hair and severely swollen bruises on her face.

I stated loudly enough for everyone to hear, "Help! We just had a major roll-over car accident and we need help!" The admitting nurses jumped out of their seats to take care of Vikie and whisked her away leaving me standing in the entryway alone.

The triage nurse stomped back into the waiting room and glowered at me and pointing towards a now available waiting room chair. "You! Go sit down over there and wait!" Puzzled by her attitude I followed her orders and sat in the waiting room for about thirty minutes. I tried to ignore all the stares being direct towards me and I was beginning to think that I had grown horns and a forked tail. It had not yet occurred to me that the general impression by everyone present was that I had beaten my wife.

I approached the nurse, "Excuse me but why can't I be with my wife?" I was startled when nurse stiffened and flashed me a suspicious frown and rudely answered my question. "You can't see her right now, so sit down and wait!" I was so distraught over Vikie that until that moment I had not considered that they may think this was a domestic abuse case. For all I knew they may have already called the police.

"No! I will not sit down. Do you think that I hurt her? I assure you that I did not beat her. We had a car accident and I have pictures to prove it." I showed the nurse the pictures and still suspicious she said sternly "Well, you certainly don't appear to be injured so you'll have to wait your turn."

It was just too much to take. "No, I insist on being with my wife!".

Another nurse heard the confrontation and came to me "Sir, may I see the pictures?"

I gladly showed her the pictures and she proceeded to do a triage on my condition and confirmed that I did have a shoulder injury. She told me to follow her and she took me to visit with Vikie and then took me to a separate exam room for a medical evaluation and X-rays.

Finally, at 4 PM and after determining that Vikie's injuries were not the result of spousal abuse we were released to go home. Vikie did not want to go back up the hill but reached deep down inside herself to get the courage to make it home after I installed the tire chains and took a slow and easy drive back up the driveway to our house.

Life continues to be an adventure but we are traveling it together.

EPILOGUE

We are comfortably settled into our new life. Elk, cougar, deer, bear, and several other types of God's creatures wander our property. Vikie takes immense pleasure in taking care of her chickens, ducks, and spoiling her feral cats and K9 friends and family. We never grow tired of taking walks, scavenging for morel and other edible mushrooms. Our two children Sassie and Skye (dogs) thrive in the environment made to order for them.

Vikie's diverse skills and talents keep me surprised every day. She is an extremely talented artist and seamstress, and an excellent cook as demonstrated in my growing gut. I cannot help but admire her pioneer spirit and she has been my strength through the tough and emotional moments that may strike me without warning. She draws her strength from her Christian faith and serves as a Deaconess in our local church.

Life refuses to follow a straight line and soon after Vikie and I were married it became obvious that I could no longer ignore my residual medical problems. My PSA numbers were still rising and I finally conceded to a prostate biopsy. The final diagnosis confirmed that it was cancer related to my exposure to Agent Orange (AO) in Vietnam.

My options were to either monitor the progression and wait or have a proctectomy. Since Russian roulette is not my style I opted for removal. Of course, my recovery from surgery was challenging. A clip had been left behind and migrated into my bladder and caused several urinary infections but now I can thankfully say that is all behind us and I am five years cancer free.

Creativity and keeping busy seem to help ease the PTSD symptoms and although I do not have the artistic ability that Vikie has, I have been successful at redirecting my mind to more positive ends. Now in my seventh decade of life I am learning to play the guitar and escape also comes through my metal art, hunting, fishing, and counseling other veterans. Donating my metal art to disabled veterans and service organizations such as fire and police departments give me a sense of purpose and peace that escaped me for many years.

I am reminded everyday of losing WK but God blessed me with three beautiful grandchildren Kali, Carlie, and Tyler. They are still living in Illinois and we stay in touch regularly. WK's fiancée at the time of his tragic death remarried and has done an excellent job raising their children. Her efforts to raise Carlie and Tyler resulted in loving, caring, mature, responsible young adults and Kali is still finding her way. I have no doubt that my son Wim looks down over them with pride every moment of every day. I look forward to the day when WK, Roy and I once again sit on the riverbank to catch King Bass.

My sister Jane lost her battle with several debilitating medical problems leaving behind a husband and three children. My brother Jim is still running the Karate schools and enjoying his passion for music. Roy's son and daughters are grown with children of their own and my prayer is that this book will give them some insight about their roots and who their father was.

I was told that my running partner, parachute jumping pal, and roommate, Ken Ritter was killed in a car accident in Detroit. The loss left a huge hole in my heart. But I have reconnected with my old friend Ken again. He is indeed alive and well. He and his beautiful wife Kathy live in Deland, FL. As long as God and life are willing, I look forward to the day in the near future to visit Ken and give him a huge, but manly, hug.

Blain, my Vietnam and Air Force brother is doing well and he and his wife Linda share at least one vacation a year. We enjoyed an Alaskan cruise and recently an eight-day Rhein River cruise ending in Amsterdam, Holland. We were able to visit my sister Maya (Dad and Stepmother Peggy's daughter) as well as my Aunt Connie and Uncle Ben (Mom's brother) and several cousins living in De Haag, Holland. It was very special for me that Vikie had an opportunity to meet them and visit some of my childhood memories.

During a reunion with Blain, I learned that Blain was never awarded the Purple Heart (PH) for the injuries he sustained from shrapnel wounds during a rocket attack in Vietnam. On his behalf I submitted a PH nomination to the Air Force including pictures of Blain showing the wounds he received during the enemy attack. "If you don't ask -you don't get."

It has been one year since I initiated the request and the Air Force recently contacted me requesting additional information. It is a frustrating uphill battle but my hope is that the Air Force Award Review Board will do the right thing.

We never found out what happened to the children that we befriended and cared for during our service at DakTo. I pray that they survived the war, married, and have children of their own and that they share stories with about Americans who they befriended. One of my bucket-list items is to return to DakTo to find them one day.

Vikie and were shopping for RV supplies at our dealership in Post Falls, WA when I saw an elderly man on crutches and wearing a Vietnam Veteran hat. Whenever I recognize any veteran regardless of service branch, I approach them with my extended hand and thank them for their service and say, "Welcome home."

As in this case after shaking his hand I asked, "When and where did you serve in Vietnam"?

"Da Nang 1967 - 1968."

"So was I. What was your specialty?"

"I was the fire department Chief,"

"Were you there when the A-6 Intruder collided with the C-141A on the runway?

"Yes, I was because it was carrying explosive materials and we were standing by with fire equipment when the collision occurred."

"So was I as the Air Freight Specialist responsible for inventorying the cargo load and offloading the aircraft. I saw the impact and the horrible fiery explosion. I was in shock and unable to move to avoid all the shrapnel when suddenly someone tackled me to the ground and covered my body. He helped me up and got me into one of the aircraft revetments."

He nodded and grinned, "That was me and I remember it like it was yesterday."

I thanked him profusely as we shook hands again and he and his wife left the store.

Recently I received word from the C-17 Weapons School that they created an award for the Loadmaster School's honor graduates. The award is titled, "CMSGT Wim Wetzel Honor Graduate Award" in recognition of my work as a Loadmaster during my Air Force career. It was an unexpected honor considering that I had worked with so many people who are highly qualified and worthy to receive that recognition.

Penny's sister Charlene is well past her training bra stage and is now a grandmother of three boys. She received a friend request on Facebook from my brother Jim and cautious about friending just anyone, Charlene asked Jim if he was Wim's Wetzel's brother.

Jim told her that he was and provided Char with the contact information she needed to reach out to me. Charlene asked my permission to tell Penny that she had found me and asked me if I would like to reconnect with her. I was hesitant to reconnect with Penny because I wanted to be sensitive to how it may make Vikie feel but I hesitantly gave Charlene the OK.

About a month later I received a nice letter from Penny that detailed what had happened during her life since we parted over 50 years ago. The long letter served to catch me up on her life's journey in the medical field and her fifty years of marriage to her husband, Bob, a genuinely nice and successful Air Force veteran. We arranged to meet them and Mike and Donna Black during a scheduled trip to Beaver, Pennsylvania in the fall of 2018 and shared a wonderful visit to Niagara Falls. It seemed that the many years since we last saw one another just disappeared like water under the bridge of time.

In the winter years of my life, I have been blessed with a wonderful wife and the best friend from my youth. Vikie and Penny are now friends and Penny's husband Bob has become a cherished friend. Vikie came into the winter of my life, bringing me hope for the future and Penny saw me through the troubled teen years catapulting me into adulthood.

I am extremely blessed by the turn of events in my life and being a participant in a circle of life that only God could have orchestrated.

ROY'S ACTUAL DEFENSE TESTIMONY FROM HIS TRIAL

The following is the actual defense witness transcript from Roy's murder trial. Whenever a defendant is acquitted in a trial in Pennsylvania the entire transcript is destroyed with the exception of the defendant's testimony. This is Roy's entire testimony exactly as copied from that document to include misspellings and grammatical errors.

OFFICIAL STENOGRAPHERS COURT HOUSE, BEAVER, PA. 15009

A - I was stationed in Guba, United States, and Vietnam.

Q - Were you in combat in Vietnam?

A -Yes.

Q - Is it true you were injured in the war?

A - Yes.

Q - How many times?

A - Three times that I got Purple Hearts for a couple other minor injuries.

Q - How many brothers and/or sisters do you have?

- I have not two brothers and two sisters.

Q - Your mother's first name?

A - Gerri.

Q - What was your father's name?

A - Willy.

Q - I would like, first of all, to direct your attention to the date of March 16th of this year. Were you in the company of your father, Willy Wetzel, on that day?

A - Yes, I was.

Q - What was the earliest time that day that you and he were in each other's company?

A - My earliest recollection is about 1:00 o'clock.

Q - And, where were you first in each other's company?

A - At the school in Beaver Falls.

Q - For what purpose, if any, had Willy Wetzel come to the Beaver Falls school?

A - I don't know.

Q - Was it customary for him to appear at the school on Sundays?

A - Yes.

Q - How many days a week is the Beaver Falls school operating?

A - It's three days a week we hold classes.

Q - What days are those classes held?

A - Tuesday, Wednesday, and Sunday.

Q - Had Willy Wetzel been coming to the school on any of those weekdays?

A - No.

Q - And, why not? Or is there a reason perhaps why not?

A - He never came during the week. He worked. He had a job at Westinghouse.

Q - Now, what time had you gone to the Beaver Falls school on that particular date of March 16th?

A - I believe it was -- I think I got there at quarter after ten in the morning.

Q - And, what was your reason for being at the school that day?

A - Instruction.

Q - Once your father arrived at the school, did you and he have any conversation with each other?

A - Very little.

Q - Do you recall what little conversation you had was about?

A - I cannot recall too much, because I am in the habit, and so is the rest of my family, and anybody knows when he starts talking, you kind of disregard it because it is the same thing over and over and over.

Q - What was the nature of that talk, even if you don't recall the details?

A - He talked about his two children to his second wife. That was the main gist of the conversation that I remember.

Q - Did you make any statements to him in response to his complaints about his two children to his second wife?

A - Yes. Well, to begin with, he had maintained all along they were not his children to begin with. And he could not understand why, since he was separated, that he had to pay support for the kids that were not even his. And he said he was going to work on the kids to get back at Peggy. I remember saying, "Don't you realize what you are doing to those children?" One of them has been to Mental Health Clinic. He is under nerve medication. He came out flatly and said, "I don't care, just as long as I get back at that bitch. I am going to get her." That is all I can recall stating to him. I said, "Don't you realize what you are doing to those kids?" We went through the same thing.

Q - As best you recall, how long did he remain at the school that particular Sunday?

A - That particular day he stayed until; I believe it was about 4:30.

Q - Was that customary once he came to the school on a Sunday, to stay that long?

A - No. He usually made an appearance, then he left. Sometimes he would not come at all. It was hard to say when he would come and when he would not.

Q - Did he make any efforts that day to supervise or instruct any classes?

A - No.

Q - And, had he been making any efforts on a regular basis say in the last year, to supervise or instruct classes.

A - No.

Q - Whenever he left the school that Sunday, were you aware of his leaving?

A - Yes, I saw him leave. I saw him go out the door. I do not know whether he left right then or not. I just saw him go out the office door.

Q - Close to the time he left, did he say anything to you?

A - No, he did not say goodbye or anything, no.

Q - Well, was there anything unusual that occurred in the normal course of events at the school that day?

A - No, sir, not that I can recall.

Q - What time did you leave the school?

A - I left -- I believe it was about close to 5:00 o'clock.

Q - And, where did you go after you left the Beaver Falls school?

A - Went to my home.

Q - Once you arrived home, what did you do? How long were you at home?

A - Long enough to come home, take a shower, change my clothes, and I took my fiancée out to Arthur Treacher' and had supper.

Q - Arthur Treacher's?

A - That's up by the Mall.

Q - Did you two have your dinner at Arthur Treacher's?

A - Yes, we did.

Q - Do you have any recollection of approximately what time you returned home after you and your fiancée had your dinner at Arthur Treacher's?

A - It is hard to pinpoint because I was not keeping track of the time.

Q - Approximately?

A - I would say we got there at 6:00 o'clock, maybe, I do not know. And we ate. I told her, that is my fiancée, I was going to do some work at home, if she wanted to go some place, go ahead, and go. She said she would go down to her mother's house and go out to a movie; I think at Gee Bee's.

Q - And, what work was it you wanted to do at home?

A - I was working on some distribution figures for the magazine.

Q - Were there any tax papers that you worked on that day?

A - That I worked on?

Q - Yes?

A - No.

Q - Now, once you were home, after having dinner with your fiancée, did you remain home the rest of that evening?

A - No, I did not. I went down and got my little girl.

Q - MARSHALL: yelled I am sorry; I did not hear that. He smiled pleasantly at Roy.

Q - How old is your daughter? Four years old.

A - West Bridgewater. That is where my ex-wife lives. And where did you have to go to get your daughter?

Q - And, for what reason did you go to get your four-year-old daughter?

A - She had called me and she was crying. She was upset. And I talked to her mother. She said talk to this kid I cannot handle her. So, the baby was upset. I told her I would keep her overnight.

Q - Had you been, from time to time on a regular basis, exercising visitation rights with your daughter?

A - Yes, I got her regularly. I would pick her up on Thursday, about noon. I would take her out to breakfast and keep her all that time, keep her overnight, and bring her back late that next day. So, I would keep her about two days a week.

Q - After you arrived back home with your daughter, did you have any phone conversation with anyone?

A - I think right after I put the baby to bed, yes. And who was that conversation with?

A - Back up. I think there were two conversations. I had a call from my sister and I had a call from my fiancée

Q - Which call was first?

A - I think my sister's was.

Q - And by your sister, you are referring to Jane Bojanic?

A - Yes.

Q - What was that call about?

MR. MARSHALL: May I ask what the materiality and relevance is of these phone conversations prior to the event?

MR. JAMES: We will attempt to show the materiality, Your Honor. They have a bearing upon Willy Wetzel.

THE COURT: You may proceed.

MR. JAMES: Thank you.

BY MR. JAMES:

Q - Would you tell us what the first phone call to you was about?

A - I got a call from my sister saying that my dad talked to her, tried to get her to pay his bills following the morning he come to the school with a stack of bill I gave him money. He said something about his car not working properly. He asked my sister and she had no car that ran. So, he then asked, as far as I can recall, he asked her what my mother's phone number was She asked me if she could give it to him. I said no, under no circumstances, because she had been harassed enough. He would arrive about 3:00 or 4:00 o'clock in the morning and rap on her door.

Q - Did your sister say anything to you about how Willy was acting or talking on the phone?

A - She told me, she said, be careful, he is acting real strange. She said, "I'm scared."

Q - Now, when did the second call come with relationship to the first? In other words, how far apart?

A - A couple hours. I would say a couple hours.

Q - A - nd, who made the second call to you?

A - My fiancée.

Q - And was that call just an ordinary call?

A - Yes, it was an ordinary call. She called me saying she had come home from the show.

MR. MARSHALL: Your Honor, again I object.

THE COURT: The objection is sustained.

MR. JAMES: All right.

BY MR. JAMES:

Q - Now, after you received the phone calls, were you still working on the papers that you talked about?

A - No, I was not actually working. I was kind of fiddling, because at that point I had just got done putting the baby to bed. We were playing games.

Q - Did you, that evening, have a visitor at your apartment? Did someone come to your apartment?

A - Yes, my father came.

Q - Approximately, as best you recall, what time was that?

A - It was after the phone call somewhere. I would say between quarter after ten, 10:30, somewhere around there. I really do not know. I was not keeping track of the time.

Q - How did you become aware of your father's presence at your apartment? How did you know he was there?

A - I was sitting in the dining area and I heard the door rattle. And I knew who it was immediately, because my father, he does not knock-on doors, he just opens them up. And I had gotten to the point where, if I knew he was coming, I would make a point not to be there. And all the rest of my family did the same thing.

Q - Did you have any idea he was coming up that particular evening?

A - No, sir, I did not.

Q - What did you do once you heard the doorknob rattling?

A - I got up because I knew who it was. And I turned on the porch light and I held the door and I let him in.

Q - Once he entered the apartment, was there any conversation between you two?

A - Not immediately. He walked in the door. He looked at me and he sat down on the couch in the corner, towards the wall where the drapes are. And he sat down. He started going to sleep. It is a habit of his. He would come to people's house. He would sit there, not say a word, and just kind of konk out to 3:00 or 4:00 o'clock in the morning. You would wake him up. He would go home.

Q - After he sat there a while, did he say anything to you?

A - When he first sat down, I asked if he would like a cup of coffee, or something, to drink. He said no. He sat back. He was rubbing his face. He said he was tired. He said no, no.

Q - After that happened, what next happened?

A - Well, during the conversation, I can recall him relating the same thing he had done at the school, about his children. And there would be no use in this country, he was going back to Indonesia. 'I said, "You cannot go back. If you go back, you will go to prison.

Q - Now, eventually what occurred with regard to your father's Income Tax papers?

A - He asked me if they were done. I said, "Yes, they are done. All you have to do is give me the name. He owns stock -- "and I need the name to fill out the back. Other than that, it's done." And I said, "Do you need it?" He said, "Yes, I want it." So, he said "Where is it?" I pointed at the table. He walked up. He sat down at the table.

Q - What did he do once he sat down at the table?

A - Well, he picked the form up and started looking at them. And he said, "I can't read this." He did not have his glasses. And my glasses were laying on the table there. And he said, "Let me see your glasses." I handed him my glasses, which he put on. He said, "I still can't see." He started looking around. He said, "Whose are those?" He was referring to the 6tagere, that is the room divider. He picked up the glasses. I said, "These are Jim's glasses." They are different than mine. They are round. He picked them up and put them on. He said, "This is a little better I can make it out now." He put the glasses down. He just sat there. He paused momentarily. I do not know how long. I said, "Do you want a pen?" He said, "Yes." So, I handed him a pen. And again, he paused for a couple seconds. He then started to sign. He signed -- I am quite sure he signed his first name. Again, he paused. And he started to sign the rest of his name. I think I said at the Preliminary Hearing, I do not know whether he ever finished signing his name or not. I do not know how he did it. He started the signing. He kind of raised his pen across the paper. He signed and went like that (indicating), and he threw the pen against the drapes in the dining room there. He took the Income Tax form, balled them up, and made a statement, you know, "Fuck it. Fuck this country," and he balled it up, threw it on the table and started to get up and walk away. At this point I did not say anything. I do not even remember. The only thing I said to him, "Do you want a pen?"

Q - Now, when he started to walk away, in what direction was he walking?

A - He walked out towards the front door.

Q - And when he was in the process of walking toward the front door, what did you do?

A - I followed him out. I was going to open the door for him.

Q - Would you tell us in what manner he walked from the kitchen area to the front door?

A - What manner? He walks extremely slow, like hunched over, like he was real exhausted or tired.

Q - Once he reached the front door, what happened?

A - He reached down -- Well, with his left hand, dropped right in front of the door, I would say six inches to a foot from the front door, he reached with his left hand and put it on the doorknob. He paused. He looked over at the Hawaiian sword, the one that is in the case down there. I had it propped up in the corner. And he looked at it. I did not think anything of it. He has picked it up before and played with it, told me it was nice. And he picked it up, turned around, and he had his head down. I could not see his face.

Q - Now, when he turned around, would his body be facing or be away from you?

A - Facing me. The sword was close enough, he was about a foot from the door, where he was, he just reached out and grabbed it and turned around and started looking at it.

Q - You say when he turned around, you could not see his face? Why?

A - He was looking at the sword. I think he was. He had his head down.

Q - What next do you recall?

A - Again he started mumbling. He said, "I'm going to lose my house, my car, everything I have got." He said, "This is it." He then lifted up his head and his eyes just literally bulged out of his head. They both bulged. He let out a scream.

Q - What kind of scream?

A - It is like a war cry, a battle cry. It is called a kea.

Q - Can you demonstrate that scream for us?

A - Not the way he did it. No way.

Q - What happened after he let out the scream?

A - I said, "Dad, what are you doing?" He started to pull out the sword. When I saw his face, then I knew what he was doing.

Q - What was he doing, in your mind?

A - In my mind he was going to do what he always told us, as long as I can remember.

Q - What was that?

A - He was going to start his thing and finish it.

Q - His what?

A - His thing.
Q - What do you mean by "his thing"?

A - As long as I can remember, all he ever talked about, if anything did not go right, he was going to take care of everyone in his family and he was going to go, but he was not going to go alone.

Q - At that point, when you saw him beginning to remove the sword from its case, what did you do?

A - I reached out and grabbed the end where he had it on the handle, and I grabbed it in the middle of the sheath.

Q - And how did you grab that, with one or two hands?

A - Two hands. I reached out like that (indicating), so he could not pull the sword out. He already had it out I would say, about six or eight inches.

Q - After you grabbed that sword in the manner you testified to, what happened with the sword, as concern you and Willy?

A - I was trying to keep him from pulling it all the way out. That sword, it is a good weapon. And he struggled against me and I had him pushed up against the door.

Q - What happened to the sword, or the condition of the sword, as a result of that struggle?

A - Well, during the struggle I saw his leg coming up to kick. He tried to kick me in the groin. I, out of reflex, turned sideways, and he hit me, and the force of the kick, I held onto the sword for dear life, and -- because I knew if I let go, it was all over. I knew that for a fact. He kicked, and the force of the kick, and my holding onto it, and my body, with it going back, bent the sword almost in half.

Q - This Exhibit K, is that what you are referring to as the sword on that occasion?

A - Yes, sir." The prosecution never presented the weapon, as evidence in their case, the defense did.

Q - What happened after he tried the karate kick on you and the sword bending? recall?

A - I used the momentum of

Q - What is the next thing you.

A - The kick. I used his force against him. That is a basic principle of karate.

Q - How did you use his force against him?

A - It was the force of his kick pushing him forward to me and it bent my body back, and the front of my body forward, and I just -- I let go with the hand I was holding the sheath with. I held onto the other hand, and I hit him with a punch.

Q - Where, on what portion of the body did your punch land.

A - Above one of his eyes. I tried to hit him in the temple.

Q - And, as a result of that punch, what occurred to Willy at that time?

A - Well, I followed up with a combination. I hit him two more. times; hit him with a right and left and right. And, what happened to him as a result of those blows?

A - He fell back against the door, slid down into the corner where the easy chair was, the black easy chair, and where the register is.

Q - After that happened, what did you do next?

A - I just looked at him because he laid there. I thought he was unconscious. And I turned around and I started walking towards the telephone --

Q - For what purpose?

A - which was in the dining room on the wall. I was going to call somebody. I was going to call the police.

Q - While you were going to the telephone, what happened?

A - I started to walk away. I got about almost out to where the room divider is, where the etagere is, and I heard him crawling. And I saw him on his hands and knees, and he was trying to reach the same sword. And he had his hand on it. And I could not reach him in time to stop him from pulling it out. So, I kicked him in the ribs.

Q - After you kicked him, what happened to him?

A - Well, he straightened up on his knees. In other words, he was on all fours. When I kicked him in the ribs, I straightened him up. He was almost straight. And I hit him again with one blow.

Q - And, then what happened to him as a result of that blow?

A - Well, actually, he was on his knees, and the force of the blow, it just literally -- It threw him back real hard and he hit again against the wall where the register was.

Q - What were you attempting to do to him by the blows you had thrown up to that point?

A - I was trying to knock him unconscious.

Q - Now, what happened after that sequence of events?

A - Well, he laid here again. I do not know how long he laid there again. I started to get up to go towards the telephone.

Q - What happened then?

A - I got -- This time I got to the phone. I started dialing the number. I could not clear my mind enough, you know, what had happened, to come to some kind of conscious conclusion of what number to call. So, I was going to go -- I looked at the telephone. I started dialing. I did not know who I was calling. So, I went to reach for the telephone book, and I heard him again. He was starting to get on his hands and knees. He screamed, "Son-of-a-bitch, you broke my ribs," and he started to come at me again.

Q - And, what was he doing on this occasion where he started after you again?

A - Well, he got up and he started to stagger. I think he was still woozy from the blows. He started coming at me. And his leg hit the corner of the glass table that is in the living room, and he reached down and grabbed his leg. And he grabbed -- He kind of walked in front of the table and he flipped up the glass and just threw it completely over, flipped it over.

Q - What glass would that be, the glass on top of the table?

A - Right, the glass on top of the table.

Q - All right. Then what next happened?

A - He lost his balance. He reached down and grabbed for support. The base for that is aluminum, chrome covered. And he picked up the aluminum thing, and I had backed away into the division between the dining room and the living room. And he threw this at me. I ducked out of the way. It hit the corner, the corner of the table hit my leg and my ankle.

Q - Did it injure your ankle at all?

A - Yes, it had a bad bruise there.

Q - What happened after he threw the bottom portion of the coffee table at you?

A - Okay. He started to stagger backwards, and I saw him looking around for something to grab. And he looked over at the television set, and I keep two swords the They are demonstration swords. I collect weapons. And I knew what he was going to do. So, I reached over. I ran over to the T.V. I tried to grab the sword he had his hands on, but it was too late. I grabbed hold of the sheath, but he already had the sword pulled out of it.

Q - Now, when you say you grabbed a hold of the sheath, are you referring to Defendant's Exhibit M?

A - Yes, supports.

Q - Of what?

A - Of the etagere. That is the room divider. It is the same thing.

Q - And, what is that room divider made of?

A - Steel.

Q - And, what are the shelves made of?

A - Glass.

Q - After the episode of him swinging the second sword at you, what did you do?

A - All I can remember, it sticks out vividly in my mind, I pulled this thing in front of me, I would say a portion of the way. He swung the sword. The sword bent around' that portion. All I did -- He lost his balance. I remember it going through my mind, I thought, "Good God, if he got me, he would have cut my head off with that thing."

Q - Do you remember what he next did?

A - Yes. He tripped over something. I think it might have been the rocking chair because it sits right in the corner. He lost his balance. I grabbed him. He was wearing a heavy aviator-type coat. I grabbed him by one of his hands. I threw him down in front of me. He tripped and fell into the kitchen area.

Q - Did he stay on the floor of the kitchen any length of time?

A - No. When he fell, ho fell and he kind of twisted around, like a top, and he landed on all fours.

Q - What did he do at that time?

A - Well, at that time, like I said, I was in a total panic. I started to look around for something, because I tried to stop him just by holding him and that did not do it. I tried to hit him. That did not stop him. I tried to kick him. That did not stop him. I have three or four sets of those sticks. I had them in the corner on the baby's high-chair, that play high-chair, and I reached out, and they were there. He started coming at me. He started spitting and screaming.

Q - What was he screaming if you recall?

A - He was making sounds like a tiger, like a panther.

Q - When he came towards you that time, what did you do?

A - Well, I waited for him to come at me. I hit him with a series of blows with the sticks.

Q - And, on what portion of his body did you strike him with the sticks?

A - In the head.

Q - As a result of those blows, what occurred to your father at that time?

A - (No response.)

Q - Did he remain standing?

A - I am not sure at that moment. When I hit him, I saw blood come out of his head, because I came with an upswing. And everything I do is in a series of blows. It is not one. I hit him, I think, at least two times in the back of the head with the same series of blows.

Q - As a result of those blows, did your father remain standing at that time, or did he go down?

A - He did not go down. He went down, but not immediately.

Q - Describe to us how he went down.

A - He staggered. He fell across the kitchen table, and he fell face down on the table. And I do not know how, but he just kind of flew back off the table, almost like he pushed himself off it, or something. It is almost like somebody pushed him off the table. He flew back and came straight down from that level to the ground. I think he landed on the typewriter, because that is where his head was when I saw him.

Q - Did he lay on that typewriter for any length of time?

A - Yes, he did.

Q - And, what did you do while he was in that position?

A - I stood there and looked at him. You know, I remember thinking, "God, please, please don't do this. Please stay down."

Q - How many times up to that point had you had him down, or had he been knocked down?

A - Once with the hand blows, once with the kicks, and once when I threw him across me.

Q - So, this would be the fourth time he was down?

A - Yes.

Q - Now, as you observed him in that position, did he say anything, or make any remarks, or facial gestures?

A - At this point there was a lot of noise going on. The stereo was on, but it was on low. But I have a Great Dane -- Well, at that time I did. He weighs about 130-40 pounds. And the dog -- The dog knew what was going on. He was throwing himself at the door. He was right at the door adjacent to the kitchen, and he was just hurtling himself against the door. And that created a lot of noise, plus the screwing that my father was doing. At this point I heard my little girl start screaming.

Q - What went through your mind, if anything, when your little girl screamed?

A - Only one thing went through my mind. I thought if he gets me, he is going to get her, then he is going to get my brother. That is the one thing now that I recall. He asked me, "What time does Jimmy usually get home?" I said, "He's home usually by 11:00 or 12:00 o'clock. I can't say for sure."

Q - When was it he asked you what time Jimmy would be home?

A - That was at the school. Then he asked me sometime when he was up at the house that night, too.

Q - Now, from the position of your father with his head on the typewriter, did he get up from that position?

A - He started laughing.

Q - What?

A - He started laughing, like jeering, cackling. I do not know how to describe it. He started laughing like a maniac.

Q - What did he do after he began laughing?

A - He started to get up and go towards the kitchen area.

Q - And, where were you at that time?

A - I was standing in the doorway. I was standing right in the doorway between the living room and dining room.

Q - Once he got up and started moving again, what did you do?
A - I stepped in front of him and hit him again with another series of blows with the stick, and the force of the blows knocked him into the living room.

Q - What were you trying to accomplish on the occasion that you hit him with the sticks?

A - I was trying to stop him. I was trying to knock him unconscious.

Q - As a result of the last set of blows that you mentioned what did he do?

A - (No response.)

Q - Did he stand, or did he go down?

A - No, he went down. He did, like a head dive into the living room, because I had forced him into that area. I did not want him anywhere near the kitchen or *the bedrooms.

Q - Now, that would be the fifth time that ho was down?

A - Right.

Q - What occurred from that point once he ended up in the living room area again?

A - Well, at that point I thought he was knocked out, because he was on his face. He was lying on his face. And I went up and I kind of sat down beside him. And I had my hand on his shoulder. I was crying. I was trying to plead with him. And he just started to roll over. He started to grab me.

Q - Well, once he was in that position on the living room floor, did he remain in that same spot?

A - No. He kind of worked his way around. He stayed basically in the middle of the floor where he was, where the stereo was. At one point he was over in the corner where the chair was and the register was. I cannot say he was there at that spot. He was all over the floor, but he was on the floor.

Q - When you got beside him, while he was on the floor, what, if anything, did you do at that point?

A - I was trying to pin his hands down.

Q - Why?

A - I was trying to hold him down. I was hoping he would pass out. I remember thinking, "Oh, God, all this blood, how can he even move."

Q - While you held his hands down, did he pass out?

A - I thought he did, yes. I do not know. I think it was just a thing to get me to relax, which I did. I let him go. And I started to move in front of him. And the next thing I knew, I ran right into a kick.

Q - What kick was it? What portion of his body struck you?

A - His foot. It is a soccer-type kick. It is called a saber kick.

Q - And, where did that saber kick land, so far as your body is concerned?

A - It hit me in the head.

Q - Would you point to the area of your head where that kick landed?

A - It hit right on this side of my head here (indicating) Right across the temple here.

Q - What effect did that kick have on you?

A - Well, momentarily it knocked me out, momentarily. Because I have been knocked out many times. I know what the feeling is. Because you are busy fighting unconsciousness, because I knew if I passed out, that was it.

Q - What is the next thing you recall after being kicked in the head?

A - I remember a few things, but as far as sequences go, I cannot remember. Like I said, I was dizzy. My head was pounding. And I could not focus my eyes. I do not know, it is hard to say.

Q - Do you know for what length of time, or approximate length of time you had been rendered unconscious by that kick?

A - No, sir, I could not tell you.

Q - Well, whenever your memory started back, what is the next thing you recall after being kicked in the head?

A - I remember a few things distantly, but in what order they occurred, I do not know. Tell us what you remember really distinctly.

A - I remember him having a severe pain in my mouth. He had his whole hand on the inside of my mouth trying to tear out the inside of my mouth, trying to tear the throat out.

Q - What else do you remember?

A - I remember him, he had one hand on my groin. He was trying to rip that off.

Q - Do you recall anything else once you regained your consciousness?

A - I remember the blows to the face. I do not remember whether it was a kick or punch, or what.

Q - And, at what stage did you experience any cuts on your body?

A - Here again I do not know when I got cut. All I know, I was -- At this point I was trying to pin him down, and I was all over him and around him. And we were just kind of rolling around on the floor, and all over I felt just like a little -- I do not know how to describe it, just like a reed, or something like a piece of grass going across my body. I did not know I was getting cut until I saw the knife.

Q - And when you saw the knife, where was it?

A - He was holding it.

Q - And, what did you do when you saw the knife in his hand?

A - I tried to knock it out of his hand.

Q - Did you succeed?

A - Yes.

Q - When you refer to the knife, are you referring to Defendant's Exhibit N?

A - Yes.

Q - After these events that you just testified to occurred can you tell us what next happened, as best you recall.

A - After I got the knife away from him.

Q - Yes?

A - Well, I laid across his body. I was trying to hold him down. I could not hold him down. I had his arms pinned to the ground, but he was picking me right off the ground. I was laying there. I could see his feet were trapped under the couch, and I looked over, and I was laying on him. I could feel my body coming off his. I could see the couch just jumping up and down. Here again I can remember thinking, how long can he even move, because it is a real heavy couch.

Q - Up to that point, did his strength seem to lessen at all to you?

A - No, he seemed to get stronger as time went on. It was just phenomenal.

Q - What did you next do, as you recall these events?

A - Well, at this point I was trying to conserve my energy, or my strength. I remember trying to hit him. I could not even get the energy to hit him with any kind of force or power.

Q - What had caused you to lose your strength, as you recall these events?

A - I do not know. I would have to say the kick to the head. I do not know.

Q - What next happened, Roy, as best you remember?

A - Well, I remember laying across him, looking for something. And I looked up. And I looked on the T.V, and I saw the sword, the other sword, a long one It is about four foot long. I looked up, like that (indicating), and I saw it, and it was going through my mind to reach up and grab the sword and stick it through him.

Q - Did you make any such effort?

A - No.

Q - And, why not?

A - Because I thought, you know, when the police did get there, they are going to see him lying on the floor with a sword sticking through his belly and it was bad enough as it was.

Q - Did you have any intention of killing him?

A - No, sir.

Q - Any other- thought go through your mind over that long sword?

A - Well, the position I was laying in, the set of sticks that I had dropped after he fell into the living room area, it was lust laying two feet away from his head. What did you do with regard to those sticks?

A - I pulled one under his neck and pulled the other over it and I laid on them.

Q - And, what was your purpose in laying on those sticks? What were you trying to do to him?

A - I was trying to render him unconscious so he could not do anything.

Is there a way that unconsciousness can be brought about by using the sticks in that manner?

Sure. You know, I thought you could do it by hitting him on the head. That did not work. I do not think I ugh. I tried to shut off his air supply.

Q - When you had those sticks around his neck, was he moving at all at that time?

A - Yes, sir.

Q - What portions of his body were moving at that particular time?

A - Well, again, I looked down and I saw his feet. His feet were going -- I mean they were, like, peddling a bicycle. The couch jumped up and down. He had one hand pulling my hair. He had pulled out quite a bit of my hair.

Q - Was there any reason why you laid on the sticks, rather than use your hands with the sticks?

A - Well, there are a couple reasons. For one, I did not have the strength. I did not have the strength that it took. I mean, to actually use brute strength, I did not have the strength.

Q - And what portion of your body was in contact with those sticks as you were laying across your father?

A - Well, I had my hands on them and I had my chest across his face.

Q - Do you recall how long you remained in that position?

A - To me it seemed like eternity. I do not know. I think it was a few minutes, because the position I was in, I know at least twice that I rolled over, and at one point I remember I looked up, and again I saw the sword, and I had, you know, I was under a lot of stress and a lot of pressure, and I can react under pressure. And there was just, like, a debate going on in my mind what should I do. Again, I looked at the sword. I visualized real vividly in my mind this thing sticking in his belly. I thought, "I have got a loaded shotgun I can run in there and get it before he gets up."

Q - At any time, did you have any intention to kill your father?

A - No, sir, it would have been an easy matter.

Q - Now, when you eventually got up from the position that you described with the stick under your chest around your father's neck, what did you next do?

A - I rolled over and I propped myself against the T.V. and the wall right next to the television, about two feet from his head.

Q - And how long did you sit in that position, if you remember?

A - I remember sitting there and looking at him and thinking, you know, I can relax a little bit. And this thing went all through my head, he got you five or six times before, he is going to do it again. My head was pounding. My pulse was going -- To me it looked like he was breathing heavily.

Q - Had you realized at that point he was dead?

A - No, sir.

Q - What did you do once you determined that it looked like he was still breathing?

A - I crawled over and I laid my head on his chest and I tried to listen for a heartbeat.

Q - And, then what next did you do?

A - Well, I could not tell whether he was alive or if he was dead, because my head was pounding and I was breathing heavy. My adrenalin was going. My head was pounding. I could not tell if it was me or him that we breathing.

Q - Did you return to the position where you had been sitting against the wall?

A - No, sir. I looked at him. I thought, "If he's not dead, he's going to get me again." I reached out and pulled the sticks out from under his neck and laid the in my lap.

Q - Why did you do that?

A - Like I said, I thought he was going to get up again. I wanted to be at least ready.

Q - How long did you remain in that position with the sticks being held in your lap?

A - I do not know. I really do not know.

Q - What is the next thing you remember doing after you were holding the sticks in your lap?

A - At some point after that, the realization hit me that he was dead. So, I took the sticks off my lap. I laid them beside the T.V. and my legs. And I got up to make a telephone call. I picked up the phone with the purpose of calling the police. And I had lived in Center Township. It was in the phone book, but I was not in a state of mind that I could look up the phone number. I tried. I must have dialed four or five numbers, and the only one that stuck out in my head was my fiancée, because I call her every day.

Q - What did you tell her when you called?

A - I do not know exactly, but I think I said, "Call the police," you know, "Willy is dead and I am bleeding to death."

Q - And, what did you do after making that phone call?

A - I hung up the phone and I went into the bedroom to see if the baby was okay. And she was asleep. She was sound asleep.

Q - What did you do after you checked on your daughter?

A - I came back in. I remember I walked in and I calmed down the dog, because he was still throwing himself against the door. And he is a huge dog. Sc, I went and calmed him down. I shut the door and I sat down in this little protrusion between the living -- I mean the dining room and the kitchen. I sat on the floor and leaned back against it.

Q - Was that the position you were in when your fiancée arrived?

A - Yes, I think so.

Q - Now, you had testified that once you saw the lock in your father's eyes, you knew what he was going to do. Can you tell us what type of childhood you had, being raised under Willy Wetzel?

A - What type of childhood?

Q - How did he treat you as a child?

A - Going back how far?

Q - Back to your younger days as a child when you were disciplined.

A - There's a lot of things I will never say about it, but the first time I can recall being mistreated is I was about five years old, five and a half years old. I will never forget it as long as I live.

Q - What did he do to you?

A - He stripped me down at the waist. He grabbed me by my feet and shoved me down in the toilet that was plugged up. He used me as a human plunger.

Q - As you became older, do you recall any physical abuse he did to you?

A - That was an everyday occurrence. The thing I do remember about him, it is so bizarre, he would, when he would beat one of us, we would all have to watch. And when he was doing the beating, he would laugh. He would lust laugh.

Q - And were those type of beatings regular occurrences, or infrequent?

A - They were regular. I mean, they were like clockwork. What would he beat you children with?

A - Like my brother testified, anything he could get his hands on.

Q - Did you love your father?

A - No, I did not. I cannot say I did.

Q - Did you respect him?

A - around 12 years old, he used to walk around stripped to the waist flexing in front of the mirror. I made the mistake of laughing at him, you know.

Q - Well, what happened when you laughed?

A - This was the time when him and my mother were not getting along, and they were still married. They had been married, and he had been going with another woman.

Q - What happened to you when you laughed?

A - That is what I am getting to. Down in New Brighton they had a swimming pool and they used to have nice swimming right on the Junction Stretch. He took us down there, me and my brother and sister, to show us who his girlfriend was. I did not know much, but I knew that was not right. So, I mentioned that to him.

MR. KELKER: Your Honor, I do not think this is really relevant.

THE WITNESS: Yes, it is. I am sorry, but it is.

MR. JAMES: Just a moment.

THE COURT: What is the question before the witness?

MR. JAMES: I am attempting, Your Honor, to have the witness testify as to what his father did to him whenever he laughed at his father.

THE COURT: And he has talked about everything except to answer that question.

MR. JAMES: Can I instruct the witness?

THE COURT: We order the Jury to disregard the response to that question.

MR. JAMES: Thank you.

BY MR. JAMES:

THE VETERANS ADMINISTRATION BATTLE EVERY VETERAN ENDURES

The Department of Veterans Affairs (VA) can be traced back-to-back to 1636, when the Pilgrims of Plymouth Colony were at war with the Pequot Indians. The Pilgrims passed a law stating that disabled soldiers would be supported by the colony. Today the United States has the most comprehensive system of assistance for veterans of any nation in the world. However, it is an understatement to say the VA has its flaws.

The layers of bureaucracy make the process of applying for earned benefits daunting, complicated and frustrating. While suffering the emotional and physical challenges brought on by serving our country too many times our veterans are forced to face humiliation, feelings of abandonment, betrayal, and the view that their loyalty and sacrifices have been forgotten.

I retired from the Air Force in 1990 and like every veteran, I felt secure that the country I fought for and loved would do the right thing for us. But I quickly learned the heartbreaking truth about how veterans were treated for their loyalty and sacrifices. My message to each veteran in my VA story that follows is that you must never give up in your quest to obtain the benefits that you are due. None of us joined the military to get medical and financial benefits for our service. However, when we are injured in that faithful service, we are all entitled to medical care without the pain and suffering the VA requires for us to get those benefits.

The reality for veterans is that the system is set up to avoid rating veterans at any rating especially at the 100% rate regardless of their total disabilities and at all costs. It has been my experience that the VA makes it extremely difficult to obtain benefits and will delay granting final decisions for as long as possible. My living examples are seven appeals that have been on their backlogged list since 2012 and still are at the time of this writing in November of 2020. Sadly, most veterans hold the assumption that the VA has an unwritten policy and is betting that the veteran will die first and will not have to pay at all.

Unfortunately, that appears to be true. Many of my Veteran brothers and sisters died without ever receiving justifiable benefits due to them or their families. One report in 2015 stated that over

300,000 disabled veterans died waiting for VA health care. A report published in 2018 states that 22 veterans commit suicide every day. My fear is that many of those suicides could be prevented if the veterans receive the mental health support that they need instead of being strangled by the broken system.

Many veterans choose not to apply for benefits for injuries suffered while serving. Those service injuries are often not reported to medical authorities so they are not entered in military records due to fear of retaliation or resulting in being medically discharged. Military flying personnel, in particular, fear losing flying status so they suffer in silence or self-medicate in order to avoid losing their flying status and flight pay.

Seeking help for non-physical injuries, such as post-traumatic-stress (PTSD) or Traumatic Brain Injury (TBI) can result in discharge and become a poisonous booby trap in the veteran's records that will follow them for life. They risk losing one of the cherished freedoms they fought for - their Constitutional right to carry and bear arms. If the VA determines that a veteran is unable to care for themselves it is, by law, required to report that to other federal agencies. The government has the power to confiscate all of the veteran's legally obtained and registered firearms. Therefore, asking for treatment for these service-related conditions is too perilous for most veterans to seek help except in the most extreme circumstances.

I was not evaluated for the traumatic brain injury (TBI) that occurred at Khe Sanh when I was blown off my forklift by the F-4 bomb run. I was not evaluated by the VA for the two significant lower back injuries I suffered in the line of duty as a C-130 and C-141 Loadmaster because they were not properly recorded in my military medical records. The back injuries eventually required two major surgeries. The VA application for benefits due to the broken back injury caused by the Marine striking me with his 5-ton truck was denied twice and the third appeal is one of the seven still waiting for a final decision.

Every person retiring from the military is required to complete a physical by the Veterans Administration (VA) within 90 days of retirement at the nearest VA hospital. Mine was scheduled at Dallas VA hospital in April 1990.

Zee accompanied me to the hospital. Entering the front door was akin to walking into a horror movie. A medic was walking through the lobby pushing a patient with a shaved head and huge fresh - looking scar on his scalp, possibly recovering from recent brain surgery. The patient appeared agitated, shifting in his chair, and yelling obscenities. The medic stopped long enough to slap the veteran/patient across the back of his head, which did not improve the patient's behavior. Then they disappeared into the nearest elevator where only God knows what happened there.

When I reported to the triage doctor's office, we were told to wait our turn. While we were waiting, a medic rolled a gurney passed us with what appeared to be a comatose patient with his arms and legs bound by retention straps. The medic locked the gurney brakes and without a word left the patient unattended.

The doctor came to the door and called my name. The gurney patient was no longer asleep and I suggested that she attend to him first. She shrugged and responded, "Oh, he's not going anywhere so please come in."

To me he was a fellow combat soldier that deserved respect and dignity but to her he was the next body that she had to contend with to get her paycheck. I asked again that she take care of him first. Obviously perturbed by my insistence she told me to follow with her.

After a lengthy and in-depth interview, she handed me a list of appointments for various departments that addressed my military medical history. I was overwhelmed by the comprehensive schedule for a single day.

The pulmonary doctor was Vietnamese with extremely poor English and she was almost impossible to understand. After a few quick questions she handed me a plastic tube covered with some unrecognizable dried food particles including a piece of dried corn and instructed me to put it in my mouth and breathe into it. I handed it back to her asked for a clean replacement. She said, "We no havey. Last one. You take and breed in it."

I refused to put the filthy thing in my mouth so she rinsed it off and cut the index finger from a rubber glove to cover the part that was put in my mouth. It was disgusting but it was obvious that any further objection would be futile and I just wanted to get the ordeal over with.

The dermatologist was also Vietnamese and her English was almost nonexistent. I have severe jungle rot that involves the bottom of both feet as a result of my Vietnam deployment. It is a condition that includes painful raw oozing, bleeding sores.

I sat on a gurney and she signaled for me to remove my shoes and socks while she sat on a doctor's rolling chair. She turned around to pick up my medical folder and I followed her instructions. When she turned around and rolled back over to inspect my feet, I lifted my right foot for her to inspect. She immediately stopped rolling her chair towards me, raised both her hands, and said something to the effect, "Dat bad. I no touchy. Chou bin Vietnam?"

"Yes." I responded.

She backed her chair away from me and said "No cure, nevah ged bettah. I give chou medachin. Someday chou lose chou legs."

The last appointment of the day was with my VA assigned primary care LPN who did much the same work as a primary care doctor. He reviewed all of the interim results from each department that I had visited and told me that my final report would be reviewed by the Benefits department and a VA Disability Benefits decision would be made and sent to me in about three weeks.

Zee was waiting for me and the first thing I said was, "If ever I don't have a choice for medical care DO NOT take me to the VA hospital. Just give me a .38 caliber pistol with one bullet and take me to my favorite hunting spot and leave me." She did not appreciate what she determined to be my typically sick military humor but I was not joking.

A month later I received my VA medical benefits report. The rating was ZERO. No department had determined that I had any military and/or combat related disabilities. Accompanying the letter was an appeal form and instructions which I immediately returned with the copies of the same medical records that were presented to them before.

My first Benefits appeals letter arrived awarding me 10% for the skin diseases.

My second appeal increased my benefits to 30% backdated to the first benefits award.

After my fourth appeal I was up to 40% and a follow-up appointment that included x-rays, the prodding of every orifice God had given me, blood tests and then I was sent on my way.

Nine months into the appeals process the VA awarded me a 50% total rating dating back to the zero-percentage award. I still was not happy but since the 50% rating covered all of my daily medications whether through the VA or a civilian pharmacy, I gave up fighting the system which was exactly what they want you to do.

Twenty-three years after my first experience with a VA hospital Vikie and I moved from Texas to Washington state and it took five months to get an appointment with a new primary care doctor at the Spokane WA VA hospital. During that time, the VA had changed dramatically. The Mann-Grandstaff VA Medical Center in Spokane, WA., its medical staff and management should be used as the gold standard for how veterans must be treated.

The medical staff in Spokane is exceptional and the Mental Health team has a thorough understanding of PTSD. Although PTSD is not curable, it can be treated and they have helped me beyond my expectations. The Dental Clinic, the Eye Clinic, the X-Ray Department, Physical Therapy, and the medical team assigned to my case is compassionate, friendly, and caring. Doctor Bloom, Lynn Alford ARNP and their nursing staff Stacy Meyer RN, Lisa LPN, and Tricia, MSA are unequaled in their competence and professionalism.

The Dermatology clinician tested me for all my Vietnam jungle diseases and jungle rot issues with my feet and provided me with treatments that manage the problems for the first time since leaving Vietnam. Everyone on my medical team greets me with respect, a smile and knows my name.

After PTSD manifested itself, in November of 2013 I submitted the medical documentation and a request for disability benefits for life altering PTSD. The VA responded in thirty days rating me at 70% for PTSD. With my previous ratings totaling 50% I had expected to be rated at 100%. However, due to an archaic and very confusing rating system, the VA's disability system calculations re-rated me at a total of 70%.

When I was diagnosed with prostate cancer and had emergency prostatectomy surgery, the VA increased my rating to 100%. Exactly one year after my prostatectomy I received another VA letter stating that I no longer had prostate cancer due to removal of the prostate and had no sign of malignancy, therefore my overall benefits were going to be reduced to 60%, even though my PTSD disability rating was 70%. The letter further acknowledged that my post-operative injuries and bladder control issues resulting from the prostate cancer surgery were not considered military related.

Per its own rules and regulations, any Vietnam veteran who files for benefits for any of the medical problems connected with Agent Orange is considered "presumptive" to be AO related. This includes prostate cancer, peripheral neuropathy, and several heart related diseases. Although the VA agreed that several of my problems are clearly Agent Orange related, the various other disabilities that I suffer have been rated at zero percent for all benefit applications.

Because the prostatectomy caused severe and irreversible damage to my urinary system, I filed another appeal and provided the additional supporting documents from my urologist. His medical assessment stated, "there is a reasonable opinion that the existing medical issues will not be resolved during the life of this patient." He recommended that my prostate cancer related disability be rated as permanent.

After waiting for over two years for the VA to address my appeals and after two attempts in eighteen months trying to get copies of my PTSD mental evaluations for one of the appeals and appealing their decision to reduce my benefits by half, I finally conceded failure and realized that I could no longer expect positive cooperation from the VA bureaucratic system without help.

I contacted my Congresswoman in Eastern Washington - the Honorable Cathy McMorris Rodgers. I explained my plight with the VA and my long-awaited appeals and the inability to obtain basic information. Congresswoman McMorris-Rodgers and her staff member, Louise Fendrich, responded within 48 hours. They contacted the VA for a request for information and a status of my appeals and active benefits requests. Within 72 hours after her request, I received a copy of the PTSD mental evaluation that I filed for twice over an 18-month period. The Congresswoman and her staff requested that I give them at least four weeks for the VA to properly respond. Compared to what I had been through, three or four weeks were like overnight express.

The bureaucratic battle that began in 2013 finally reached a conclusion on July 20, 2015. My total disability rating will be retained at 70% due to the prostate cancer surgery and its many peripheral medical problems and with the addition of my life-altering PTSD, the rating has been changed to 100% permanent and total (P&T) rating. This rating means that I will no longer have to go through the constant and recurring re-evaluations again. But the VA can change this decision at any time, even though the letter specifically states that no future evaluations are scheduled. I am still waiting for my back-related injury appeals to be resolved so that my final rating can be back-dated to the original benefits denial date thereby paying me the benefits I was denied.

I extend my eternal gratitude to Congresswoman Cathy McMorris Rodgers and her staff for delivering me from this long-fought nightmare.

The VA overall service and its value to our nation's veterans cannot be overstated. Prior to the intervention of President Trump, Disabled Veterans had to go through abhorrent, inhuman, and degrading requirements to get help.

I thank God and ask Him to bless this great country and all that she provides its citizens. My family was blessed with the opportunity to immigrate here because of President Eisenhower's initiative to bring displaced people into the country. I thank the American soldiers, airmen, marines, and sailors that gave of themselves and their lives to free my parents and relatives from the Japanese internment and prison camps. I commit and will endeavor to repay her for the honor to serve our nation until the moment of my last breath. Even at my age, I would serve again if given an opportunity.

NEVER, NEVER TEACH THEM EVERYTHING YOU KNOW

NOTE: This informational chapter was added at the expressed request by hundreds of the students and instructors of the Wetzel style of Poekoelan.

Over the years since leaving home, practitioners, and loyal followers of the Willy Wetzel family's teaching style of Poekoelan, Kenpo, etc. approached me for more information about how our training evolved over time. They are confused and expressed their dismay about why many of the schools started by our students are different in the way the Art is taught and practiced. A brief explanation of the history and constantly evolving methods of teaching in our schools is appropriate here. But I will caution you that this explanation defies and clearly contradicts what practitioners thought they understood about the martial arts and Poekoelan in particular.

Since the mid-1950s the secret art of Kung Fu became a national phenomenon in the Unites States and finally accepted for training to the American public by the Chinese. Eventually Bruce Lee and other movie stars displayed their skills in numerous movies. Everyone wanted to be a karate expert and schools flourished all over the country. Public competitions became the rage and there was a lot of money to be made.

There is a great deal of confusion or misunderstanding about the current state of Poekoelan and the Martial Arts in general. This confusion about the current status and various existing teaching styles or versions are shared by literally everyone in the Indonesian Martial Arts community.

Poekoelan is a living, breathing and constantly evolving form of martial arts. All martial arts styles i.e., Korean, Chinese, Japanese, Indonesian, etc. have changed significantly since their first inception over the centuries. So, I am asked; Why does my school teach Poekoelan differently then another school whose owner or head teacher completed exactly the same training at the Wetzel schools?

That is the beauty and ultimate secret in all the martial arts styles across the eons and the globe. "Your' style is described in the following way: "You learned what you have and you do not and never will have what Jim, Roy, or your competitors and I learned."

When the Asian styles were first developed, they were basic self-defense moves and responses based on the defensive movements of birds and animals. The different Asian nations held their styles close to the vest and did not allow them to be shared outside of their scope of influence. That is where the high-level of secrecy began. People died because they shared the closely held secrets.

Over the centuries as fathers passed on their knowledge and styles to their offspring, as my Dad did with us, they and we fine-tuned the moves to suit our individual desires and goals. The Poekoelan of my father does not exist today and it should not in your schools either. That may sound sacrilegious to you and many martial artists will argue and challenge me about that. But if they are true to themselves, as you also should be, you will admit that you modified, no matter how minor, almost all the moves and methods that you have ever been taught. Why?????? Because the modifications you made allowed you to beat your opponents since they never saw the changes you developed before and were not ready for them. The end result is that YOU BEAT THEM!

Martial Arts masters and teachers are seed sowers. They plant the seeds, water them regularly and trim the growing plants to suit their visions of perfect plants. Then they harvest them and watch as their new seeds grow independently or cross breed with other similar plants to develop a new species or breed.

Dad's so-called Golden Boys today cannot and would not survive in competition, even using what they learned from Dad because they did not modify and evolve to improve their skills over time.

Roy and Jim are the perfect examples of experts who will continue to beat their opponents. They continued to modify and fine tune what they were taught by our father and that is why no one ever beat them in competition and never will.

They and I do not look anything alike if you were to watch us work out or spar in the same room. This fact holds true even today because Dad made sure of that in all our training. On many occasions Dad would train us separately. The other two bothers would never know what we learned in private unless we shared the newly learned skills.

What Jim, Roy and I often tell out students, visitors or interviewers about our individual styles is appropriate and correct: "this is what my father taught me!" We are not being rude or evasive in that response. We are being factual in our positions and you should accept it as the truth. There is nothing for us to gain or to do otherwise.

My Dad had a moto that was unquestioned and unchallenged by us: "Teach your students what they need to know to be good and to be champions; BUT never, never teach them everything that you know! Because if you do, they will ultimately beat you." He actually said" "They will kick your asses!"

Asian parents across the globe in every field of expertise or endeavor live and breathe by that mantra. That is one reason why the Asian nations often beat us in the technology and business communities. To them business and industry are battlefields that require the best fighters, who can think and perform on their feet, and to win in competition.

Americans often follow the exact and opposite philosophy and teach our competitors everything, including top secret information, in every field of business, industry, etc. Then when the opportunity arises, they use that knowledge to ultimately beat or outperform us.

If you research and study any subject where Asian countries outperform us; we taught them how to build the best cars, electronics, etc., etc. Once we realized what had happened to our market share in almost any business, because we shared All our knowledge with them, it was too late, and we ALWAYS ended up playing catch-up. We catch up and they continue to steal our ideas, Top Secrets, technology, send their children to our best schools and outperform us in every area where we once led. Until we change how we deal with our competitors in every field of endeavor, they will always kick our asses.

The same process is true in the Martial Arts.

In this autobiography, I share and describe a specific event in 1957 when my Dad's life was threatened by the Chinese in Roy's and my presence. For the martial arts practitioner reading this book, this event should be a lesson to you, your colleagues, and students. Your personal style of how you practice and teach will and must evolve if you are to survive in the martial arts.

In my humble opinion based on many years teaching and practicing the martial arts, there is not a single martial arts master of any style in the world who teaches just what they were taught. Any martial arts master worth a damn will admit my position and statements to be true. But because of Asian close-held norms and secrets they are prevented from admitting these facts. All of them will without hesitation may call me a liar and blasphemer for divulging this information. So-be-it!

I will just suggest to you to stop looking for what should be the same in everyone's school. Develop, modify, and continuously change your style while keeping the basics the same for every student -BECAUSE if you do not, they WILL kick your ass in the end.

IN MEMORY OF TSGT HAROLD R. (BOB) LEAVITT (1948 – 1984)

I met Bob when we were stationed together at the Edwards AFB Test Pilot School. Bob's job was to track test flights through a system of aircraft to ground electronic systems. He wanted to become a pilot and I often took him flying, sometimes letting him take the controls. He caught the flying bug and soon obtained his pilot's license and purchased a Cessna 150. We logged many flight hours together sharing fuel costs.

He always wanted to become a Loadmaster. I encouraged him to follow his dream and helped him apply for cross training before I left Edwards for my new assignment. The next time I saw him was at Altus, AFB sitting in the front of a class that I was monitoring. We reconnected during the break and I learned that while he was assigned at Norton, AFB in California he received approval to cross train as a loadmaster and had flown his Cessna to Altus Municipal Airport to attend the school.

Since I was an FAA Flight Instructor by then Bob asked me to conduct his Biennial Flight Review (BFR). Bob's BFR went smoothly and I was amazed at Bob's flying skills. One of the key elements every pilot for whom I conducted the BFR was to have them conduct engine out or failure and aircraft spin procedures. Upon completion of all my assigned tasks I confidently signed off the BFR in his logbook.

Bob graduated from the Loadmaster school and flew his Cessna back to Norton AFB enroute to Norton. He found himself flying at night and on descent to the approach to San Bernardino and Norton AFB through the notorious El Cajon Pass in California.

Bob entered a smog and fog layer on his descent and crashed the Cessna adjacent to Interstate 15. He called me the next day and told me that if we had not practiced the engine out procedures at Altus, he more than likely would not have survived the impact. He remembered the training to slow the aircraft to Best Glide speed, keep the wings level using the instruments despite what his brain was telling him about being level, unlock the door, open the window, turn off the fuel, and tighten his seat belt.

Bob crash landed without ever seeing the ground above and to the left of the freeway and walked away to safety. He suffered minor scratches but no major injuries.

Later Bob became a C-130 pilot and at the age of 37 he was assigned to the 37th TAC Airlift Squadron in Peoria, IL. The aircraft and crew he was assigned to was sent to Rhein Main, Germany to fly an airdrop missions out of Borja Spain. On the night of February 28, 1984 Bob was one of 18 Americans who were killed in a C-130 crash in the snow-covered mountains of Spain during a combat personnel airdrop training mission. A permanent memorial listing the entire crew was installed on the base at Rhein Main, GE. He will be dearly missed.

The memory of his loss haunts me to this day. What IF I had not encouraged him to become a Loadmaster?

THE MOONEY MITE N4140 WARBIRD FINAL FERRY FLIGHT

Early in the morning of June 11, 1988 I received an interesting call from a friend of a friend. His name was Colonel Tom Jones and he had a unique out of the blue request that I could not say "no" to. After introducing himself he told me that he was calling me from the Frederick Regional Airport in Oklahoma and he needed a favor.

Colonel Jones was in possession of a Mooney Mite with tail number N4140 that needed to be ferried to the Liberal, Kansas Mid-America Aviation Museum. He contacted numerous other pilots about ferrying the aircraft but they all turned him down because of the unique characteristics of this Warbird and that there were no pilot manuals available for them to study.

He told me that I was referred by another pilot as someone who always liked challenges and that I never turned down flight time and experience.

He came directly to the point and asked, "Are you interested?"

My answer was immediate and without restrictions or argument, "Absolutely! Where is the aircraft and what time and day do you want me there?"

"The bird is at the Frederick Regional Airport and I need the plane to be delivered to the museum in Liberal Kansas tomorrow. It is co-located at the Liberal Municipal Airport and one of their pilots will fly you back here to Frederick. Can you be here at about 09 hundred?"

"I will be there promptly at 9."

Early the next morning I flew directly to the airport and met with Tom who immediately introduced me to the 1954 Mooney M-18C C/N 307 N4140 and the local aircraft mechanic who had prepped the bird for the trip. The mechanic had fueled the aircraft and ensured that it had fresh oil. I did the normal preflight and got into the cockpit to get familiar with the cockpit and controls. The mechanic briefed me on rudimentary information and how to start it. He made a point of telling me what I had already determined. There were no navigation instruments beyond the whiskey compass. However, the engine instruments were all in place and worked properly – according to him.

Tom accompanied me to the terminal where I called for a weather briefing and planned my route on the navigation map for my route of flight. It had to be a "Dead Reckoning" (DR) route which meant that the flight had to be accomplished with a floating compass and lots of good visual identifiers on the ground. I identified several highly visible points of interest with the Quartz Mountain State Park just North of Altus as the first one. Several other highly visible ground markers would make the DR flight simple and direct. I filed the visual flight plan and completed a thorough pre-flight of the strange bird.

N4140 was clean and damage free and the fuel drain test was clear. The fuel tank was full and all the parts were where they should be.
Since no pilot manuals were available there was no mandatory information available for a pilot to fly safely. What was the takeoff speed, best glide speed, cruise speed, landing approach speed, etc., etc.? Oh! -There is a sticker on the panel with a short note. "Don't fly below 45 mph!'

Tom suggested that I take a short test flight in the pattern and a couple of touch and go's until I was comfortable with the aircraft and its unique characteristics. I agreed with him, got in and started the aircraft. Starting was simple and standard for most single engine aircraft and I taxied to the runway after announcing my intent.

After the standard engine runup and engine checks I taxied onto the runway, trimmed the aircraft for takeoff and applied power. Like any aircraft if it is trimmed properly N4140 rotated for takeoff at about 38 mph. I reached for the manual gear handle to raise it but it was frozen or locked in place. Rather than fooling with it I completed two touch and go's, landed, and taxied to the parking ramp and shut her down.

The mechanic came over and said, "Oh by the way. The landing gear handle does not work so you will have to fly her dirty (gear down). Keep an eye on your fuel level because of the increased fuel burn with the gear down."

I had him top off the fuel before leaving on the 3-hour flight.

Takeoff, departure and getting to cruise level with the correct departure heading went smoothly and I was feeling cocky. I was just flying over the southern edge of Quartz Mountain reservoir when without warning the engine quit. Without hesitation I split the difference between the posted 45 MPH and the rotate (take-off) speed of 38 and set it as my best glide. I immediately went through the start procedure and the engine stuttered and started again but indicated it would not stay that way. I pumped the primer and the engine started to run smoothly. It remained that way after I completed some fine-tuning throttle adjustments. Now I had to find a place to land and change my "panties."

About two hours enroute I landed to refuel just for insurance since I had no manual to determine the fuel burn rate. It turned out to be a smart move as I only had a third of a tank of fuel. I departed immediately and landed without further incident at the Liberal airport. I requested taxi instructions to the museum and stopped in front of the hangar where I was met by the pilot who flew me home.

It was a challenging opportunity to fly a unique and historic aircraft using my own wits and experience as an FAA certified flight instructor.

N4140 Displayed at the Liberal, KS Mid-America Aviation Museum

ABOUT THE AUTHOR

Wim Wetzel is the proud and eldest son of Willy and Gerry Wetzel who both survived over four harrowing years in Japanese Prisoner of War camps in Indonesia during WWII. Wim and his family emigrated to America in October 1956 and in 1966, at nineteen years old, he followed his lifelong dream and joined the United States Air Force. He is a decorated Vietnam veteran and served his beloved country for twenty-four years and retired honorably as a Chief Master Sergeant.

Chief Wetzel holds three training and. airport management related associate degrees, a bachelor's degree in Technical Occupational Education, a master's degree in Human Resources Development and a PhD in Business Administration. Wim is an FAA certified Multi-Engine Flight, Instrument and Ground Instructor. After retiring from the Air Force, he dedicated the remaining years of his working life to designing, developing, and delivering organizational development and training programs for civilian business and industry at Hughes Training, Inc., Raytheon Training, Citizens Communications and NEC.

After a successful military and civilian career, as a 100% disabled veteran, he continues to dedicate himself to helping other combat veterans in obtaining their duly earned Veterans Administration benefits.

ABOUT THE COVER ARTIST

Kathryn Stepp is a young aspiring artist from the equestrian community of Wellington, Florida. Kathryn's lifelong dream to sell her art became a reality through the unlikeliest of circumstances. When the whole world shut down during the COVID-19 pandemic, Kathryn spent her time in quarantine painting watercolors.

Her animals were the favorite subjects to paint during those harsh-stressful times. Social media followers expressed strong interest in purchasing her art and as a direct result, the online art shop KathrynsWatercolors was born! Kathryn's most popular art pieces are her custom pet portraits. These unique projects are one-of-a-kind paintings that celebrate the life of her customers' loving and special companions.

Kathryn's Art Gallery can be viewed at: kathrynswatercolors.com.

Made in the USA
Middletown, DE
04 March 2021